COME TAME SOMEONE LIKE ME

A Love Story

Christy Gerrell

Copyright © 2025 Christy Gerrell

All rights reserved.

No part of this book may be reproduced, stored in a retrieval system, or transmitted by any means, electronic, mechanical, photocopying, recording, or otherwise, without written permission from the author.

ISBN (Paperback): 979-8-9989661-2-5

Dedicated to:
My Grandpa – Spencer Thomas Kinard
And my Grandma – Merrill Celeste Anderson

Dedicated to:
My Grandpa – Spencer Thomas Kinard
And my Grandma – Merrill Celeste Anderson

Come Tame Someone Like Me:

I was the wild one,
Running free.
No one could tame me
I had the world to see.

Confident and happy,
My life was an easy ride.
Never any worries,
My content I could not hide.

And then I saw her,
The beauty that she was
And I could understand
Why she did the things she does.

So lovely, sweet and true
To her I gave my heart
She told me she couldn't loved me
Then tore my world apart

She was every dream I had come true,
My love in her heart she felt.
I couldn't live without her,
Into my body I had her melt.

She joined me at last
In being wild and free
She forgave herself the past
To come and tame someone like me

Synopsis:

A tale of a man who was meant to be a hero. Set in the time of World War II he will learn that sometimes you don't have to fight in order to win. Allen Roston Tucker is the strong willed handsome grandson of Allen Blackburn and Levi Tucker. He grows up in the shadow of his Grandfathers and his Uncle Doctor Lang Taylor. Known as Tucker, he is smart and determine to make his mark on the world. And then he falls in love with beautiful Jessie Fairchild and she's in trouble and needs a hero and that is what he is, a hero. Unable to stay with Jessie, Tucker is on the USS Northampton when Pearl Harbor is attacked and he has to serve his country during World War II. This is the heartbreaking and triumph conclusion to the Blackburn Family again set on the beautiful St. Marks River near Tallahassee, Florida. Allen and Alicia Blackburn fight to keep their family together despite the ravages of war.

The Blackburn Legacy:
Come Love Someone Like Me – Allen and Alicia's loves story
No Sound the Silence Makes – Levi and Cecily's love story
A Return of Innocence – Lang and Holly's love story
Come Save Someone Like Me – Shane and Shaun's love story

PART ONE

THE MAKING OF TUCKER

Chapter One

Riverbend, Florida
Late November 1919

She lay on the bed in an agony of pain wondering when this torture she was in would come to an end. The whole pregnancy had been this way, she thought. The baby had beaten her up on the inside and was now protesting to come out. Everything about carrying this baby had been difficult, Bethany thought as she screamed in pain and gripped the covers of the bed. At first she had been so sick, even sitting up had made her dizzy and nauseous and that hadn't been the worst. The absolute worst was her cousin's Shaun's wife, Sarah was also expecting and Sarah was small and well rounded and looked beautiful carrying her baby. Bethany, in her physical build was smaller than Sarah and she was not beautiful carrying her baby, she was huge, but she looked like she had swallowed a large watermelon whole. She waddled around before the fifth month and often could be found just sitting down somewhere and miserable.

Bethany lay back lost on the bed unable to see over her huge stomach thinking this was all his fault, him being her husband Ethan Tucker who stood at almost six foot four inches and was solidly built. This is what she got for falling in love with a man that was built like a mighty oak tree when she was more likened to a dainty dogwood tree. She saw him standing beside, he had been sitting next to her on the bed, but now he was standing and he honestly looked ready to run at any given moment. With each scream coming from her, her husband looked worse than she felt.

"You may leave," Bethany spoke to her husband and saw him nod his head before pushing past his mother to get out of the room. "Why did I marry that monster? I didn't realize how huge he is," Bethany moaned and saw her mother move to sit where Ethan had been sitting before.

"All the men in our family are tall," Alicia Blackburn said as she wiped her daughter's head and looked at the doctor at the foot of the bed.

"You'll be fine, Bethany," Cecily Tucker said as she sat on the other side of the bed and like Alicia, she stared at the doctor wanting his assurance that everything was going to be as they were saying, all right and fine.

Doctor Lang Taylor looked up at Bethany and told her to push harder with the next pain that she had and then turned to his wife Holly as she reached down with a cloth and wiped his face to keep the sweat from rolling into his eyes. "You folks sure keep the house hot here at Riverbend," Lang said as he saw Bethany grab a breath and push, her face turning red as she screamed loud and long.

"Allen had gas heating put in," Alicia said to Lang when her daughter fell back onto the bed and was still. "Holly, might you open a window?" Alicia asked Lang's wife and watched her go and crack the window open so that the doctor wouldn't be so hot.

"Bethany, I think just a few more pushes and this little one will be here," Lang said gently thinking that as large as Bethany was, this baby wasn't going to be little.

"Thank you God," Alicia prayed hoping the doctor's words were true. Her poor daughter had been battling to give birth to this baby for more than a day, for Alicia, it felt like her daughter had been carrying this child for a year instead of only nine months. Alicia looked back up at Lang and knew, he and his wife Holly had only come to Riverbend to accompany their daughter Charlotte back to their home in Fernandina Beach where she would give them a grandchild in a few months. The Doctor and his wife hadn't meant to stay more than a few days, but Bethany had been having a difficult time and their daughter's sister in law Sarah was also due almost any day now. So Doctor Lang Taylor and his wife Holly had generously offered to stay until the two babies were born so that Lang could deliver them both.

"She's almost done," Lang said to Alicia and Cecily as they saw Bethany lift up off the bed again and push, the scream this time from Bethany was ear splitting and then drowned out by the baby's screaming.

Alicia saw Cecily hug Bethany as the younger woman fell back onto the bed and smiled in relief before Cecily's eyes met Alicia's and they reached out to hold one another's hands. They were now grandmothers. Allen and Alicia Blackburn were the parents of Bethany and Levi and Cecily Tucker were the parents of Bethany's husband Ethan. "We're now related by blood," Alicia said joyfully to Cecily and both women fought not to cry.

"My baby," Bethany lifted up to see Lang silent at the foot of the bed, Holly helping him as they appeared to clean the baby.

The room was too quiet, Alicia thought as she sat up to see that the baby was blue. She had to look away and as she did, she saw Cecily's face. Cecily had her hand over her mouth and looked ready to burst into tears. Alicia knew; Cecily had seen how blue the baby was and the grandmothers were both aware that this wasn't going to be the happy ending to a long day that they had hoped for.

"Give him a minute," Lang said to Alicia and Cecily right before Bethany sat up and saw her new baby in Doctor Lang Taylor's arms, once glance and she knew her baby wasn't all right.

"Oh no, my baby," Bethany cried out and then cried out again louder, her voice filled with horror and pain.

Allen Blackburn stood in the hall with the man that was his business partner, friend and his daughter's father in law, Levi Tucker. Both older men watched Ethan Tucker, Levi's son and Allen's daughter Bethany's husband pace the long hall of the upstairs breezeway at Riverbend and wring his hands in worry. Every scream from his wife that came from the bedroom she was in caused him to jump and run to the end of the hall. Allen knew that this affected Ethan differently than most men as Ethan was suffering from shellshock, the after effects of the Great War which the young man had fought in as a Marine. He had fought and survived and come home to Allen's daughter Bethany and in the end, that was all that Allen Blackburn really cared about because he loved Ethan like he was his own son.

Allen heard his daughter scream and felt like his heart was beating down in his stomach instead of in his chest where it should be. He had thought that becoming a Grandpa would be a wonderful thing, but he had forgotten how difficult a birth could be. He peeked into the room and saw Doctor Lang Taylor taking care of his daughter and was thankful the man was here with them. They were blessed to have the Taylors as a part of their family and soon the Taylor's daughter Charlotte would have a baby by her husband, one of the twins, Shane Blackburn. Shane's brother Shaun's wife Sarah was also due to have a baby any day now and Lang was going to stay and help when that baby came into the family as well.

"I wish this baby would come," Levi Tucker worried and watched his son amazed to see how calm his friend Allen Blackburn was. Every time Bethany screamed, Levi felt like he was going to hit the floor head first, it was beyond words to describe her screams. And then everything went quiet in the room, too quiet.

Allen peeked back into the room where his daughter was giving birth and saw his wife's face, his beautiful wife that he adored and was more than thankful for every minute of every day, his wife that had given him their beautiful daughter while he was dead to her. Alicia's eyes met his from the room and he knew things were fixing to become heartbreaking for his family. He saw Levi come to stand next to him, Levi seeing Cecily with her fist in her mouth trying not to cry and yet tears falling onto her cheeks and he knew his friend knew they probably wouldn't be Grandfathers today.

"Damn," Levi said and offered his wife a loving look knowing that he would comfort her in his arms soon. They would comfort one another and their son and daughter in law over this sad loss.

Allen saw Ethan before Levi did and both men grabbed him by the arms when he cried out for Bethany and kept him from running into the room. Doctor Taylor looked busy; they didn't want to bother the man while he tried to save the baby.

"Ethan!" Bethany screamed and reached out for her husband and saw her father and father in law let him go. Cecily moved aside for her son and went around the bed to comfort Alicia who lay with her face on the bed not looking at anyone now. Cecily knew that Alicia knew the baby wasn't going to make it, that as good as Doctor Taylor was as a doctor, he couldn't give life to this baby.

Allen saw his wife with her face on the bed and her shoulders shaking and knew she was crying herself sick and felt like joining her in those tears. He and his Alicia had lost several babies, they couldn't survive birth and as a couple they remembered each loss. They never dreamed their beautiful daughter would lose her first baby; the thought had never entered their mind, though now, Allen thought of how difficult a time Bethany had these past months and he knew how difficult pregnancy had been for his wife, for his Alicia.

"I'm so sorry," Lang said as he handed the baby wrapped up in towels to his wife Holly and turned to Bethany, the baby had been so big it had torn her and he knew he was going to have to put in stitches. "I'm so sorry," he said again softly. "Would you like to hold your baby?" he saw Bethany nod her head with tears falling and Holly come to stand beside Ethan sitting on the edge of the bed and handed the new mother her still and blue baby. "Bethany," Lang said and saw her looking down at her baby, "I'm going to have to stitch you up some, can you be still for me?" He saw her head nod but she never took her eyes off of her baby.

"Ethan," Bethany said her husband's name but never looked away from her baby. "I'm sorry," her voice broke and the floor of tears came. Lang knew the tears needed to come; the happy event had now turned into a tragedy.

"I'm done, Bethany," Lang said and reached to cover her up. "I need you to be still for a few days. Your baby was big." Lang looked down at the baby and thought that this was the largest baby he had ever delivered in all his years as a doctor.

Allen and Levi came into the room when Lang motioned that it was all right to do so and they stood around the bed looking at Bethany with her lost baby in her arms. "We need to pray," Allen said gently to his daughter and reached out for Levi's hand and Holly who stood next to him. "Shall we hold hands?" he asked and saw the rest of his family claps hands, only Bethany, who held her baby, didn't join the circle that surrounded her and her baby.

"Allen, you want me to say a prayer?" Levi asked and Allen nodded his head.

"You can start us off Levi," Allen said in a voice filled with sorrow.

"Dear Father in Heaven, thank you for hearing our prayer," Levi began and didn't feel less of a man for the tears that dropped from his eyes. "Thank you for this family, for the love that is filling this room," he stopped and swallowed hard, he couldn't go on and he squeezed Lang's hand and Lang knew why.

"Be with our family at this time of sorrow and loss," Lang continued the prayer for Levi. "Protect this young mother and father as they struggle through the coming days, help them to be strong." Lang realized he couldn't go on, this family inspired him; they had welcomed him and his family as a part of their own. They were the strongest family he had ever met in his life and so close that they all felt the same way about the same things.

"Dear God," Allen Blackburn picked up the prayer, "please, be with my daughter and her husband as they struggle through the loss of this most precious baby. Be with all of us as we love and support them and know with certainty that his baby is with you and waiting on his mama and daddy to join him. In Christ's Holy and Loving Name, we all pray this prayer together." Allen let go of Holly Taylor's hand and moved to the bed laying his hand on the lost baby's head. "May Christ's healing hand be laid upon you in heaven, little one. We all love you." Allen looked up and saw his sweet daughter crying, her husband Ethan holding her close. These two had survived so much with the war, they were young and their love was strong, God bless them and keep this strong through this Allen prayed silently.

"Daddy," Bethany said and her aqua eyes looked into her father's grass green eyes as she gasped. "Daddy, the baby isn't blue any longer." Allen moved his hand from the baby's hand and saw chubby cheeks that were pink and the baby's chest moving as though he were breathing.

"Lang?" Allen moved back and watched his very dear friend, Doctor Lang Taylor move to the edge of the bed where he had stood. Allen saw Alicia look from the baby to her husband with huge hopeful eyes. Something had happened, something had changed.

"Dear God in Heaven," Lang said in a serious and prayer like fashion. Everyone in the room watched Lang take the baby from Bethany and unwrap him from the towels he was in. Lang then examined the baby from head to foot and when he was done rewrapped and handed the baby to his mama. The baby screamed long and loud as he had when he was born. "Dear God in Heaven," Lang said again. "I've never seen anything like this happen." He turned shocked eyes to his wife and then smiled and grabbed Holly's hand. "He looks perfect." He laughed and hugged Holly and then hugged Allen and Levi. He noticed everyone was hugging everyone, Cecily was laughing and crying at the same time and her husband Levi was doing the same. This was something he had never heard of happening; Lang shook his head in disbelief. "The baby screamed and was well when he was born," Lang said as he looked again at the baby. "And then he fell silent and I lost him and now look at him, screaming his head off."

"He's alive," Ethan said to Bethany and felt her hand on his cheek and saw her head nodding. "We have a son," he added and his wife gently handed him the baby. "He's huge," Ethan said looking at Lang for verification.

"He's the biggest baby I've ever delivered," Lang said firmly while showing everyone that the baby was long, probably two feet. "Tallest baby I've ever seen as well."

"What are you going to name him?" Holly Taylor asked as she saw the shock still on all the faces in the room.

"A miracle just happened in here," Allen said looking at Holly with a smile. "The miracle needs a name."

"Ethan and I already chose his name," Bethany said looking at her father. "We're naming him Allen Roston Tucker, after you Daddy." She saw her father smile and nod his head in a humble pose and knew she was honoring him and he felt honored.

"What are we going to call him?" Alicia asked looking from her husband Allen to the baby. "We can't call him Allen, I won't know if I'm talking about my grandson or my husband."

"We were thinking of calling him Little Allen and Daddy Big Allen," Bethany said and saw her mother's frown.

"I don't want my husband called Big Allen," Alicia frowned and saw her husband smiling and nodding his head in agreement.

"That name won't work anyway," Levi said and looked at Allen and Ethan. "There's no way that baby, the size he is now, is going to be seen as little for long. Between his daddy and his Grandfathers, we're all well over six feet," he laughed and shook his head, "He isn't going to be little anything for long. I think you should call him skeeter, I always like the name skeeter." Levi Tucker saw his wife's face and knew he might be the only one in the room that liked skeeter for a nickname.

"Don't you dare call this baby skeeter," Cecily said in a deadly serious voice first to her husband and then to Bethany and Ethan.

"If we're looking for a good nickname," Allen offered giving Alicia a wink, "I like the name Lucky. You can't go wrong giving the little fellow the name Lucky, more so since he died at birth and came back to life." Allen saw Cecily looking at him and shaking her head with an expression that told him he wouldn't get lucky and have this baby called by that name.

"What about Ross?" Alicia asked in her gentle voice. "It's a part of his middle name, though I do admit, he doesn't look like a Ross."

"Tucker," Ethan said looking at his newborn son holding his finger in a tight fist. "He looks like a Tucker," Ethan said firmly.

"So his name is Tucker Tucker?" Lang asked with a laugh and saw Ethan shaking his head.

"His name is Allen Roston Tucker," Ethan asserted, "and his nickname is Tucker. We're calling him Tucker." He looked up at his mama and saw Cecily nod her head.

"He fits the name," Bethany said taking the baby back from her husband and hearing the baby cry loud again. "And he needs feeding," she said with a blush.

"In other words, we need to leave," Allen said giving his daughter a wink.

"As her doctor," Lang said, "I'm staying and making sure the baby is eating all right and swallowing well. I'm going to stay around a few days to watch out for this little man."

"Tucker," Alicia said softly, touching the baby's head before she walked out of the room leaving only Ethan, Lang and Holly with Bethany and the baby.

"We're Grandparents," Allen said lifting his glass of ice tea up in the air and pointing to his wife Alicia and his friends Levi and Cecily Tucker. "I think it's time we had a serious talk about our family," Allen said to Levi and both men nodded their heads.

"What do we need to seriously talk about concerning our family?" Cecily sat down in a chair next to Alicia in the drawing room and looked from Allen to Levi.

"Since the war ended things have changed a lot," Levi said to his wife. "Florida is starting to grow here in his region, mostly because of the capital. Our area in Madison County is slowing down. Allen and I have talked about our moving here; the sawmill, our whole operation. The timberland we own over there can ship the logs here on the train and we can ship the lumber out east on the railroad and west via the Gulf of Mexico. It's time to move, Cecily. The money is here, the land is here and most of the trees are here. In the past year I've bought up almost a thousand acres in Jefferson and Leon County preparing for our future. Ethan and Bethany belong here darlin', and this river has grown on us." Levi saw the look on his wife's face and gave her a few moments to process what he was saying to her.

"You want us to leave our home?" Cecily asked in a choked voice and saw her husband nodded his head. "I love our home."

"I do as well, darlin', but we belong here now. Look at us, you and the girls and I are here all the time, we rarely go home." Levi saw his wife's eyes tear up. "I want to watch that baby up there," Levi pointed to the ceiling, "grow up and we can't keep imposing on Allen and Alicia, we need to build our own home here." Levi winked at Allen and then Alicia.

"I know you're right," Cecily said to her husband and felt Alicia take her hand. "And we're all family now. That new baby is the tie that binds us together."

"Uncle Allen," Allen turned and saw one of his twin nephew's in the doorway. "I need Doctor Lang," Shaun gasped. Allen knew it was Shaun because his wife Sarah was expecting any day now. "The baby is coming."

Allen left his chair and went to the stairwell. "Lang!" he yelled up and saw his friend appear at the top of the stairs. "Another baby is coming today," he smiled and saw Lang hurry away only to reappear within seconds with his coat and bag.

"Holly girl," Lang called up to his wife and saw her hurrying with her coat, "another baby," he smiled and took his wife's hand pulling her toward the door.

"Uncle Allen," Shaun said in a hurry. "I ran over here, can Doctor Lang use your car to get to my house?" Allen nodded his head and watched his nephew run out the door and it slam hard behind him.

"He could have waited and gone with you two," Allen said with a smile to Lang and Holly. "I bet you pass him on the road."

"If we do," Holly said with a laugh. "We'll be sure and pick him up."

"Two Blackburns born on the same day," Alicia said with a contented smile. "Cecily, why don't we go up and see that new baby? Neither of us got to hold him." Levi watched his wife follow Alicia to the stairs where Cecily stopped and looked back at him.

"I love you, Levi. I've loved you most of life and I'll follow you wherever you want to go. And you're right, we have friends back in Cherry Lake, but our family is here." Levi nodded his head toward her and she turned to find Alicia on the stairs waiting for her, a smile touched her eyes as she reached for Alicia's hand. "I feel like you and I were meant to be sisters," she said and Alicia hugged her close.

"I've always wanted a sister and if I were to get to choose Cecily, I would choose you."

Allen watched his wife turn at the top of the stairs and turned back to Levi. "My Alicia," he said to his friend as they sat back down in the drawing room. "She went through a lot when she was young, she was hurt. She's delicate and sweet. I see that in your Cecily."

"One day Allen, after you finish helping me build my house here, I'll tell you the story of my beautiful wife and how blessed I am that she forgave me and loves me."

"I bet that's a short story," Allen teased and then saw the serious look Levi gave him.

"I was a bit of a bully in my younger years," Levi reached for his glass of sweet tea. "And she still married me." Levi took a long drink from his glass.

"I understand in a way," Allen said looking back at the stairs thinking of his wife. "I feel blessed every single day that Alicia married me."

"Your father and I witnessed a miracle today," Holly Taylor said to her daughter Charlotte while her husband examined Sarah. "Bethany delivered her baby today," Holly continued seeing the twins Shane and Shaun looking at her and listening closely to what might have happened to Bethany today. "The baby came out screaming, he is the biggest baby your father ever delivered. And then he went still and silent and within seconds he was blue. Your father couldn't get him to revive in anyway and he tried for a long time."

"Bethany's baby died?" Sarah cried from the room that Holly was standing outside of with Charlotte, Shane and Shaun. "Oh no," she cried and Lang rushed to assure the baby was alive.

"No, the baby didn't die. That's the miracle," Holly continued looking into the room and at Sarah. "We all stood around praying for the poor little thing and holding hands, your Uncle Allen put his hand on the baby's head and prayed and then we looked down and the baby was pink and breathing."

"If I hadn't been there and seen that happen," Lang added to his wife's words. "I wouldn't have believed it. Truly and without doubt what I saw today was a miracle." He looked up at Sarah as she fought off another pain. "This baby is coming fast, Sarah. Don't fight the pain, I want you to push. The rest of you go downstairs and wait. Holly girl, I need you." Lang saw his wife come into the room and ready for the baby's coming.

"I can help you, Daddy," Charlotte said coming into the room and saw her father shake his head hard and give her a firm look. Then she saw all the blood coming from Sarah. "Daddy?" Charlotte spoke to her father and he clearly heard the alarm in her voice.

"Honey, can you go down and pray with Shane and Shaun. It's a day of miracles." He gave his child a look that left no doubt in her mind that he wanted no more questions and she didn't need to be here for this birth.

"Shane," Charlotte rushed into the kitchen and grabbed her husband's hand pulling him outside. "Sarah's bleeding too much," she whispered to her husband not wanting Shaun to hear his wife was in trouble. "We have to pray." She went to bow her head and saw her husband's twin brother coming out the door, Shaun was pale and worried and Charlotte knew he had a right to be.

"Something is wrong," Shaun didn't ask this, he made it a statement.

"Dear God, be with our loving Sarah, guard her and guide her in this hour of her need. Protect her and keep her safe from all harm. In your name we ask this humbly. Amen," Shane prayed taking his brother and his wife's hands just as the screams of a newborn baby came from inside. Shaun took a deep breath and his brother felt his fear. "We trust in Jesus that Sarah will be all right," Shane added in prayer looking inside the house, hoping that Holly Taylor would appear with the baby and tell them that Sarah was fine.

"I can't wait any longer," Shaun said after standing on the porch for several long minutes. He went back into the house not seeing that Shane had pulled Charlotte into his arms and they both were crying. Shaun hurried up the stairs to his bedroom and looked in, "Sarah," he said her name from the doorway and Holly turned with the baby in her arms.

"Lang is working on her," Holly said while coming to him to show him his baby. "It's a boy." She didn't hand the baby to Shaun, he was looking to afraid for his wife and hardly noticed the baby.

"Sarah," Shane called his wife's name not looking at their baby, his voice broke and he knew he was crying, he hadn't known he was crying.

"Don't be afraid, Shaun," Sarah said from the bed and reached a hand out to him which he rushed to take into his own. "I'm going to be fine." Sarah had her eyes closed, her breathing was shallow and she was pale.

"Doctor Lang?" Shaun looked at Lang's face, saw the older man was working hard and lost his breath, his Sarah was in trouble.

"I love you, Shaun," Sarah said and became still and quiet, too still.

"Sarah," Shaun cried her name and looked again at Lang Taylor.

"It's all right Shaun," Lang took a deep breath. "She's asleep and she needs to sleep." Lang met the grass green eyes of Allen Blackburn's nephew and nodded his head. "She needs sleep, son."

"Hold your baby, Shaun," Holly said while bending down to Shaun and handing him his new baby. "It's another boy," she said with pride. "Two Blackburn boys born on the same day."

"And my baby will follow in three months," Charlotte said from the doorway.

"Sarah said we're naming him after our fathers," Shaun said looking in wonder at his little baby.

"Seth Thomas," Shane said with a smile.

"We're going to call him Tommy while he's little," Shaun said looking back at Sarah lost in the covers and pillows. "Sarah said so. And when he's a grown man, we'll call him Thomas."

"A good solid name," Charlotte said and touched the baby's hand. "What did Bethany and Ethan name their baby?"

"Allen Roston Tucker," Holly said the name with a laugh. "Levi wanted to call him Skeeter,"

"Skeeter?" Shane laughed out loud.

"Cecily put a firm stop to that name. And Allen wanted to call him Lucky," Lang joined the conversation. "Someone suggested little Allen but that baby won't be little for long. He's at least thirteen pounds." He reached down and touched Shaun and Sarah's new baby. "I bet this one isn't half the size of Bethany's baby."

"What are they going to call the baby?" Charlotte asked looking at her parents.

"Tucker," Lang said looking at Charlotte. "They're going to call him Tucker."

"I think I like Thomas better," Shaun said looking back at his Sarah lying still on the bed.

"Thomas and Tucker," Holly said going to her husband. "What will you name your baby, Charlotte?" Holly turned to her daughter and saw Charlotte give her a caring gentle look filled with compassion and love, a look that mirrored the look that Lang had given to Holly often.

"A girl will be Amy," she saw her father turn around quickly and their eyes met. "We can't forget your first daughter," she said moving to her father and taking his hand. "Mama told me everything last night, Daddy. The whole story. I know all about Amy and you and Mama. And Daddy, you were always my hero, but learning what you did to save your family, Daddy I love you all the more today. I want to be just like you, as loving and as giving." Lang pulled his daughter into his arms and looked at his wife.

"You told her everything?" he asked and saw his wife nod her head.

"It was time Lang," Holly said looking at Shane. "These two are making a happy and strong marriage, they'll have grandchildren someday and I want our great grandchildren to know how great their Grandfather was."

"You made me great Holly girl." Lang pulled his wife into his arms while holding his daughter and saw Shane smiling at him. "Well what will you name the baby if it's a boy?"

"Lang, I guess," Shane said seriously

"I'm not going to be called big Lang while the baby is called little Lang," Shane heard his father in law say firmly and laughed when Charlotte left her father's arms and went into her husband's embrace.

"We'll call him Taylor," she said and saw her mother nod her head.

"I love it," Holly said looking up at her husband. "I really love that name."

Chapter Two

Rockhaven, Florida
June 1927

Alicia Blackburn saw her grandson running toward the house, he was barefooted and even from a distance she could see his shirt was torn. "Oh no," she moaned and knew Allen, Levi and Cecily heard her. "He's been in another fight," Alicia turned away quickly and looked at her husband. "Allen, where is Ethan?"

"He's at the sawmill, we have a load of lumber going to Tallahassee on the train tomorrow and he and Shane and Shaun are working hard to get it ready to go the train station in an hour and have it loaded. Where's Bethany?" he asked his wife seeing his grandson jump up the steps of their porch.

"She's with Sarah, they're canning some peaches Shane and Charlotte brought when they came back from Fernandina Beach," Alicia bent to examine her grandson's black eye. "Well, that's the worst one yet."

"His parents are going to find out about this with one glance," Cecily said shaking her head hard. "Tucker, why do you keep coming home beaten up son?" she asked him seriously and saw his smile with the deep dimples and his aqua eyes meeting her clear eyes.

"I'm just trying to be like Grandpa Allen," Tucker said to his grandmother Cecily and went to sit on Allen's lap.

"How are you being like me by getting into all these fights, Tucker?" Allen asked looking at his grandson. The boy bore his name of Allen Roston but that wasn't all they shared. The young Tucker looked just like Allen Blackburn, deep dimples, cowlick in his hair, bangs that fell forward, eyes that were slanted down and wide, thick lips. Allen stopped looking at his grandson and then up at his wife, the boy had her aqua eyes and that made him beautiful to Allen.

"Grandma Alicia told me," Tucker swung his legs and jumped down off of his Grandpa Allen's lap going to his Grandpa Levi and climbing on his lap then laying his head on his shoulder.

"Your Grandma Alicia told you what?" Allen asked trying to be stern with the boy; he couldn't keep fighting like he was.

"Yes, young man," Alicia said trying to give the boy a stern look like her husband but he looked so much like Allen that Alicia knew she failed. How could she be stern with this smaller version of the man she adored? She knew she couldn't be. "What did I tell you?"

"I found your headstone in the river, Grandpa," Tucker said innocently and Allen frowned, he had thought the tombstone bearing his name was long ago swallowed up by the river. "I asked Grandma about it cause I read the date and your name and you're not dead." Allen looked to Alicia who slowly nodded her head.

"How does a tombstone with my name on it justify you're constantly getting into fights, Tucker?" Allen leaned forward and looked at his grandson closely on Levi's lap.

"Grandma said when I asked her about that tombstone being yours that you had died for her. That you were a man that would fight for your family and for all women." Allen looked to his wife and half smiled.

"So Grandma Alicia told you that, huh?"

"Yes, she told me since I'm you made all over again that when I fall in love someday I'll know it because I'll be just like you and die for the girl." Tucker said with confidence.

"Good grief," Levi Tucker said looking at Alicia Blackburn who was a lovely shade of red.

"So why were you in a fight today, Tucker?" Cecily asked smiling at Alicia.

"Cause old Johnny Morris told the teacher she was fat," Tucker said in a mad tone.

"Your teacher is fat," Levi Tucker stated to his grandson.

"Don't matter that she is," Tucker asserted. "It hurt her feelings when he said that and she cried. So I took him down in the school yard and beat the stuffin out of him. Just like Grandpa Allen, I'm protecting the women."

"Good grief," Levi Tucker said again not seeing his wife had doubled over in a fit of laughter.

"I won't ever let anyone mess with my family or any girl I like," Tucker said and Allen stared at the boy with pride. Alicia saw the pride on her husband's face.

"I think it was a good reason to stand up for the teacher," Alicia said carefully to Tucker. "And Grandpa Allen would certainly have stood up for the teacher," Alicia looked at her husband and saw him nod his head in agreement. "But Grandpa Allen would never have beaten anyone up; he would have sat them down and had a firm talk with them."

"Fighting again!" Bethany said as she came out onto the porch. "Allen Roston Tucker, what am I going to do with you? For Shame. And you tore your new shirt too."

Tucker jumped down from his Grandpa Levi's lap, "Time to go," the little boy said and took off running from his mother.

"You come back here young man, I'm not finished with you."

As Bethany came past Levi toward the steps intent on catching her son Levi grabbed her arm and stopped her by holding her still.

"We need to all have a talk about that boy," he said looking from Allen to Alicia to his wife and to his daughter in law who looked at him with a frustrated look on her face.

"Ethan and I are at our wits end," Bethany confessed and went to sit on her father's lap. "Daddy, he's just a handful."

"He's certainly has kept us all on our toes," Allen confessed. "But this fighting might not be his own fault. We have to remember he's only seven years old. And I think Alicia might have had a hand in the way he's behaving." Bethany looked at her frail and fragile sweet mother with shocked eyes.

"Mama? Mama wouldn't hurt a bug," Bethany said and her mother nodded her head in total and complete agreement.

"I am tenderhearted," Alicia confessed. "But Tucker just explained why he's fighting. Hear what your father has to say." Bethany turned away from her mother and looked at Allen.

"Why am I cleaning up your mess, Alicia? You're the one that told the boy that story." Alicia shook her head hard.

"It's not a mess," Alicia said gently which was her way of speaking at almost all times. "A while back Tucker found the old headstone with Allen's name on it in the river," Alicia said to Bethany. "He wanted to know why his Grandpa was dead in the river. I had to explain that to him, so I told him that his Grandpa had died for me one time, that his Grandpa protected our family and all the women in the area. And that headstone was a reminder to me of the hero my husband is." Allen put his daughter from his lap and reached for his wife, she climbed onto his lap and snuggled up to him.

"What does that have to do with Tucker fighting everyone?" Bethany asked her parents and Allen pointed to a rocking chair for her to sit down in.

"Apparently some boy at school called their teacher fat," Allen said looking at Bethany sit down in the rocking chair.

"So? His teacher is fat. Who cares? She a fantastic teacher," Bethany said looking at her father.

"Tucker saw the teacher crying, he didn't like his teacher crying so he went after the boy that made her cry and he beat him up." Allen had the look of pride on his face again as did Alicia and Bethany saw that Levi was looking proud as well.

"Your grandson is a bully and constantly fighting and all of you are sitting out here looking pleased as punch. And I am sorry that the teacher cried, that's sad," Bethany stopped speaking when she saw her cousins coming down the road. "Look at Tommy," she said to her family; Tommy was her cousin Shaun's only son and he was a very good boy. Born on the same day as Tucker, the boys could be brothers by appearances. Both looked like her father, the only difference was Tommy had her father's grass green eyes and her son had her and her mother's aqua eyes. "Tommy never gets in trouble; he does very well in school,"

"Our Tucker does very well in school also," Alicia jumped in to defend her grandson who was very intelligent.

"I know he does, Mama but he's not like Tommy."

"Thank God," Allen muttered. "That Tommy is as serious as a Judge." He saw Levi burst into laughter and Cecily cover her mouth as she giggled.

"Daddy," Bethany said severely but smiled at her father knowing he was right. "Well, look at Taylor," she pointed to her cousin Shane's son coming up into the yard. Shane and Charlotte had Taylor only three months after Tucker and Tommy were born. "He's not just smart, he's well mannered and always calm and level headed." Taylor Blackburn was as Bethany described and he looked just like his cousins Tucker and Thomas the thing that set him apart was his eye color which was a deep dark brown like his mother's.

"He's pious," Allen muttered of Taylor. "He'll be the first Minister in our family, mark my words." Bethany nodded her head in agreement. "He's still not perfect Bethany. Look at your brother Shaun Allen," at that moment Bethany saw her ten your old brother running toward the house, he jumped up onto the steps in one giant leap and kissed their mama causing Alicia to smile.

"We're supposed to be talking about Tucker," Levi said and watched Shaun Allen bounce into the house. "That boy never stands still. I get worn out just watching him." Levi looked at Bethany with a serious face. "If Tucker is a bully, I guess he did inherit something from me after all," Levi confessed and looked at Cecily. "In my younger years, well someone made a move against Cecily and I gave him a whole new nose." Bethany looked at Levi with disbelief.

"It's true," Cecily confirmed. "Levi was the nicest boy and man I ever knew," she looked at her husband and took his hand. "But if you did a wrong in his eyes, well I did one time and he made me pay." Levi nodded his head looking at Bethany.

"Excuse my truth, but I was a bastard toward my wife and I've spent years atoning for my actions and behaviors." Levi looked out into the distance and remembered that time long ago and felt sorrow for the way he had behaved.

"He redeemed himself," Cecily said gently squeezing her husband's hand.

"My point is," Levi said looking back at his daughter in law, "I was a bully and I became a good solid man with the guidance of my wife. Tucker's almost eight years old. He's fighting for the honor of a lady; he thinks he's a hero. And in a way, he is." He saw the look Bethany gave to him and held up his hand. "I'm not saying the boy is right. I'm saying his heart is in the right place."

"He's right," Allen said and Alicia nodded her head.

"So what are Ethan and I suppose to do? Just let him run wild fighting everyone that he doesn't agree with? If it's someone calling the teacher fat today, what will he be fighting over tomorrow? We have to come down hard on him."

"Why not just have a talk with him?" Cecily said and saw the look Bethany gave her. "Well, Alicia's talking to him is what got him into the mess in the first place."

"I didn't mean for him to go around beating up everyone in the county," Alicia defended her reasons for telling her grandson what she had.

"I agree Alicia," Cecily said. "I'm not saying you did anything wrong. In fact, I think what you told Tucker was romantic."

"Good grief," Levi said shaking his head. "Allen is the great communicator of our family," Levi turned to Allen Blackburn and spoke firm. "The boy looks like you, he acts like you and he bears your name, deal with him."

Allen held Levi Tucker's eyes and thought how close they had grown in the past years since Levi and Cecily had moved from Cherry Lake to Riverbend. They had built a home for Levi and Cecily right near the edge of the river and their home could be seen from the second floor of Allen's home. Levi was like a brother to him and he respected Levi greatly. "I know you're right. Someone needs to talk to the boy and he does have a misplaced admiration for me," Allen said looking at his wife who still sat on his lap. "I'll talk to him Bethany," Allen turned to his daughter. "I don't know if I can do the boy any good, but I'll talk to him. As soon as I figure out what I should say."

"He's just so wild, Daddy," Bethany moaned.

"Wild isn't a bad thing," Alicia said to her daughter. "And he makes sure our life is never boring."

"There he goes, Allen," Levi pointed to their grandson Tucker running off into the trees at the edge of the river. "Good luck catching him to have that talk."

"I'm not catching him," Allen said in a firm voice. "He'll come home when he's hungry and that won't be much longer." Allen leaned back in the rocking chair and rocked his wife in his arms. "I think one of us," he spoke to Levi, "should go check and make sure the boys have that lumber ready to take to Woodville? If they don't, they'll miss tomorrow morning's train." Levi shook his head and laughed.

"By one of us, I take it you mean me?" Levi looked at Allen comfortably holding his wife on his lap and Alicia wrapped up into her husband.

"Since you don't have anything else to do," Allen smiled to his friend and saw Cecily stand with her husband and take his hand.

"We could take a walk along the river," Cecily said to her husband and Allen saw Levi pull his wife close.

"Or we could go home," Levi bent his head and kissed his wife.

"I'm surrounded by old people kissing and hugging and carrying on," Bethany said in a disgusted voice. "The way you and Mama behave, and Ethan's parents, they're just as bad and don't even get me started on Dr. Taylor and Mrs. Holly, those two are too intimate in public."

Allen and Alicia laughed as they watched their daughter leave the porch and walk toward her own home before Allen stood up with his wife standing next to him. "Where do you think Shaun Allen is?" Allen breathed against his wife's cheek.

"He's in the kitchen getting something to eat and then he'll be down on the river playing with the other boys until dark," Alicia said with certainty.

"Do you want to go upstairs with me and act like we're young again?" He saw his wife's head nod and smiled showing his deep dimples. "I fell in love with you the second I saw you," Allen lifted a curl of his wife's red hair which was now lighter than it had been when he married her. "And I'm as much in love with you now as I was with you then."

"We're not that old, Allen. You just turned fifty one and as hard as you work, you're in good shape. And I'm only forty three. Even when I'm old, with you I'll feel young." Alicia took his hand and started leading him into the house.

"I'm still in good enough shape to carry you up the stairs, Alicia and make love to you all afternoon." Alicia laughed as her husband swung her up into his arms and started up the stairs.

"So Tucker," Allen said walking out into the river, "where did you see my old headstone, son? I need it now." Tucker came running by his Grandfather splashing him with water as he went.

"It's over here Grandpa Allen," he pointed and Allen went to the headstone seeing the green algae that covered most of the beautiful marble stone. He remembered when he had been separated from his family, when he had to appear for all intent and purposes to be dead and buried. The pain he had felt was something he had never known before and he hoped that he never would know that pain again.

"You wanted us Uncle Allen," he turned to see one of his twin nephews standing on the bank of the river nearby and wondered for a moment, was it Shane or was it Shaun? "The water looks inviting; I hope you wanted us to go swimming." Allen saw the twinkle in his nephew's eye and knew this one was Shaun.

"Yes, I hope you have your shorts on," Allen said as he turned back to his grandson who was now standing on the old headstone. "Where's Shane and Ethan?" he asked trying to push on the stone and see how loose it was knowing the thing had been laying here in the river for twenty five years.

"We're here!" Ethan called out and sat on the root of a huge tree to take off his shoes and socks. "You never invite us to go swimming and it's hot as fire out here."

"This is real thoughtful of you, Uncle Allen," Shane said as he too removed his shoes in a hurry and pulled off the rest of his clothes as well.

"Yes, thoughtful is my middle name," Allen said looking at the three men he had watched grow up in the past ten years. Shane and Shaun were Allen's younger brother Seth's oldest sons and Allen felt they were like his own children; he loved these boys and would lay down his life for them knowing they would do the same for him. Shane had married Dr. Langston Taylor and his wife Holly's daughter Charlotte and Shaun had married Sarah Cartledge who they had known all of her life as her parents ran the general store in Rockhaven. And Ethan, Allen looked at his son in law, Ethan was Levi and Cecily Tucker's son and he had married Allen and Alicia's oldest daughter Bethany. All three of these younger men had gone off to the Great War and come home changed, but they were faithful husbands and loving fathers and he was very proud they were his family.

Tucker laughed as his father came running toward him, scooped him up in his arms and jumped out into the deeper water of the river causing them both to go under. Allen loved Ethan like a son, he was a good man and devoted to his wife and his children, if only Tucker were more like his father and less like him, or less like he thought Allen to be.

Allen dove into the river and cooled off with the younger men, the sun was at a noon day high and the crickets were loud down near the water and the current was not as swift today as it usually was. "The water is always cold here, even in the heat." Allen said as he swam past Shaun to get back to the headstone. "The shade of these towering trees makes it stay cool year round in this spot."

"I know you didn't just drag us out here to swim," Shane said as he joined Allen and Shaun, all three were watching Ethan throw Tucker into the air and land in the water as the little boy swam back to his father to be thrown again. "Whatcha need Uncle Allen?"

"Well Shane," Allen said seeing Taylor, Shane's son on the bank chucking off his clothes along with Thomas, Shaun's son, "I think we can take a little while to swim." Allen pointed to the bank and saw Shane start to swim that way grabbing his son Taylor's leg and pulling him under the water.

"Daddy," Taylor cried out right before Shane ducked him under the water again and they both heard Thomas scream as he ran from his father who chased him into the deeper water and the grabbed him up throwing him toward shallow water.

"Can anyone join this party?" Allen laughed when he saw his brother Seth and friend Levi taking off their clothes.

"Heaven help us if any of our ladies decide to take a walk down here today," Allen said with a smile.

"Sarah and I have our own private little swimming place," Shaun said as he threw his son to his father Seth who was now in waist deep water.

"The place you and Sarah swim isn't private," Shane laughed throwing his son into the air and catching him. "It's right out the front door of our home at Twin River. I cannot tell you how many times we've had to put a halt to Taylor going fishing because of you and your wife." Shaun burst out laughing with his brother.

"Don't think Sarah and I don't know you and Charlotte spend time in our private place," Shaun said and saw his brother nod.

"This river is in our blood. It's a part of who we are," Seth said looking to Allen who agreed with him. "Our mama use to say that we were born on the river and grew up in the river."

"I'm wondering why Allen brought us down here," Levi said catching Tucker in his arms to keep the youngster from going out into the deep current of the river.

"I need you younger fellows to help me get this headstone out of the river," Allen said and went up to where the headstone rested.

"What in the world do you want that headstone for?" Seth asked only seconds before he saw their friend Doctor Lang Taylor sitting on the bank and pulling off his clothes. "Hey Doc, what are you doing here?" Seth called out.

"Holly and I came to visit Charlotte and Shane for a bit. Aaron has finished medical school and he's home trying to decide where to open a practice and I just thought we needed a vacation on the river." Allen listened to Lang as he stared at the headstone and then saw Lang swimming out to where he stood. "What do you need the old headstone for, Allen? You aren't planning on using it, are you?" Allen laughed softly and nodded his head.

"Actually, I am going to use it. That's what I wanted to talk to you boys about." Allen sat down on the old headstone and let the water cover him up to his chin while everyone became still around him. "Lang, I'm glad you're here because this involves you as well since you're heavily invested in our operation here." Allen looked at Levi and Seth hoping they didn't think he had lost his mind in what he intended to do. "The nearest bank is in Tallahassee, every time we need money; I have to go to town. Now it's not that far driving my new car, it doesn't take so long to get there, but the fact is, it's a huge inconvenience and the roads are hard to travel on. I want to go back to living like my father did," he looked at Seth and saw his brother nod his head. "He kept a safe in the house with all our money in the safe, we never used a bank. After a lot of thought, I realized us being out here so isolated from the rest of the world, we really needed to make this move."

"If I can interrupt you for a moment here, Allen," Lang said and Allen turned to the doctor. "I have a safe in my home, not all our money is there, but a large part of it is. I've never been too fond of banks."

"I'm glad you understand, Lang. We really need to make this move. But I don't want the safe in our home. I think it needs to be somewhere that no one can find it and only we fellows here know about it." Allen looked at Ethan, Shaun and Shane who put their sons down and told them to go get dressed and run home.

Allen watched his grandson Tucker pulling on his pants and running ahead of his cousins leaving his shirt and shoes on the bank. His nephew Shane's son, Taylor was pulling on his pants and shirt and grabbed up his shoes and ran while Thomas, Shaun's son sat on the bank carefully dressing, buttoning up all the buttons of his shirt before putting his shoes and socks on.

"That boy isn't anything like you Shaun, or me," Seth said watching his serious grandson dress himself. "I swear I've never seen him smile once in his whole life."

"He's unique, Daddy," Shaun said watching his son with pride and joy. Thomas was his and Sarah's only child. She had nearly died giving birth to him and despite their trying; no other child came after Thomas. "Sarah says still waters run deep," Shaun watched Thomas slowly walk away from them and wondered what his son was thinking, he often wondered what his son was thinking.

"He's family," Allen said of Thomas. "He loves his Grandma Mary's rolls, so that alone makes him a Blackburn." Shaun and Seth both laughed knowing everyone loved Mary's yeast rolls. "Anyway boys, back to what I was saying. My plan is to remove our money from the bank and put it in a safe. I think we should bury the safe in the cemetery, not deep, shallow and then put my old headstone over it, that way the money will be safe with just us having the combination."

"You don't think we should keep the safe in the house?" Lang asked with a confused frown.

"I don't think we should. If someone were to find out we had money in a safe out here, we'll as I said before; we're very isolated out here." Allen looked at the faces around him to see if they understood, and saw the younger mens look of confusion so he knew he had to spell this out for them. "Someone might try and rob us and hurt our families to get the money. If we burry it in the cemetery no one will know we have a safe. My goal is to keep us all safe."

"Sounds like a good idea to me," Levi said. "Allen, I have a lot of personal funds in the bank. You know my father left me well off." Levi saw Allen nod his head. "I think I'll buy a safe and bury my money in the same grave."

"As I said," Lang looked at Levi and Allen, "I never did care for banks and I have a safe in my office with my money already there. I know this new age we're living in everyone is going toward banking, but I feel safer knowing where my money is. Holly has some cash in our mattress just for emergencies."

"Most people do have their money in their mattress out here in the country," Allen said before turning to Shane, Shaun and Ethan. "So boys, I need you to get that stone out of the river and up to the cemetery."

"You're kidding?" Shaun said looking at the stone.

"Son," Seth said seriously and the three younger men looked at him. "Allen and I along with Heath brought that stone down here twenty five years ago, we were just about the age you boys are now. I have full confidence you can get it back up to the family graveyard." Seth didn't see Allen looking at him and smiling.

"Boys," he spoke up with a laugh. "What Seth isn't telling you is that twenty five years ago, we had a wagon that we came to the edge of the water with and tossed that stone in from. I'll go up to the house and hitch the wagon up and be back in a," Allen stopped talking when he heard the child's cry and saw every man in the water move to grab their pants as the child screamed again.

"Daddy, help us!" one of the boys cried out and Ethan turned to Allen and Levi who were running behind him toward the noise of the crying.

"That's my Tuck!" Ethan yelled and called out for his son.

"Over here, Dad!" Allen looked and saw his son Shaun Allen on the bank about two hundred yards away, the ten year old was waving his arms so his father would see him.

"It's my Thomas!" Shaun pushed past Allen who had stooped to grab Shaun Allen close and see if his son was hurt.

"Doc!" Seth cried out for Lang who was running slower than the rest of them but saw he was needed, there was blood everywhere.

"Hold still Thomas," Lang said as he bent over the boy.

Shaun stood up and walked to the edge of the river, his hand was over his mouth and he turned around seeing his son bleeding badly and then looked back out at the river. This was his and

Sarah's only child, nothing could happen to his son. He ran his hands through his hair and looked back at his son lying still on the ground in Doctor Taylor's arms. "Oh God," he cried over and over not seeing his Uncle Allen come to him.

Allen knew, in his gut he knew that Shaun was aware his son was hurt badly and that this was Shaun's only child. The emotions playing out on his nephew's face were easy to read and Allen reached for him afraid he was going to fall off the bank into the water. "Uncle Allen," Shaun said with his eyes not looking at his Uncle. "Is he dead?"

"No," Allen said not sure if Thomas was alive or dead. And then Shaun was holding on to his uncle.

"Please, Doctor Taylor, please don't let me lose my son," Shaun cried holding tighter to Allen who had him steady despite the fact he was swaying.

"Shaun," Lang Taylor spoke in his gentle way, "I'm doing all I can, just pray." Allen turned and saw Lang tearing his shirt and asking Levi to tear off the hem of his own shirt before he tied a bandage around Thomas' eyes. "I think Riverbend is closer," Lang lifted Thomas up into his arms, "we should take him there." He started toward the house, the afternoon sun beating down on his head and he knew everyone was following him. "Shaun Allen," Lang called out to Allen's son. "You run faster than these littler ones. I want you to run to Twin River and get my medical bag, tell my wife Holly and my son Aaron to come quick, I need her and Charlotte too."

"Sarah," Shaun said and saw his young cousin look at him and then his Daddy.

"I'll get Sarah without scaring her," Shaun Allen assured his cousin. "I'll tell her Doctor Lang needs her too. Don't worry none Shaun."

Allen Blackburn watched his only son run toward Twin River, it was about a mile down river and he knew as fast as Shaun Allen was, he would be there within ten minutes. He looked and saw Lang cradling Thomas and realized that Thomas, Taylor and Tucker looked so much alike that when Alicia and Bethany saw him coming with the child that wouldn't know which boy it was. "Tucker," Allen motioned for his grandson to come to him and Shaun and looked down at him as they walked to the house. "Skedaddle up to the house and tell Grandma Alicia that Thomas has been hurt and we'll be there soon." He saw Tucker nod his head and then run through the trees toward his house.

Lang stopped and went to his knees with Thomas seeing the boy was bleeding more than he wanted the child to bleed. "Taylor," he said to his grandson, "give me your shirt." Every eye watched as Lang wrapped the shirt around Thomas' head and tied it tight sitting still and applying pressure. "Head wounds always bleed a lot," he said in his calm gentle way to everyone but he was looking up at Shaun. "Let's give this a few minutes to slow the blood down." Lang looked at his grandson and saw Taylor looking at Thomas. "Can you tell us how this happened?" Lang touched his grandson's arm and saw the boy's head nod.

"We were pretending to be river pirates, Granddaddy," Taylor said and started to cry.

"It's all right," Shane bent down to his son and put a supportive arm around his shoulders.

"We all had sticks we were playing with like swards and Thomas tripped and fell and his stick went into his eye and he fell," Taylor leaned into his father, "and his head hit a big old lime rock and it cracked. Tucker, me and Shaun Allen heard it and started screaming for help."

"You did the right thing, Taylor," Lang said with a hint of pride in his voice he hoped the child heard. "I think the bleeding has slowed down, let's get this child to the house." Lang stood and started walking again seeing the house off in the distance.

"Doctor Lang," Ethan reached over for Thomas, "it's a long way to the house and we've already come up river a long way. I'll carry him and you can hold the bandage on his head to control the bleeding." Ethan saw Lang agree and took the boy holding Thomas close and knowing but by the grace of God, this might be his own Tucker.

Alicia caught Tucker by the arms as he ran up to her, his hair in his eyes and his face red. "A bear after you, sweetie?" she teased and saw Cecily coming out of the house and onto the porch.

"Something is wrong with this child," Cecily stated and knelt down before her grandson. "Everything is all right Tucker," she said in a soothing voice but saw the boy shaking his head and then Bethany came to the doorway and her son broke free of his grandmothers and ran to her burying his face into her apron.

Bethany looked down at her son and then up at her mother and mother in law with a questioning glance and quickly saw neither woman knew why Tucker was upset. "Darling baby," Bethany said knowing that Tucker was not a baby but he seemed so frightened it was the right thing to say now to him. "You're all right, I'm here." Bethany gasped when Tucker looked up at her with a tear streaked face and terrified eyes.

"I think Thomas is dead," he cried out before burying his face back into his mother's apron.

"What happened?" Bethany knelt down to her son and demanded to know. "Mama, go find Daddy, something bad has happened."

"Grandpa, Doctor Lang and Uncle Seth are with Thomas, Mama. And Daddy and Uncle Shaun and Uncle Shane." Bethany looked again at her mother who; with Cecily was now turned looking toward the river. "Thomas fell hard Mama and he cracked his head," Tucker said while more tears fell.

"I see them coming," Alicia cried out and Cecily and she rushed down off the porch with Bethany staying still with Tucker.

"I didn't know Lang and Holly were visiting," Cecily said in relief and then heard the car coming down the road and stop by the porch. "Aaron is here as well thank you Jesus," she said to Alicia as they met the men in the yard.

"Dad," Aaron called out to Lang and had his bag and his father's bag in his hands. "How bad is it?" Lang met his son's eyes and shook his head before looking back at Shaun.

"Charlotte," Lang called out to his daughter. "Take our bags to a room upstairs," he looked at Alicia who hurried with Charlotte into the house. "Ethan, give the boy to Aaron. Where's his mother?" Lang looked for Sarah and was relieved she wasn't there.

"Shaun Allen asked Sarah to walk here with him and he took her hand and was walking slow. He's a smart boy," Holly said as she rushed into the house with her husband by her side and her son in front of them.

"Allen, Levi," Lang called out to his friends and didn't look to see if they were listening to him, he knew they were. "Take Shaun for a walk to find Sarah, she's with Shaun Allen coming this way. And have them take their time getting here."

"Daddy," Tucker said as he ran to his father and Ethan bent down and picked the boy up. "Is he dead?" Tucker asked and Ethan hugged him close.

"He's not dead," Ethan said as Bethany came to him and he wrapped her in his arms with Tucker between them.

"Let's all go up to the house and pray," Bethany said as she took Shane's hand and reached down for his son Taylor's hand. The house seemed so still and silent, she thought, she had never known Riverbend to be so silent.

Sarah Blackburn laughed at Shaun Allen as he ran around her while she walked down the road leading to Uncle Allen's house. Her husband had been missing in the Great War and presumed dead and her Uncle Allen and Aunt Alicia were expecting a baby, they named that baby after her husband. And when he returned to them alive everyone started calling the boy Shaun Allen to differentiate him from his cousin. The family was so large that all the little ones called the older ones Aunt and Uncle even if they were cousins and sometimes even just friends of the family were called by the name of Aunt or Uncle. A child saying the name 'Grandpa' around here would see many older men turn their heads. They were close, this Blackburn clan, they never let one another down and they were always open and honest.

"Aunt Sarah," Shaun Allen said in a casual way, "don't be mad at me, but there's something I need to tell you." He saw Sarah stop and look down at him and he went to hug her. "Uncle Shaun is coming and he might be crying because Thomas fell down and got hurt."

Sarah looked up and saw her husband in the distance and then back down at Shaun Allen. "That's why you came for Aaron and Doctor Lang's bag," she said in a voice filled with panic and then she ran past the little boy named for her husband screaming her husband's name and saw he was running to her with Uncle Allen and Levi Tucker behind him.

Shaun ran into Sarah's arms and lifted her off the ground and held her close. "Please, please, tell me my child isn't dead," Sarah sobbed and Shaun told her he was hurt badly.

"Sarah," Allen grabbed her hand as she broke free of Shaun and started to run to Riverbend. "Lang and Aaron are with him, you can't be with him right now; they're trying to help him. Take Shaun's hand and let's all walk together to the house."

"Daddy," Allen turned to see his youngest child standing in the middle of the road looking afraid and he left the others seeing them walking away as he went and knelt down to his son. "Is Thomas going to die?" Lang reached and brushed the tears from his son's face. "He fell hard Daddy, real hard."

"I'm sorry you saw him fall, son. We just need to pray and stand together for the women, they're frightened. Let's go home and comfort them, all right?" Allen saw his son nod his head and slip his small hand into Allen's larger hand and they started down the road. "Look, here comes your sister Jenny," he said gently hoping seeing his sister would help Shaun Allen be strong.

Jenny Blackburn was an old maid, that's how she described herself. Her sister Julie had married Jon Brooks and lived over in Jefferson County now but Jenny had never met anyone she wanted to marry. She was now twenty two years old with no desire to find a husband and settle down. In fact she had talked to her father about finding a college for girls for her to attend and hoped that soon she could go away and just disappear from this perfect family she was a part of. They didn't know this, but she was imperfect and just didn't fit in.

Allen saw Jenny stop and speak with Shaun and Sarah and Levi before she skipped on to him and her brother. "Any word on the boy?" Allen asked his daughter as she took hold of his free hand and started walking.

"Doctor Lang hasn't come out of the room, but his son did. I don't know his name but he said the boy was in serious condition and it would be at least until tomorrow before we know if he'll get better." Jenny said in a concerned voice.

"Did you tell them that?" Allen motioned ahead of them and saw Jenny shaking her head.

"No, I just told them that Thomas was in a room upstairs and the doctor hadn't come out with any news yet." Jenny looked at her brother Shaun Allen and saw him crying. "What's wrong?" she let go of her father's hand and walked to her brother and he hugged her tight. "Did you see Thomas fall and get hurt?" she asked and felt him nodding his head. "Tucker and Taylor are all broken up too, Daddy," Jenny said to her father. "Ethan and Bethany have them on the porch rocking them. Shaun Allen, you run to Bethany and let her cuddle you too honey. She'll make you feel better. She always does." Jenny saw her brother nod his head and run fast down the road to his older sister Bethany.

"Good thinking, Jenny," Allen took his daughter's hand back into his own. "Bethany and Shaun Allen are close, she mamas him."

"Daddy, I didn't want to say this in front of Shaun Allen, and I didn't tell them," she pointed up the road to the others, "but Doctor Lang's son told me that Thomas probably won't live through the night."

"Dear Lord," Allen prayed and lowered his head. "And he's Shaun and Sarah's only child."

"It's really sad, Daddy." Jenny felt her father pull her close. "Poor little Thomas, he was always so serious and never smiled or laughed or anything." Allen nodded his head thinking of the little boy that he secretly referred to as 'the judge' and prayed with all his heart the boy would pull through this.

Chapter Three

"Dad," Aaron said his father's name and saw Lang turn to him. "I don't like dealing with emotional parents." Lang nodded his head and put his hand on his son's shoulder. Aaron had turned into a fine man and a good doctor, but he felt things too deeply and sometimes people didn't think he felt at all because he would pull into himself instead of sharing how he felt. Lang knew that he showed too many emotions as did Charlotte, but Aaron was like Holly and held things inside keeping his own counsel.

"Just be honest, be gentle and it's all right to feel like crying with them, I've done so with grieving parents in the past." He stood from the side of the bed and left Charlotte to sit with Thomas. "We'll go down and face the family together." He couldn't help seeing the relief on his son's face.

"Daddy," Charlotte's speaking to him stopped Lang at the bedroom doorway. "Can you ask Mama to come sit with Thomas so I can see Taylor and Shane?"

"Certainly sweetie, I should have thought to do that on my own," Lang replied before going out the door seeing Charlotte's sorrow filled eyes as he went. He hadn't thought of her, she lived with Shaun and Sarah in that big house at Twin River. His daughter took care of Thomas as though he were one of her own. He should have had Holly with the boy from the start. "Aaron, I'm going to

let you handle the telling of this, I'll be here to support you, but you can do this son, and these people are our family."

Allen stood in the doorway of the drawing room of his home and looked out at his family gathered together. Seth, his brother stood with Mary and their three sons, Shane, Michael, and Shaun who was clinging to Sarah and Sarah to Shaun. They were also surrounded by their young grandchildren. Allen's eyes met his wife's eyes from across the room and she gave him a worried look as she held Tucker on her lap and Bethany's smallest child, a little girl they named Ali. Bethany sat with Ethan and their heads were together, Allen could see they were talking in whispers and felt glad that they had found one another and had been happy all these years. Allen then looked at his sister Emily and her husband Heath, their daughter Heather wasn't in the room and Allen was relieved. Heather was not a happy presence at the best of times; she was moody and often said things that just didn't need to be said. Allen felt someone touch his arm and turned to find Levi and Cecily standing in the hall.

"There's food on the table for anyone that wants to eat," Cecily said in a tender way and Allen nodded knowing no one would eat right now.

"Allen," he heard his name said from the stairwell and saw Lang and Aaron coming toward him, his wife Holly peeked out from the dining room. "Holly, can you go upstairs and give Charlotte a break, please?" Lang spoke to his wife before drawing Allen near to him and Aaron and away from the room full of family. "Aaron is going to talk to the family," Lang said and turned to his son and saw Aaron take a deep breath before they entered the drawing room.

"Doc," Seth was the first one to see Lang enter the room with Aaron beside him and Allen behind him, Levi and Cecily had stayed in the hall, both watching and listening and praying the little boy would be better.

"Thomas?" Sarah left her husband's arms and came to stand in front of Lang who gently touched her arm.

"I'll let my son explain, Sarah," he spoke gently to Sarah as he regarded as very nearly as a daughter. "Aaron is fresh out of school and knows things I don't know."

"I doubt that," Aaron said in a low voice before looking at Sarah. "He's lost his right eye, Sarah," Aaron saw Shaun had come to his wife and was listening to what he was saying and when he looked up and out into the room, he saw everyone was straining to hear what he was saying. This wasn't just parents he was talking too, this was a family. "I was saying," Aaron raised his voice, "Thomas has lost his right eye. He's suffered a blow to his head and hasn't regained consciousness; we know he has a concussion. Right now, all we can do is wait."

"Will he die?" Sarah pleaded to know in a broken voice as she bowed her head.

Aaron looked back at his father for help and his father place a firm hand on his shoulder. "We don't know, Sarah. But he might." Aaron wanted to cry with Sarah as she turned into her husband's arms and he held her close.

"Allen," Levi spoke to him and Allen turned around. "Let Cecily and I take all the children home with us for the night, that way you adults can comfort one another without worrying over the children seeing and hearing what's happening." Allen looked up and saw Taylor in his father's arms sobbing hysterically and Tucker in a corner facing the wall. All of the children had heard the grim reality for their playmate and cousin Thomas and it was overwhelming. His Shaun Allen was lying on the stairs behind him with his face in his hands sobbing uncontrollably.

"I need all the little ones to come here," Allen spoke loud and except for the babies, all the children came to him. "We're going to hold hands," Allen said gently yet firmly and took the hand of his son and the hand of Charlotte and Shane's little three year old daughter Cora. "Bow your heads," he said and watched every child do as he said as well as the adults in the room. "Dear Father in Heaven, thank you for hearing our prayer. Father, please take care of our Thomas, guard him and guide him, protect him and keep him safe. In Christ's holy and loving name we pray. Amen." Allen looked up at the children and patted several heads. "Now, we've done all we can for Thomas and if you get afraid for him tonight, I want you all to bow your heads and pray, hold hands like we just did here. Now, you're going to a sleep over with the Tuckers and you're going to be good for them and have fun because that's what Thomas would want and what we want. Can you do that?" Allen saw all the heads nod except for his Shaun Allen who was shaking his head.

"Daddy, I can't go." Shaun Allen was holding on to his father's arm. "I can't go."

"Cecily, Levi," Allen moved so they could get all the children out the door and into their car while Allen picked up his son in his arms and went to the dining room not seeing Alicia coming in behind him. Once all the children were safely out of the house, Allen cringed as he heard Sarah scream and her sobs fill the downstairs as well as Shaun's.

"I did it!" Shaun Allen screamed and Allen bent down to his son who was now hysterical and crying louder than Sarah and Shaun in the other room.

"You did what?" Allen pulled his son onto his lap and held him close with Alicia kneeling in front of the chair they were sitting in. "Calm down Shaun Allen, it's going to be all right."

"I made Thomas play river pirate, Daddy. He didn't want too. He wanted to lie in the grass and look at the clouds. It was going to be Tucker and Taylor battling me and Thomas, I gave him a stick and told him to stop being a baby and to play. He didn't want too but he did because I called him a baby." Shaun hid his face in his father's shirt and continued to cry while Allen looked at Alicia.

"It wasn't just Shaun Allen that made him play, Grandpa," Tucker stood in the dining room doorway. "I won't let you take all the blame Shaun Allen," Tucker, not yet eight years old spoke like a grown man. "I called Thomas a baby too."

Levi came into the room and put his hands on Tucker's shoulders. "This little man got away from me," he said to Allen and Alicia.

"Come here Tucker," Allen said in a low calm voice and Levi let go of their grandson's shoulders and Tucker went to his Grandfather and climbed onto his lap. "You and Shaun Allen weren't very nice to call Thomas a baby, and you'll tell him you're sorry when he wakes up. Accidents happen, boys. You didn't push Thomas or cause him to fall, he tripped and fell. No more crying. God will take care of Thomas." He put both boys off of his lap and gently pushed them to Levi who looked at him and nodded, the nod told Allen he handled this situation well.

"They're suffering from what they did," Alicia said as she watched her son and grandson leave the room. "That tells me they'll learn from this and be kinder boys." Allen nodded his head and pulled Alicia onto his lap.

"I'm sorry I called Thomas a judge the way I did," Allen whispered to his wife and she leaned into him. "None of us is perfect, no not one."

Jenny Blackburn looked out at the star filled sky and worried about her brother and nephew. They had both seen Thomas fall and get hurt, and now she knew that they both had made him play a game he didn't want to play and because they did, Thomas got hurt. Poor little boys, they were just being boys, she thought as she looked back into the dining room at her parents. Her father held her mother on his lap and her mother was hugging him tight. They were the perfect couple, just like all the couples in this family, Jenny thought. The only one that wasn't happy with a spouse was her cousin Heather, and Heather wasn't happy with anyone.

Jenny jumped down from the porch rail and went out into the dark yard thinking she didn't want to be like Heather and felt herself wanting to cry. Maybe she wanted to cry for Thomas, or for herself for being an old maid, or maybe for Shaun Allen and Tucker for having called Thomas a baby. She wasn't sure why she wanted to cry, only that she really needed to cry.

She wasn't ugly, Jenny thought as she walked beyond the house and near the trail that led to the river. She just looked different than her sisters. She was taller and slimmer than her sisters, her hair wasn't dark red but more the color of carrots and she had freckles on her nose and cheeks and her Daddy's grass green eyes. She didn't have the dainty, delicate, fragile look of her mother, her father said she looked like a fairy and all she needed was wings.

Jenny stopped and stood still listening to the noise that was nearby in the darkness she stood in. A chill came over her and she stepped back afraid, someone was out here with her, she was not alone and that terrified her. Daddy and Mama were right there, in the dining room, she thought and turned to see them still holding one another in the light that spilled out the door which now seemed a million miles away. The clouds that had covered the moon for a few moments suddenly moved away and Jenny started to run for the porch with her heart in her throat, she was too afraid to scream.

Arms came around her and a hand covered her mouth just as she was going to scream her head off and she was lifted off the ground. "Don't scream, you'll frighten everyone in the house," a male voice said near her ear and she started kicking for all she was worth causing her and the person that held her to fall to the ground. "Please, I mean you no harm, I just don't want anyone to know I'm out here," the man said as he held Jenny down on the ground with his hand still over her mouth. Jenny looked up into dark brown eyes and the young man she knew was Doctor Lang's son.

"You," Jenny said in shocked surprise. "What are you doing?" she hissed when Aaron moved his hand from her mouth. "Get off of me."

As though he just now realized he was laying on top of her, Aaron moved quickly away from Jenny and stood up waiting a full minute before reaching down to help her up. "I am sorry. I saw you in the dark and I didn't want to bother you or have you bother me so I was being quiet and still. Then I realized you had sensed me there and were afraid. I just wanted you not to bother everyone in the house." Aaron reached down and started to brush the dirt and dust off of Jenny's dress, his hand coming close to her breast and yet unaware that what he was doing was very incorrect.

The slap nearly knocked him down as Jenny went up the porch steps looking down at Aaron. "Don't you dare touch me like that again!" she screamed out and ran into the dining room past her parents not seeing her father had stood dropping her mother to the floor from his lap and then he hurried out the door to see Aaron holding his left side of his face.

"Aaron?" Allen said coming out onto the porch and seeing his confusion.

"She had dust on her dress, I was just trying to brush it off, sir." Allen looked down at the younger man believing him completely, he didn't look the type to lie.

"What happened?" Charlotte asked running out onto the porch.

"Oh Charlie," she heard her brother moan. "I just wanted to be alone to think about little Thomas and that girl walked up in the dark on me and I'm afraid I frightened her. I'm so dumb around girls, you know I am and now that one hates me and thinks badly of me."

"What girl?" Charlotte asked Allen and Alicia while looking at her brother, her beautiful awkward brother.

"He's talking about our Jenny," Alicia answered Charlotte who nodded her head.

"You can tell her you're sorry in the morning, Aaron. Jenny's a sweet soul, she'll forgive you." Charlotte watched her brother come up the steps of the porch and give her a miserable look.

"I wanted to find a safe place to be alone and cry over the little boy," he said in a low tone unaware that Allen heard him clearly. "I don't know if I can be a good doctor Charlie, I see things like this and I want to fall apart in sorrow. I'm not like Dad."

"You're too much like Daddy," Charlotte said softly. "I'm glad you feel things deeply, that you care so much. By the way, if you want to be alone, you'll have to wait until you get home. This place is always busy. But you'll be loved here Aaron. Let's go back up to Thomas and relieve Mama and Daddy." Charlotte took her brother's hand and pulled him into the house.

"There goes a good man," Allen said pulling his Alicia into his arms.

"You dropped me on the floor," Alicia said seriously and saw Allen frown down at her before she leaned into him. "It's all right," she hugged him close and he held her tight.

"It's going to be a long night," Allen breathed in the damp night air as he stared out into the darkness hearing the river flow off in the distance. "I don't think anyone will be sleeping in this house."

Lang escorted Shaun and Sarah up to their son and watched Sarah crawl into the bed on one side and Shaun onto the other side and each took a hold of one of his hands. There wasn't anything anyone could do now but wait, wait and see if Thomas would wake up and heal. Lang touched Holly's shoulder and they left the room going out onto the upstairs porch leaving the parents alone with their son. "Aaron," Lang saw his son by the porch rail. "Are you all right?" Aaron turned to his parents and saw his mother come and hug him.

Lang realized in that moment that the son he thought was like his wife; the son that kept everything inside as his mother did was more like him than he had known. Aaron felt far too much. "I don't think I can be a good doctor, Dad," Aaron confessed. "I see someone in pain and I hurt physically. Facing the fact that I'm going to lose a patient is agony, and then losing someone, it takes me to my knees dad."

"Aaron, you make me so proud that you have this compassion and empathy. I went through something similar early in my career." Lang moved to his son, his wife was still hugging him on one side and he put his arm around him on the other side and smiled at Holly. "Be just who you are, you will make a great doctor someday. Don't change anything about yourself, and don't ignore your feelings. If you need to cry over a loss; then cry over the loss."

"I was out in the dark tonight wanting to cry for our little Thomas in there," Aaron confessed. "And that girl, the freckled face girl walked up on me and I'm afraid I insulted her." He closed his eyes and shook his head. "I'm twenty seven years old and I still have no clue how to behave around a girl." Holly hugged her son close and laughed softly.

"He gets that from me," she said to Lang. "I'm the awkward one."

Jenny Blackburn sat small and still on the upstairs porch outside of her bedroom door hearing every word said by the Taylor family. When Aaron had called her the freckled face girl she had burned inside that he saw her that way. There was so much more to her than her freckles. She thought of him touching her as he brushed the dirt from her dress, dirt that was only there because he had tackled her to the ground. Awkward, yes, he certainly was she thought narrowing her eyes to see him in the dark. He looked like his father, dark hair and large round eyes with a face more pretty than handsome like her father. She couldn't find a flaw with him to even think of and kept thinking over and over in her mind that she was only a freckled faced girl and the more she thought this, the more upset and angry she became.

Come Tame Someone Like Me

"Doctor Lang," Jenny jumped up when she heard Sarah cry out and saw the Taylor family move into the room little Thomas was in. Carefully she moved down the porch and peeked into the room through the door and saw Thomas moving on the bed.

"I can't see Daddy," she heard Thomas saying to Shaun and heard Shaun telling him to be still and let the doctor look him over.

Aaron Taylor removed the bandages over Thomas's eye and head and saw the stitches he had put into the young boys forehead. "Can you see me now?" he asked gently sounding just like his father.

"Uncle Aaron," Thomas said with a half smile, "I didn't know you were here."

"It's good to see you little buddy," Aaron said and pulled back from the bed. "Dad, can we talk outside?" Aaron stood with his father and saw Shaun coming with them onto the porch neither seeing Jenny run down the porch to her bedroom doorway.

"Thomas looks real good for a boy that took a fall like he did this afternoon," Aaron said to Shaun and his father. "And he's alert and aware of us all." Aaron turned to Shaun who he saw was looking much better than he had been. "We're going to have to keep him awake for the night, his one eye he can see out of I can tell he has a concussion. We'll take turns sitting up with him, can he play checkers?" Shaun nodded his head.

"I saw his eye when you took the bandage off," Shaun said in a weak voice. "The eye?"

"It's destroyed Shaun," Aaron said trying to keep his voice from betraying his intense sorrow. "We'll get him a patch to wear to keep it covered. It'll heal some and we'll, time will tell us what we need to know. He's a strong boy, amazing really considering the bump on his head." Aaron saw Shaun nod his head and go back into the room to his wife and son.

"You handled that very well," Lang said to his son and patted his back. "You'll be fine, Aaron, I promise."

"I need a few minutes alone out here," Aaron said to his father and walked to the far end of the porch looking out at the moon high in the sky and all the stars shining down upon the earth. He leaned his head in his hands and breathed in the night time river air.

"There's more to me than my freckles," he heard her voice, the girl that he had frightened outside earlier.

"Freckles," Aaron said looking at Jenny and not seeing, due to the lack of light, that she was upset with him.

She slapped him hard again and Aaron grabbed his cheek completely unaware of what he had said or done to deserve this slap, unless she were still mad at him from before. With no warning, with no thought as to what he was about to do and taking himself by complete surprise as much as her, Aaron reached out to Jenny and pulled her into his arms and kissed her. He hadn't even realized he had wanted to kiss her ever since he first saw her until he was kissing her. At first she was pushing on him, but he held on tight to her and then she was moaning into his mouth and melting into his arms and her arms were around him pulling him close. Aaron couldn't stop what he was doing, he never knew that kissing someone like this could feel so good and he didn't know that a kiss could go on and on as this one was. His tongue darted in and out of her mouth and met her tongue and he heard her cry out and moan all the way into the back of his throat. She wasn't pulling away from him, she was kissing him back and he wanted to cry out in the joy her kissing him back was giving him.

"Don't stop," she begged him when he moved his lips down her neck and then back up to her cheek and around her ear. "There's more to me than my freckles," she cried when circled her ear with his tongue and breathed his hot breath down her neck.

"I think your freckles are the most beautiful freckles I've ever seen in my life and I don't know how I've kept from kissing you for as long as I have. Every time I come here with my parents and see you," his mouth covered her mouth again and she moaned and he bent her in his arms to better hold her, to deepen the kiss. "I want to hold you and kiss you and I stop myself because I'm not nearly good enough for you."

"What?" Jenny pulled away from Aaron and tried to look into his eyes but it was too dark. "You're too good for me," she said seriously.

"I'm awkward and clumsy and I never know the right thing to say," Aaron touched her cheek and her nose and put his forehead against hers. "You're so graceful and beautiful, you always know what to say."

"Do you really like my freckles?" she asked Aaron and saw him nod his head. "Kiss me more, please," she begged him in a pleading tone. And he did.

The breakfast table was overflowing with food and family as the sun came up the next morning. The children's table in the kitchen was noisy despite the fact that Taylor, Tucker and Shaun Allen sat still and quiet unaware that Allen Blackburn was watching the boys. He had already spoken with Aaron and Lang and knew that Thomas had a rough night with a lot of pain and crying and was still struggling.

"We have a situation," Allen spoke to Lang and Aaron seeing that Aaron seemed distracted and wasn't listening to him. "The other boys, Taylor, Tucker and my Shaun Allen, they're feeling pretty badly. Apparently Tucker and Shaun Allen told Thomas he was a baby for not playing pirates and he only played because they picked on him." Allen saw Lang nodding his head while Aaron seem to be looking for someone or something.

"So the boys need to see Thomas to let him know they're sorry because they're blaming themselves for his accident," Lang said softly understanding the situation completely as Allen knew he would. "So Aaron, do you think Thomas is up to company this morning?" Lang asked his son who turned with a confused look on his face.

"What?" I'm sorry Dad, I wasn't listening." Lang gave him a puzzled frown and saw his son didn't even notice the look.

"Can you go see if Thomas is up for the other boys to come in and visit him?" Lang saw Aaron was again back to looking for something and not listening and his frown deepened.

"I can't Dad," Aaron said in a voice that clearly let his father know he was completely distracted and his patient was not on his mind. "I'll be back." Lang and Allen watched him wander off apparently looking for something.

"What in the world has his undivided attention?" Allen asked as they followed Aaron out onto the porch and saw him running across the yard. "Oh," Allen said seeing Jenny going toward the river and Aaron running after her.

"Another one of my children in love with a Blackburn," Lang said watching his son chase after Jenny Blackburn. "Charlotte married to Shane," Lang muttered, "and now Hannah engaged to Michael,"

"What?" Allen interrupted Lang. "My brother Seth's son Michael is engaged to your daughter Hannah? I didn't know." Lang nodded his head and turned back to Allen seeing his son had almost caught up with Jenny.

"I have three children," Lang said with a laugh. "My two daughters are married to two of your brother's sons and now it looks like my only son is sweet on your youngest daughter."

"Well, Lang," Allen said in a serious voice, "If I had been able to choose a man to be my brother, you would have been the first man I chose behind Seth." Allen turned to see Aaron grab Jenny's arm and spin her around and saw his Jenny slap Aaron's face. "Oh dear," he laughed knowing Lang had seen the incident between their children.

"If he's anything like me," Lang laughed as he saw Aaron pull Jenny into his arms, "that slap will just make him love her more."

"What are we talking about?" Holly Taylor came up to her husband and Allen taking her husband's hand.

"I was just going to tell Allen that I fell in love with you at first sight, but I didn't fall deeply in love with you until you slapped me." Holly's mouth fell open and she looked from Allen to Lang who was laughing and hugging her. "Jenny Blackburn just slapped our Aaron." Lang pointed toward the river and Holly saw Aaron holding on to Jenny's arm one second and then he was kissing her the next.

"Oh, I see," Holly said and leaned over the rail watching her only son lost in a kiss. "He kisses as well as his father," she said in a serious tone and Lang saw Allen backing away as he moved closer to his wife.

"Let's see if I'm still that good," Lang said and turned his wife around in his arms knowing Allen was watching them from the doorway and not minding. He and Holly had a deep love for one another, they were only content and whole and happy when they were together and he smiled in the kiss he gave his wife, she was everything that mattered to him and he knew, he was everything that mattered to her.

Aaron ran after Jenny, he had seen her at breakfast and she had glanced at him and then away from him quickly as though she didn't even know him. When he had tried to approach her, she had gone to her mother and Aunt and was talking, completely ignoring him. He didn't know what he had done to make her reject him, last night on the upstairs porch she had kissed him as long and as hard as he had kissed her. He had felt right with her in his arms and he knew, he didn't want to leave here because he wanted to be with her. He had lain awake most of the night thinking that he would become a country doctor, never be rich and yet be contented to live here and be with her and a part of this loving family for the rest of his life.

He had seen her leave the house and walk toward the river, she had thought she had slipped out unnoticed but he had been watching her even while speaking with Allen and his father. And he knew, nothing mattered to him at this moment but to be with her, he had to be with her. He had left the porch unaware of what his father and Allen Blackburn were discussing and chased after Jenny who had a good head start on him, as he was taller than she was, he caught up to her pretty quickly and grabbed a hold of her arm. "Freckles," he said her nickname as he held on to her and she spun around and slapped him in the face again. "Are you going to make a habit of hitting me?" he asked feeling his cheek sting and burn from what her hand had done.

"If you keep touching me," Jenny said in a breathless whisper shocked that she had slapped Aaron again. He was so handsome and tall and then he was pulling her close and she was only an inch away.

"I have to keep touching you," he breathed before his mouth came over hers and then she was moaning and molding herself into him. "Forgive me Jenny, I know I just discovered you but I want only to be with you. Please, don't push me away."

"I was afraid you would think ill of me for my forward behavior last night," she cried and he tilted her chin up to look into his eyes.

"Be yourself, don't change one thing. We're alike, you and I." And Jenny knew that was true.

"I don't always fit in, I'm awkward and I'm uncertain all the time," she lay her head on his chest and wrapped her arms around him.

"That's me," Aaron said seriously. "And we feel too much."

"Sensitive," Jenny said only seconds before he kissed her again and she knew she finally had found her place in the world, she no longer wanted to leave home and fade away from the perfect family. She now fit into her family, she had a lover too.

"Lang just came in and said we could take the boys up to see Thomas," Alicia said to Allen as he stood looking out of his study window. "Allen," she said his name and saw him point out the window.

"Oh thank goodness," Alicia sighed as she saw her youngest daughter walking hand in hand with Aaron Taylor. "I knew this morning she was just miserable." Allen turned and looked at his wife wondering what she knew that he didn't. "I saw them kissing last night upstairs," Alicia laughed at the look on her husband's face. "She was slapping him in the yard one minute and kissing him the next. I knew there was something brewing between them. They're made for one another you know." Allen shook his head and looked back at his daughter. "She's insecure and uncertain and Allen, she's always felt she lived in Bethany and Julie's shadow, Jenny never had her own place. And him," she nodded to Aaron, "he's very sensitive and he's like a fish out of water, if you know what I mean. But look at him now." Alicia smiled looking at the young couple as they stopped in the yard and kissed. "That fish has found his pond in our daughter and my goodness, does he know how to kiss."

Allen laughed and pulled Alicia into his arms. "Reminds me of Lang and Holly kissing all the time, those two are the perfect couple."

"Like us," Alicia turned into her husband's arms. "The boys need to see Thomas," she breathed as he bent to kiss her.

"They can wait another five minutes." Allen pulled Alicia close and knew that he would never be too old to kiss his Alicia.

Tucker lead the way into Thomas' room followed by his cousin Taylor and his Uncle Shaun Allen. He saw Doctor Lang motion for them to come in and onto the bed gently to sit next to Thomas and then the doctor backed up and stood with Tucker's Grandfather.

Tucker could see the two older men were talking in low voices, probably about Thomas.

Tucker looked up and saw his cousins Sarah and Shaun on the porch outside holding on to one another and he was aware enough to see that they were both tired. If he had been older, he thought, he would have told them to go take a nap, but he couldn't boss them around yet because he was still a child. He then looked to his cousin Thomas and saw the little boy he shared the same birthday with laying still and lost in pillows. "Do you hurt bad, Thomas?" Tucker asked and saw his cousin look at him with his one good eye.

"Yes," Thomas spoke trying not to cry. "Don't tell Mama and Daddy, they're both real worried."

"I can see," Tucker said and saw Taylor and Shaun Allen looking at Thomas' parents.

"I'm sorry," Shaun Allen started to cry despite the fact that he had promised his father he wouldn't cry in front of Thomas.

"Why are you sorry?" Thomas looked at his older cousin that led them in their play and in their adventures. "I fell down, that's all."

"You didn't want to play pirate," Shaun Allen said. "And Tucker and I called you a baby and you played." Thomas lay in the bed and frowned at his cousin.

"I didn't want to play pirate," Thomas confirmed. "I wanted to play as the four musketeers. Remember, you called me a baby because pirates are more fun than boring old musketeers."

"I wouldn't mind playing musketeers," Taylor said sitting up taller on the bed.

Lang smiled at Allen when he saw his friend sigh in relief; the boys were going to be all right. "I still need them to get that headstone in the cemetery and everyone is after me to talk to Tucker about why he gets into all these fights with other children," Allen said right before Shaun and Sarah called for him to come out onto the porch and Lang as well.

"Jenny," Shaun said with a smile and Allen went to the porch rail to look down at his daughter and Lang's son.

"Good grief, they've been out there kissing by that river all morning," Allen said in frustration. "This won't be a long engagement. Alicia caught them kissing last night too." He ran his hand through his hair and turned to Lang. "So do you think Aaron will take her away from here?"

"I don't know," Lang said looking out at his son and Allen's daughter, they were still kissing. "At this rate I don't think they're ever going to move from right where they are."

"At least they're not in the river," Shaun laughed and hugged his wife who blushed.

"One of us needs to go down and talk to them, tell them to cool their heels." Allen looked at Lang who was shaking his head.

"Not me," Lang held up his hands and went back into the bedroom with the children.

"Hey, I'm not getting involved," Shaun said as he and Sarah looked back to where Jenny and Aaron were.

"I'll let Alicia handle them," Allen muttered before turning to Shaun. "How about we all get together and go get that headstone? Thomas is a Blackburn through and through, he'll be up and playing with the other boys in days." Shaun nodded his head with a smile, yesterday had seemed bleak for his son and now the boy was talking with his cousins.

"Shane, Ethan and I can get the stone out of the river, Uncle Allen. You're getting kind of old now, you and Doctor Lang and Mr. Levi, find a rocking chair on the porch to rest in." Allen laughed as he popped Shaun on the butt as the younger man ran out of the room laughing.

"Hey Lang," Allen called out as he walked past Sarah and gave her a wink. "Shaun thinks we're too old to pull that headstone out of the river. Let's go get Levi and show those young pups how it's done." Lang fell in beside him.

"What about Aaron and Jenny?" Lang asked as Allen found Levi and told him what Shaun said, Levi had a twinkle in his eyes and was ready to pull the stone out of the river.

"I'll deal with Aaron," Allen smiled and nudged Lang. "We need to get a move on boys."

Chapter Four

"Grandpa," Tucker sat in the front of the boat holding his fishing pole and watching his cork bob up and down in the water. "Why didn't you bring Shaun Allen with us today?" he asked without looking back at Allen who was sitting in the back of the boat.

"I wanted to spend the morning with you," Allen said looking at the back of his grandson's head, the sun just rising up and the clouds were pink and gold in the distance. He was proud of the boy who wasn't quite yet eight years old. Tucker was different, he had a wild side to him and he was gentle and caring as well, being with Tucker you never knew what to expect from him. "I wanted to talk with you about your fighting," Allen said gently and saw Tucker turn around and face him."

"I only hit Sammy Messer this past week," Tucker started to defend himself. "And I wouldn't have had to hit him had he not pinched Eliza." Allen took a deep breath and leaned back in the boat feeling all of his fifty one years of age.

"Tuck, if you keep hitting people for doing something you don't like, you're going to wind up in big trouble son. Now I'm serious and so is your Mama and Daddy. You can't keep hitting people. You must stop now. If you see something happening and you don't like what you see, then say so, speak up. But we just don't hit son."

Allen held Tucker's eyes and saw the defiant look in his eyes. "You could have stood up for Eliza when Sammy pinched her," Allen tried to reason with the boy. "You could have turned to Sammy and told him it's wrong to pinch anyone, which it is, and that you were going to tell the teacher what he was doing and she would speak to his father." Allen saw Tucker's facial expression change, the boy was starting to understand; Allen was making sense to him.

"But Grandpa," Tucker said looking at Allen's hands. "We all know that all the holes in the front hall wall are from you wanting to punch someone in the face."

"Who told you that?" Allen felt his face heat up with the truth. He had hit that front hallway wall a lot and those marks were from him. He took his frustration out on a wall or door and he sat here now remembering a night long ago that he married Alicia and saw what had been done to her and punched a hole in his Aunt Julia's bedroom door.

"Daddy told me, and Mama told me and Shaun Allen told me, and Uncle Seth," Tucker would have continued only Allen held up a hand and stopped him, the child had made his point.

"Hitting a wall and hitting a person are two different things," Allen asserted to his little grandchild. "And that fish on your line is going to pull your pole in son," he said gently and saw Tucker pull in the fish. "You need to find a tree that's all your own Tuck," Allen said as he pulled the fish off the hook and put it in the bottom of the boat. "Good catch," he said of the fish and saw Tucker put a worm on his hook and drop it back in the water.

"What am I going to do with my own tree, Grandpa?" Tucker lay back in the boat like Allen and watched his line.

"When you feel like punching someone, go punch the tree. Like I have my hallway wall." He saw Tucker's head nod and was so thankful for the boy. Thankful that Ethan Tucker, Levi and Cecily's son had married his beautiful daughter Bethany and that they had given him this child that was so like himself. He felt his legacy would continue, Tucker would carry on.

"I'll find my own tree," Tucker said firmly. "And I won't hit anyone anymore, Grandpa. At least I'll try not to." Allen smiled and ruffled his grandson's hair.

"I need you to do me a favor," Tucker turned and looked at Allen with the aqua eyes of Alicia Blackburn. "Shaun Allen, I want you to promise me you'll always watch out for him, Tuck. He's my only son and I want him to grow to be an old man like me. You're strong and sturdy. Watch out for him for me. I love him so much. Like I love you, boy." He saw Tucker smile and nod his head as he pulled in another fish.

"I love you too, Grandpa. I'm going to remember this day forever, fishing with you and talking. You're my best friend."

"You're my best friend too, Tuck. And it's time we got these fish up to the house; maybe Grandma will fry them up for our breakfast." Allen rowed to the shore with Tucker splashing in the water with his hand and Allen knew he would cherish this memory forever as well.

Tucker helped his Grandfather pull his boat onto the bank of the river and tie it to a tree thinking Grandpa hadn't seen what he had seen. He smiled and skipped ahead toward the house hoping Allen would follow him. "Get married," Allen said in a firm voice as he passed the tree causing Jenny to pull away from Aaron and gasp. "Too late to be shocked, daughter of mine," Allen gave the couple a serious look. "This has been going on for days, people are beginning to talk. The Fourth of July picnic is next week and everyone will be out here visiting, a good time for a wedding."

"Then I have your permission to marry Jenny?" Aaron ran alongside Allen pulling Jenny behind him by the hand.

Allen stopped and stood still a long moment before turning to face Aaron. "With what I know you two have been up too,"

Allen said looking from his daughter to Aaron, "get married on the Fourth. And where are you planning to live son?"

"There's no doctor in this part of the county, sir," Aaron said looking at Jenny smiling at him. "I'd like to set up a practice here in Rockhaven. We'll need to find a place to live until I can have a house built." Allen looked at his beautiful freckled faced red haired daughter and reached to pull her close thankful he wasn't going to lose her, she was going to stay here near her mother and him.

"The Morris place is for sale, Aaron," Allen said still looking at his daughter. "The house is not far from the church and across the street. It's a nice size house." He let his gaze leave his daughter and looked at the man that would soon be his son in law. "Let me get changed out of my fishing clothes and we'll drive into town and you can look the place over. If you want it, then it'll be a wedding gift from Alicia and I."

"Oh Daddy," Jenny cried and flung herself in his arms.

"I'm in my fishing clothes, girl," Allen said in a rough voice but hugged her close. "So no more talk of going away from me and your mama?" Allen's voice changed to a gentle tone as he hugged his little Jenny close.

"I belong here Daddy, you were right. This place is where I was meant to live forever." Allen nodded his head as he hugged Jenny and looked at Aaron.

"He belongs here too," Allen said and reached for Aaron's hand and shook it. "You'll never know what you've done, son. You've helped us more than you'll ever know."

Alicia stood on the porch with Holly and they clasped hands. "We'll, the ties will bind us in more ways," Alicia said to Holly and smiled at Lang as he joined them on the porch looking out at Allen hugging Jenny and shaking Aaron's hand.

"Michael and Hannah just arrived for the long Fourth of July weekend," Lang said. "They don't want to wait for a big formal wedding and invited Michael's friend out here to perform the ceremony. I guess we're going to have another wedding," he nodded to his son who was grinning from ear to ear. "A Taylor to a Blackburn," he laughed, "and a Blackburn to a Taylor."

"We are a circle," Alicia looked and saw Bethany and Ethan coming from their home up the river with Levi and Cecily, she could hear Levi's laughter when Tucker ran up and jumped into his arms, probably bragging of the fish he had caught this morning. Shaun Allen was running to his father and Alicia could hear Shaun and Sarah upstairs talking to Thomas who was still in bed healing from his fall. "I hope Mary brings her rolls on the Fourth," she sighed and waved to her husband who had an arm around Jenny and an arm around Aaron.

"We're going to have a wedding," Allen called out and saw all the happy faces around him, Levi meeting him in the yard and tossing him Tucker who he caught with ease while Jenny and Aaron ran to Bethany and Ethan to talk. "I love my family," he said looking up at his wife. He remembered a time long ago, a time that he was leaving this river and his home behind and going to start again because he didn't want to marry the girl his father had left for him to marry. He didn't want to marry Alicia and then he had married her and he came home, home was with Alicia.

The night was hot and dry, heat lightening lit up the sky all around, the darkness was even darker because of the night lightening. Somewhere far off in the night a screech owl called out and joined the noise of the crickets and frogs and the river flowing by. "What are you doing out here?" Holly asked her husband seeing him sitting in the ladder back chair with his feet propped up on the porch rail. She climbed onto his lap facing him in the chair and he laughed pulling her close into his arms.

"Actually, I was thinking of you," Lang said and tilted his head back so his wife could kiss him and she did. "Holly girl, you know I love you more than life itself," he saw her head nod. "And I've loved our home on the beach and the joy we've had there raising our children." He saw his wife nod her head again before she kissed him and he pulled her close and held her tight while he deepened the kiss knowing he would never get enough of holding his wife like this, he was as in love with her right this minute as he had been thirty years ago.

"We belong here," Holly spoke for him. "We loved our home on the beach and our lives there. But our family is here now and we need to be with our family."

"Uncle Sam left us enough money to never have any worries and I'm invested in Allen and Levi's operation here. People always need lumber, Holly girl. We have the bank of Blackburn right here," he laughed thinking of the safe with all their money buried in the cemetery. "I'm ready to retire. I know I'm a bit young to do so, but I'm ready to settle down. How about a little cabin on the river? Just you and me and all our children and grandchildren surrounding us?"

"I would be happy with just you," Holly said and laid her head on his chest. "Do you remember the first time we met?" she felt her husband head nod, his arms pull her close. "I'm so thankful you made everything all right for me Lang. I just wish Amy were here."

"Amy," Lang breathed his daughter's name. Even after all these years, he ached just thinking of her. She had filled his heart when it had been empty. "Everywhere I've gone, every breath I've taken, every minute of my day, Holly girl, our Amy has been with me. She's here now, surrounding us with her love and goodness. We were so blessed even for the short time we had with her."

"Amy, Aaron, Charlotte and Hannah, we have been so blessed, Lang. I love you always. Even in heaven, I'll love only you."

"I may be old and retired," Lang teased her as a screech owl called off in the distance. "But right now I want to take my wife to bed, lay her down, and love her all night long." He watched Holly stand, her long hair falling forward as she offered him a hand and pulled him up, both laughing right before he swung her up into his arms. "I'll carry you in heaven," he breathed and heard her gasp as he walked into their room, the night dark behind them, but their lives together always bright.

The fourth of July saw two weddings take place as Hannah Taylor, Doctor Lang and Holly Taylor's youngest daughter married Michael Blackburn, Seth and Mary Blackburn's youngest son who had a law practice in Tallahassee. And Jenny, Allen and Alicia's daughter married Aaron, Lang and Holly's son. Shane and Shaun were turning the hog over the fire pit while Charlotte and Sarah added the sauce that would make it tangy and sweet and the other women were in the kitchen cooking.

"What in the world is Allen doing?" Mary asked as she went and looked out the window with Allen's sister Emily.

"They have a new material for the screen and Allen's making all the men help him screen in the porches," Alicia said laughing.

"So he had a party to get everyone here to work," Holly laughed and saw Shane and Shaun run up to the house climbing the porch rails with hammers in hand. "I know what Shane can do," Holly watched her son in law Shane Blackburn climb up to the upper porch of the house and remembered a time when she and Lang and Charlotte only knew him as their soldier after the Great War, he had no memory of who he was and he had put a new roof on their home and painted the place from top to bottom. "Shane alone will have the screen on before the day ends," Holly said with pride in her son in law and confidence.

"He has his twin beside him," Mary, the twins mother said, "everything they do together they have to compete, the job will get done quickly."

"Allen is a smart man," Cecily said watching her Ethan climb the roof. "He was just a baby not so long ago and now he's as big as his Daddy and he survived that war Shane and Shaun survived." Only Ethan had come home scarred on his face from a bayonet. "I remember when I had him," Cecily said in a dreamy way. "I almost died having him, and then I almost died again to make sure his Daddy knew him." She hugged herself remembering Levi and her rocky relationship early on.

"I feel there's a story in these words," Holly said and came to stand next to Cecily.

"We all have our own story," Cecily said seriously. "Each one of us has been through something hard in our lives, and it made us better when it was past. For Levi and I," she turned back and looked out in the yard at Levi now at the fire pit turning the hog, "we made a mistake early on and almost lost one another. Secrets have no place in a marriage," she said firmly and then laughed. "Look at Michael trying to outdo his older brothers," she pointed at Michael climbing up the porch rail like a monkey.

"There goes my Aaron," Holly laughed. "Oh no, he is not. That man is fifty five years old," Holly screeched as she ran out the door and stopped her husband from climbing the porch rail to the second floor. "Lang Taylor, if you want to get on that porch you'll take the stairs," she ordered her husband who climbed up the rail anyway.

"I'm not dead yet, Holly girl," he called down to her and laughed when Allen and Levi joined him on the porch.

"Let's get these porches wrapped in screen, boys!" Allen called out. "Last night I killed seven mosquitoes in one slap!" Allen looked over the rail of the porch and grabbed Tucker with one hand and Shaun Allen with the other, pulling them up to the second story. "Seth!" Allen called out to his little brother who waved up to him.

"Someone has to tend this meat," Seth yelled back at his brother while turning the hog for Sarah and Charlotte to season over the fire pit with Heath and Emily standing beside him helping. Allen wondered where Heather was and scanned the yard; he knew she wouldn't be nearby. His niece Heather was difficult at the best of times and mean at the worst. Every family had one unhappy member that no one could please, that family member in his family was

Heather and he breathed as sigh of relief that she wasn't anywhere to be seen. She wouldn't be inside in the kitchen with the ladies helping, he knew that, she avoided helping in the kitchen. Allen was certain, Heather hadn't come today.

Allen saw Sarah's parents arrive and join his brother at the pit and then Eddie, sweet Eddie came running toward the porch ready to climb as the others had and Allen saw Heath hurry to give the younger man a boost while Allen reached over the rail to pull him up.

"You won't let him fall!?" Ester called out to Allen as he was given a hug from Eddie.

"Never!" Allen called back seeing Eddie join the little boys in Thomas' room.

"Seven in one blow," Taylor said as his Grandpa Lang pulled him up over the rail. "That's a lot." The boy ran past Allen and into Thomas' room with Shaun Allen and Tucker.

"Allen," Lang said his name and took hold of his arm before they went to help putting up the screen. "Holly and I have been talking," Lang saw Allen nod his head. "Our children are here, our grandchildren are here. We feel we belong here. With the money I have invested with you and Levi, we'll if you have some land to sell me, Holly and I want to stay here. We're Blackburns now."

"You and I were meant to be brothers," Allen said taking Lang's hand into his own. "The three of us," he turned and saw Levi beside him reaching out to shake Lang's hand and welcome him to Riverbend. "The lines are fallen unto me in pleasant places, yea I have a goodly heritage. Psalm sixteen six," Allen breathed softly before turning to help his nephews wrap his porches in screen thinking of how much he loved his family and how very blessed he was. He might not be here now but by the grace of God. He thought of his mother, of her faith and he knew; his mother had passed on to him the value of family. As long as he lived and breathed, he would not forget to value each member of this large clan or as Levi called them, 'a crowd.'

"Who called this meeting?" Ethan asked as he looked around the table at most of the family surrounding him. He saw Allen at the head nod toward Lang and wondered why the older man wasn't bone weary. They had spent the day putting screen on Allen's huge wide porches and then eaten half a Bar B Q hog and Mary's rolls and now it was dark and everyone was tired and ready to go home.

"I wanted to let everyone know that Holly and I have decided to retire here. We'll be needing help with building a small home for us." Lang saw all the smiling faces around him and smiled at everyone at the table. "I also want to talk about something else, something I've been giving a lot of thought too." He saw everyone looking at him and knew he had all the attention in the room. "We're a family now, by marriage and tied by blood. It's not just the Blackburns or the Tuckers or the Taylors, we are all one family. In years to come," he predicted, "our offspring will want to know of their heritage, something Allen quoted from the bible to me today. And for Holly and I, we lost a child, a little girl and we want her to always be remembered. So I'm proposing that we all take time out in the evenings and write down our life story. When our great grandchildren look back at the old photos and paintings of their ancestors, let them read our stories. I know Holly and I have a love story that we want our children to know of and tell and our grandchildren. We want them to know what we survived and that our love carried us through, like you Ethan, and Shaun and Shane, coming home from the war scarred and having to heal and the women that helped you boys move on with life because of their love.

"All of us need to tell our own story. We need to leave behind the life lessons we've learned for our children so that they can learn from what we've gone through. And they'll know they have a goodly heritage," Lang finished speaking looking at Allen.

"You never know," Allen said holding Alicia's hand. "In one hundred years from now, will my great grandson be living here? Will my great grandchildren be swimming in that river out there the way we all have? That river flows on forever, so will our family." He turned to Alicia and held her hand tight. "I know it might be hard to tell our story, but what we survived there's no shame in. What brought us together made us both whole."

"Oh Daddy," Bethany said softly and looked at her mother who had tears falling on her face. Bethany and Ethan knew her parents story, they knew the courage Allen and his Alicia had to have to gone through all that they did.

"And write about Mary's rolls," Allen laughed meeting his sister in law's eyes from across the room. "They make our life sweet, Mary." Allen saw his brother's wife smile and thought of how she was as much as sister to him as Emily was, and she was a good and kind little sister.

"Cecily and I have a story as well," Levi said softly looking down into his Cecily's eyes. "I think people can learn from my mistakes with my beautiful wife. I won't lie to anyone; I was not good to her at the start of our marriage. I'm ashamed at how I treated her." He felt Cecily's fingers cover his lips and saw her head shaking before he gently took hold of her hand and moved it away from his mouth. "Future generations can learn from our story, darlin'. Look at little Ali and Tucker and Bethany fixing to have another baby for us." Levi saw Bethany blush and winked at her.

"Levi wasn't bad," Cecily insisted to all sitting at the dining table. "I can say this; the lesson to learn from our story is to always communicate. Secrets have no place in a marriage, and when you start keeping secrets, you have to lie. So yes, because of that, we'll write down our story Lang." She saw Lang nod his head and lean back in his chair.

"Doctor Taylor," Ethan spoke from the end of the table looking from his father Levi to his father in law Allen then back to Lang. "I've been building a bigger home up river from Shane and Shaun," he heard Bethany gasp and lean into him. "We'll our family is growing," he smiled pulling Bethany close. "The house is almost done now and we'll be moving in soon. That'll leave our home empty if you and your wife might want to move there to live." Lang nodded his head and smiled.

"Everything works our around here," Lang said looking at Holly. "This is what family is all about. And I'd like everyone to not call me Doctor Taylor any longer. We're all adults here at this table, let's use first names. And the children, if we're not a Grandpa or a Grandma, let's have them call us Uncle and Aunt, it'll make us closer." Lang looked at Allen and saw him smile. This man, Allen Blackburn had been a stranger to him, Lang thought and then the Great War had happened and it brought their families together and now Allen Blackburn was the brother to him that he never had. Next to Allen was Levi Tucker, another man without a brother, until Levi met Allen Blackburn. Allen was the man that tied them all together, Allen Blackburn was Riverbend.

PART TWO

TUCKER AND JESSIE

Chapter Five

Riverbend, Florida
February 1941

Most people that met and knew Jessie Fairchild saw her as someone that they knew was sweet, every once in a while a person would come along and mistake that sweet for weak and Jessie would not be treated fairly. There were even times that she would be targeted and treated in a rough way. It didn't help that Jessie was tiny; she wasn't small, that word didn't describe her because Jessie wasn't small, she was tiny and she was cute, everyone said so.

Tucker came into town with his cousins Thomas and Taylor and his Uncle who was only a few years older than he was, Shaun Allen. The young men saw the children on the playground at the school and Tucker shook his head before he broke into a run followed by his three companions.

"Not again," Shaun Allen sighed as he moved to keep Jessie from falling hard to the ground but saw that his nephew Tucker had her safely in his arms. The girl had been flying through the air being tossed around like a rag doll by the older boys at school; they had done so many times in the past. Poor little Jessie, Shaun Allen thought as he saw Tucker holding her safely in his arms.

Shaun Allen frowned as he stared at Tucker standing with Jessie in his arms and felt like he had never seen his nephew look as he was now before in his life. As he stood looking at Tucker Shaun Allen glanced to see that Thomas and Taylor were also staring at Tucker as he was. Tucker, all six foot three inches of him, solid built, his hands as big as Jessie's whole head was holding her like she was a doll in his arms, a china doll and the look on his face was one that made Shaun think that Tucker only had eyes for Jessie. Right at this moment there was no one else in Tucker's world beyond Jessie Fairchild. He had thought that he knew Tucker better than anyone; they were best friends, but right here, right now he felt only shock that he hadn't seen that Tucker was in love with the girl everyone called a pixie fairy because she was so tiny and her face was so cute. The four of them had saved her several times from the older boys at school bullying her and Shaun Allen had been clueless that Tucker felt anything more for her than any of the rest of them might feel. But now, he remembered the times he had seen Tucker holding the church door open for her on Sunday, when they had dinner on the grounds how he had sat next to her and teased her and talked like they were brother and sister, the times he met her in the general store and helped her reach something on an upper shelf, and Tucker was always interested in what she had to say. And Shaun Allen was seeing now the look on Jessie's face as she stared at Tucker, she admired his nephew. She was only fifteen years old, Shaun Allen thought and Tucker was twenty, she was still a baby, far too young for Tucker to be so serious about.

"Hey, let's go get a coke," Taylor said taking Shaun Allen by the arm and pulling him to the general store. "There's Eddie!" Taylor waved and ran to him as Thomas and Shaun Allen followed.

"I miss Taylor," Thomas confided in Shaun Allen. "I'll be glad when he's done with his studies, now that the Reverend Farmer has passed on, the church has been offered to Taylor as the roll of pastor." Shaun Allen smiled; soon they would all be together again, soon Taylor would be home to stay and his education complete.

"I'm working full time at the sawmill, that's my life," Shaun Allen said knowing that he had been blessed, the whole family had been blessed by his father, Allen Blackburns plan to not use a bank. When the market had crashed more than ten years ago, all of their money had been buried in a safe in the family cemetery and though they had a few lean years, everyone needed lumber and now business was booming. "Shaun and Shane and Ethan have taught me all I need to know and I'm happy there. The only problem I have is Heather," Shaun Allen thought of his mean cousin that managed the accounting books and wished a tree would fall on her. Heather made everyone miserable, his father said she was just a difficult person and they had to put up with her. Since her mother and father had passed away, she had gotten worse. If his Aunt Emily and Uncle Heath were still here, Heather wouldn't be as hateful to everyone as she was.

"Daddy wants me to work in the sawmill as well," Thomas said as he opened a bottle of coke and hugged Eddie. Eddie was his Uncle, his mother Sarah's brother that had nearly drowned in the river and Uncle Allen had pulled him out and saved way back when Eddie had been just a boy, but sadly Eddie had never returned to the boy he had been and forever Eddie had remained forever sweet and hugging. Everyone knew and loved Eddie and protected him, Thomas more so as Eddie was his flesh and blood. "I won't be working there though, Shaun Allen," Thomas said in a serious voice. "I was just hired to be the deputy sheriff for this end of Leon County. I was worried with this patch on my eye when I met with the Sheriff he wouldn't even consider me for the job, but he said the patch made me look like a bad ass and hired me in part because of my last name. He said my Grandpa Allen could get me hired because of him being one of the richest most well known men in all of the state."

"Daddy is pretty important," Shaun Allen agreed drinking a coke. "You're going to be our new deputy, huh?" he said to Thomas in a teasing way. "And a bad ass too." Thomas started laughing with Shaun Allen and both men looked at Tucker still holding Jessie Fairchild. "Did you have any idea about that?" Shaun Allen asked pointing toward Tucker with his coke bottle.

"None," Thomas confided. "But hey, I'm blind in one eye so I don't always see everything."

"I think it's good that one of us is going to settle down soon," Taylor said coming out of the store and hugging Eddie.

"Tuck is as wild as they come," Thomas said and Shaun Allen agreed. "I'll be shocked if that little gal can settle him down, or anyone for that matter."

Shaun Allen pointed again with his now empty coke bottle. "Daddy says that boy has wanderlust in his soul, he's not going to stay here. I'll settle at the sawmill and work alongside Ethan and Shaun and Shane and have sons of my own take over for me someday, Thomas will be the deputy that takes care of bad men in this end of the county and you Taylor, you'll be the minister to us all. But Tuck, he ain't staying around here, Daddy's certain he won't. When Bethany was crying over Daddy's words he told her that Tuck was full of the river like all of us kids, that one day Tuck would be back, but not for a long time." Shaun Allen saw his nephew Tucker take Jessie's hand and walk toward the river and wondered if his Daddy, Allen Blackburn knew of this budding romance, would he still think that Tucker was going to leave here.

"Well, I'm for home," Thomas said to Taylor and since they both lived with their parents at Twin River they started the walk home together. "You gonna wait on Tuck?" Thomas yelled back to Shaun Allen and within a minute Shaun Allen was with them walking home.

"What are we going to do about girls?" Shaun Allen asked with a laugh and broke into a run. "Beat you fellows to the house."

Tucker had caught Jessie in his arms with ease and then looked down into her cute little face and smiled. She was the size of child but he knew, she was not a child in any way. Jessie was smart and well read, she could converse on almost any subject and she knew the river like the back of her hand. She loved to fish and swim and skip rocks, she could shoot a gun as well as he could and she was little like his mama and both of his grandmothers.

"Thank you for catching me again, Tucker." Jessie Fairchild looked up into Tucker's aqua eyes and knew that he was her hero. She didn't love him like a girl loved a boy, he was too old for her, he was the hero in the story that slays the dragon and saved the day, then rode away to find another dragon to slay and more people to save from the dragon.

"Want to take a walk?" Tucker asked her and she wondered if he was going to carry her like an infant on this walk.

"I can't walk unless you put me down, Tucker." He loved the way she said his name, Tucker thought with a smile and lowered her to the ground. Jessie looked up at Tucker as they walked toward the river and thought he was handsome, he could even be called pretty. The story around Rockhaven was that all the men in the Blackburn family looked just like Allen Blackburn had when he was young. She didn't know how Allen Blackburn looked when he was young, but if the story were true, then she knew he had been pretty back then. Jessie closed her eyes and pictured Allen Blackburn as he was the last time she had seen him in church, he was handsome with gray hair at his temples and a few lines on his forehead and when he smiled he had deep dimples like Tucker. If Tucker grew to look like him in later years, then Tucker would still be awful handsome, she thought.

Jessie opened her eyes and frowned when she saw her mother pull up to the general store in their car and saw her mother looking at her walking with Tucker. Her mother had told her one Sunday months ago after church that Tucker was sweet on her and ever since her mother had kept pushing for her to be nice to him. Her mother said that her dream was that at least one of her daughter's married into the Blackburn family saying that it would increase their social standing. Jessie didn't know why that mattered to her mother but she knew she didn't want any part of Tucker beyond his friendship. Jessie was going to live alone and grow old alone and be happy alone.

"Hey Jessie," Tucker said her name and she turned to give him her attention by turning away from looking at her mother. "What are you going to make for the box social? Grandma Cecily said she's organized for all the girls to make a box we fellows have to bid on, and all the money goes to the new church roof." Tucker looked down just as Jessie looked up at him, her huge blue eyes met his and he thought she was beautiful beyond words. Tucker knew, without any doubt, that he was in love with Jessie Fairchild, and it wasn't a puppy love, his was a forever love.

"I've not thought if I'd even do a box up yet, Tucker. My mother said she would make up mine and my sister's boxes because she cooks better than we do." Jessie stopped walking and saw Tucker had as well. She knew she had to be honest with him; it was her way, to never lie. She thought of all the times he had saved her from the bigger boys at school tossing her around and pulling her hair and she was grateful. But Jessie knew something about herself no one else knew. She was stupid and she was weak and some had even called her dumb. The girls at school teased her constantly and they picked on her for her hair and her clothes and even her size. They let her know they hated her and she couldn't understand why, if she was nice to them, they laughed at her. The boys were often mean and aggressive toward her, Tucker knew that and he tried to keep her safe, but the fact was, she had no friends and she didn't want Tucker as a friend, she didn't want to hurt him.

Jessie's father had told her it was like their chickens in the chicken yard, there was this thing called the peck order. The big chickens would peck the little chicken to death just because it was little and couldn't stand up for itself. She was that little chicken, and she didn't want to be around anyone because eventually they hurt her and she knew Tucker for a hero, she wanted to keep him in her heart as her personal hero, she never wanted him to hurt her. And if she spent any time with him she was certain she would do something that would make him mad at her or hate her. Jessie Fairchild knew the only way for her to be safe was for her to be alone.

"What are you thinking, Jessie?" Tucker asked looking down at the only girl he would ever love and he wanted her to be his sweetheart always.

"I'm thinking I have to tell you the truth," Jessie said in a quiet voice and looked away from Tucker. "I'm never going to like any man Tucker." She heard him suck in a deep harsh breath and she looked back up into his clear aqua eyes. "It's true Tucker. Everyone I meet I make them hate me in time. My Daddy, he's been mad since the day I was born because I was a girl and then I stopped growing too soon, and now he has no son to run the farm. He's not mad at Elise because she's older and she's more sturdy than I am and can do chores I can't. And then there is Mama, she's always disappointed in me, always fussing at me. I don't even think she loves me at all Tucker, in fact, I know she doesn't love me." She saw the look of shock on Tucker's face that her words had caused and knew he didn't believe her.

"It's true Tucker. Look at all the boys in school always tossing me around and picking on me. And the girls are just as bad, if not worse. The only person that doesn't pick on me is Elise and she's my sister. I'm that little chicken in the chicken yard, I'm being pecked to death because people see me as weak, and maybe I am weak."

"I would never be mad at you Jessie, or mean to you," Tucker stopped speaking when Jessie put her hand on his chest and he lost his breath just because she touched him.

"Yes, you would, I would do something to make you mad or to make you hate me Tucker," she said in a firm voice. "And being so much bigger than me, you'll break me in two. My mind is made up Tucker, I'm not going to ever love anyone and I'm not going to stay here. As soon as I'm old enough, I'm going to go to Tallahassee and get a job. The teacher has spent extra time with me and taught me shorthand and how to use the typewriter, I can be a secretary or work in the library. I'm going to stay as alone as I possibly can for all of my whole life, I swear on that, I'm going to be alone." Jessie looked back up at Tucker and moved her hand from his chest. "My mind is made up and nothing will change my mind ever. I am always going to remember you as my hero and I thank you for all the times you've saved me. I thank you with all my heart." Tucker started laughing and turned to walk away from Jessie not seeing that she ran alongside of him working hard to keep up with his long legged pace. "What's so funny?"

"The workings of your mind Jessie. You're fifteen years old, you're the size of a minute and there's no way you're mother will ever let you leave here." Tucker was thinking he had all the time in the world to make Jessie love him and she was silly about everyone being mad at her or hating her when he knew she was the sweetest girl in the county.

"You think I don't know what I'm talking about." Jessie stopped running beside him and Tucker stopped and looked back at her with a surprised look when he saw her crying. "I'm telling you the truth, Tucker. Everyone I meet eventually hates me or gets mad at me over something. I can never please anyone, I'm serious. And I don't want you to join the crowd that can't stand me." Tucker took the steps that separated him from Jessie.

"If anyone hurts you, they'll answer to me, Jessie." Tucker took her chin in his hand and forced her to look up at him. "I could never hate you," he said in a gentle and kind voice.

Jessie knew in that moment that Tucker was her savior, that he had helped keep her safe for years. She didn't want to lose his kindness, she didn't want to do something wrong to earn his hatred. But she couldn't ever allow him for one minute to think there would ever be anything between them. "I don't love you Tucker," she said firmly and saw him back away, letting go of her chin. "I won't ever love you. You're too big for me. Look at us, you're a giant and I'm the size of an ant." She saw the hurt touch his face and shook her head hard. "I won't ever love anyone like you!"

Tucker stood still as Jessie raced away from him, he didn't turn and see her get in her mother's car, he didn't move for a long while. There was no other girl in the whole state he wanted to be with other than Jessie Fairchild and she had just declared her true feelings for him. He wasn't a giant, Tucker thought as he turned and started to walk home. He had been trying to decide what to do with his life, he didn't want to stay in the sawmill, he was smart and he wanted to go to college but he wasn't sure he could concentrate on studies for that long, he was too wild and he needed to be free, he wanted to be outdoors, he wanted to see the world.

"Want a ride home?" Tucker hadn't heard the car until his Grandpa Allen spoke to him and he turned. "Where are you?" Allen teased and Tucker opened the door to the car and got inside.

"Suffering from a broken heart, I guess." Tucker rolled down the window despite the cool weather and let the wind hit him in the face.

"I didn't know you were in love to get your heartbroken," Allen Blackburn said to his grandson that was the spitting image of him nearly forty years ago. He had lied to Tucker, Allen thought. He knew that Tucker was in love with the little Fairchild girl, he had seen the longing looks Tucker gave to her in church, Allen had hoped in time that Jessie Fairchild would notice Tucker, but the girl was awful young. "How old is Jessie now?" Allen asked glancing over at Tucker.

"I thought you didn't know I was in love?" Tucker teased his Grandfather well aware the older man knew everything that went on in their family, his Grandpa Allen even knew some things before they actually happened. "Jessie will be sixteen next month," Tucker said and sat back as the car swung onto the Riverbend road. "She told me today that she won't ever like me. I'm too big for her. I think her exact words were that I'm a giant and she's an ant."

Allen Blackburn worked hard to not burst out laughing at the description Jessie gave of the differences between herself and Tucker. "Well," he finally spoke when he knew he could. "Shaun towers over Sarah and you know Shane makes Charlotte look delicate. Look at your Mama and Daddy and Grandma and me. Even Uncle Lang and Aunt Holly and Uncle Levi and Aunt Cecily. Women in general are just smaller than their men; it's the nature of things. Now to be fair, little Jessie Fairchild isn't grown up yet, she might yet fill out and not be so little. Give her time to see you Tucker, really see you. If she's meant to be your girl, she'll be your girl."

"I have time," Tucker said seriously. "I talked to Dad about going to college and becoming an engineer but I don't feel ready to go. Maybe next year." He saw the look on his Grandpa's face, the hurt fill his green eyes and he felt sorry about talking of leaving. Tucker knew that his Grandpa favored him and didn't want him to ever leave the river.

"Tuck, I know Shaun Allen is going to stay here forever, he'll inherit the house and the mill and he'll keep it running. I know he'll grow trees and for generations to come my offspring will harvest this land. But Shaun Allen works best with you. He needs you, he always has. Remember that time I asked you to take care of him for me?" Tucker nodded his head, they had been out fishing and

Grandpa had told him to find a tree to punch. "I feel in my bones that Shaun Allen will need you one day. Please, be here for him."

"No matter where I am in the world Grandpa, if Shaun Allen needs me, I'll be home. You have my word on that." Tucker promised.

"I want to take a walk in the cemetery," Allen said and stopped the car next to the family graveyard. "When I was your age there were no cars out here, we rode our horses everywhere or a buggy or wagon. The new cars make things easier and they are faster but I miss the days my Mama was alive and my Daddy." Tucker followed his Grandfather into the cemetery and he knew why when Allen handed him a shovel.

"What are we going to buy now?" Tucker asked as he went to the stone with Allen's name carved onto it, the stone that Grandma Alicia had said was made because Grandpa died for her. The family safe was buried in this grave and they only dug down to open it when there was a large purchase.

"Levi and I feel it's time to put some cash back in the bank," Allen said as Tucker uncovered the safe. In nineteen twenty seven Allen had buried all their cash here in this safe in the graveyard, at that time Lang and Levi had moved here to live and with all the families together and the bank so far away in Tallahassee that seemed the smartest thing to do. And they had survived the depression because they buried their money in the cemetery. "We're not going to put it all in the bank, we probably never will in our lifetime or maybe even your Daddy's lifetime, but it's time to have some in Tallahassee for trips there and we need a large sum of money."

Allen stood watching Tucker rebury the safe, being close to the river grass never grew here, only white powder sand was here so the grave would never look disturbed. "I miss the old days," Allen said softly looking at his Aunt Julia's grave and next to her Greg Martin Steel's grave. "I didn't know time was going to go by so fast. I was young and carefree one minute and an old man the next."

"Come on Grandpa," Tucker said heading back to the car. "You're not that old."

"I'm sixty four," Allen told Tucker to drive the car and got in on the passenger side. "Grandma Alicia will be fifty six this year and heaven knows she doesn't look a day over forty."

"You're in great shape Grandpa," Tucker said kindly. "You still work with all of us and for the whole day and you can out ride and out hunt any of the younger ones." Allen laughed, he knew that was true. He loved to ride his horse and jump the fence and round up the cattle and he could still us a hoe with the best of them. He worked hard physically and for his age, he knew he was in very good shape.

"Lang says we have to keep moving or we'll get stoved up," Allen laughed.

"Grandma is waiting on you," Tucker pointed to his grandmother Alicia on the porch and waved to her when his Grandfather left the car. "I'll park her in the carriage house," Tucker called out as he drove the car to where they use to keep all the horses and now the former stables held two cars. He didn't see his Grandmother walk into his Grandfather's arms or the way they kissed, but Tucker didn't have to see them together now, he had seen them a million other times in the past. He knew his grandparents were in love and so were his parents and he wanted that sort of love someday. He thought of Sarah and Shaun and Shane and Charlotte and Uncle Lang and Aunt Holly and he couldn't forget his other grandparents, Cecily and Levi were more than in love, they were devoted to one another. He had wanted that with Jessie and he still wanted that kind of love with Jessie. His whole world was Jessie and depending on her was how he would plan his future. He was just waiting on her to show him the way.

Alicia watched Tucker in church on Sunday as he stood leaning against the wall staring at Jessie Fairchild. He was so obvious, she thought. The girl would never notice him as long as he was showing her he was sweet on her. Men didn't understand women; she thought and leaned over to whisper to her daughter Bethany. "Get that son of yours to come over here," Alicia said gently as she always spoke in a gentle way and Bethany searched the church for her son. When she saw him she motioned for him to come to her and saw him push off the wall he was leaning on and head her way.

"What's the matter, Mama?" Tucker asked and saw his Mama point to Grandma Alicia. "What can I do for you Grandma?" Tucker asked politely and Alicia forced him to look at her.

"Stop mooning about after that Fairchild girl," Alicia said firmly yet still in a gentle way. "She's made it clear to you that she doesn't want anything to do with you,"

"She has?" Bethany asked looking at her beautiful son that she knew was sweet on Jessie.

"She said I was a giant and she's an ant and to leave her alone." Bethany couldn't help but laugh at what her son said and leaned over onto her mother.

"As all the men in our family tend to be huge, every woman will be an ant," Bethany laughed harder as she pointed to Ethan who was standing with his father and her father. "You were meant to be big with the men in our family."

"Is that all you two called me over to tell me?" Tucker asked in an exasperated tone. "Nothing new in what's been said here," he moaned.

"Tucker," Alicia said and took his hand in her hand. "Every time you look at that girl she notices you looking at her. Leave her alone. Cecily's fixing to start the auction for the box lunches and your sister Ali has no one to bid on her lunch and she's fifteen too. Be a good big brother and eat lunch with your sister." Tucker looked at his little sister Ali; she had grown up while he wasn't looking. Just like their mother, his sister Ali had a mass of dark red curls only she had his Daddy's crystal clear blue eyes and looked like a photo he had seen of Grandma Cecily when she was a girl.

"I'll bid on her lunch and eat with her too," Tucker assured his mother and leaned back as his Grandmother Cecily went to the front of the church.

"We need a new roof on this church boys, and I'm depending on you all to bid well." Tucker smiled at his Grandmother Cecily knowing she found it hard to speak in public and was only doing this because it was important to her.

Tucker sat still and watching the boxes of lunch with the girls being auctioned off. If a girl didn't get a bid he was seeing her brother or father bid on her lunch, but that didn't happen very often, most of the boys were bidding well. And then he saw his sister's box lunch and heard her name and saw her smiling sweetly. He started the bid off at twenty five cents and saw her give him a hateful look to which he smiled and winked at her. Then Steven Jerrold bid on his sister's lunch and Tucker had to bid higher. His sister's lunch was up to three dollars and he counted what was in his pocket and leaned over to his grandmother.

"Grandma Alicia, can I borrow some money." Alicia slapped Tucker's hand and in a not so gentle voice ordered him to stop bidding on his sister's lunch and let the Jerrold boy win. "That's the highest any lunch has ever sold," Tucker said with pride and Bethany hit him hard in the arm. "What?" he asked and his mother rolled her eyes. Tucker saw Ali walk by him and stick out her tongue and kick at him and he was confused as to what he had done wrong.

Tucker saw that Thomas had won Elise Fairchild's box lunch and he saw them walk out of the church, he didn't know that Thomas liked Elise, Thomas hadn't shown any interest in any girl. And then he saw his cousin Thomas hand the box lunch to Taylor and the girl, Taylor turned bright red and looked ready to faint but managed to walk off to have lunch with Elise.

"Well, if he hadn't done something," Alicia said to Bethany who was watching Thomas come back into the church while Taylor walked off with his lunch and the girl, "Taylor would be an old man still staring at Elise and she'd be married with a house full of babies and even grandbabies to a man capable of telling her he's sweet on her."

"I had no idea Taylor was sweet on Elise," Bethany said and felt like she had missed something important.

Tucker saw that it was his little fairy's turn to be auctioned off and he saw that Jessie looked terrified out of her mind. "Grandma, Mama, what's the matter with her?" he leaned over to ask.

"She's scared," Bethany said and Tucker shook his head at her hard.

"I can see that Mama," he said in frustration.

The bidding had started and no one bid. Tucker looked around for her father and he wasn't in the room. Jessie had no brother, the younger men were almost all gone except for him and Thomas and Thomas had spent all his cash on Taylor's lunch. Tucker sat frozen waiting for someone to bid and no one did, the silence went on. And then her eyes met his, her eyes were huge, frightened and pleading with him to help her and he knew he would. Despite her prediction that he would hate her, he knew he never would. "Three dollars and a quarter," Tucker bid and looked at his Grandmother Alicia. "I need a quarter, I couldn't bid less on her than I did on Ali's lunch," he explained and his Grandmother handed him that quarter with a smile.

"Well," Bethany turned to her mother with a serious look. "Your plan was to have him bid all of his money on his sister's lunch mother. Then he would be gone and not here to see this beautiful girl humiliated so Jessie would then come to him and be humbled and give him her heart."

Alicia Blackburn looked at her daughter shaking her head. "That's what I said to you, Bethany. But my real plan just worked out fine." Alicia smiled and her whole face lit up. "Who do you think gave the Jerrold boy five dollars to bid against that big thick son of yours?"

"Mother, you did not."

"Yes, I did. Steven Jerrold was expecting to keep a few dollars of what I gave him, but it went to the roof instead because of Tucker." Alicia smiled at her grandson as he walked by holding the lunch and his little Jessie next to him. "She's a sweet girl," Alicia said. "Very misguided in her thinking though. Tucker told me that she confided into him that she makes everyone hate her and mad at her and she doesn't want to be around him because she wants to remember him as her hero, not another person that hates her."

"Oh dear," Bethany said watching Tucker hold the door open for Jessie. "That's so sad. Whatever happened to Jessie to make her think like that?"

"I don't know but I can understand," Alicia said standing when she saw Allen coming toward them with Lang and Holly beside him and Levi who was holding his hand out for Cecily as she rushed to get to them. "You and Ethan knew from the second you laid eyes on one another that you were in love, the same with Shane and Shaun and Charlotte and Sarah and even Mary and Seth. And our dear Emily and Heath. But some of us don't find love right away." Alicia walked into her husband's arms. "Some of us need time to realize what love is." She looked up at her husband who was smiling down at her.

"Telling Bethany our love story again?" Allen asked his wife and she nodded her head. "We need to finish writing that down."

"We can't finish it until one of us leaves the other," Alicia said. "We go on loving more every day." She saw Lang wink at her as they left the church, true love lasts a lifetime.

"So what happened with the plan for Tucker to have lunch with Ali?" Allen asked as the family sat down at their picnic table on the church grounds.

"Mama happened," Bethany said looking at her mother. "She paid that Steven Jerrold to have lunch with our Ali and to bid against Tucker.

"No matter what she did," Allen nodded his head toward Tucker and Jessie, "they look about as happy as a horse that picked up a stone half way home."

"He does look miserable," Levi said of his grandson. "I guess we won't know until we get him out on the river and a few good shots of whiskey…." Allen hit him in the shoulder and Levi became quiet looking to see if his wife was listening to what he had just almost said.

"So that's how you've been finding out about his relationship or lack thereof with Jessie," Alicia said with wide eyes. "What time are you going out the river? Oh I wish I was able to come with you." Allen was staring at his wife in disbelief and then looked at Holly, Cecily, Bethany and Mary and all the women looked at him and Levi like they were brilliant for getting the boy drunk to find out his thoughts and feelings. "Wait, how drunk do you get him?" Alicia had narrowed her eyes and was staring hard at her husband.

"Good and drunk," Levi answered and Cecily slapped his shoulder. "Well do you want to know what we need to do to help the boy or not?"

"Get him drunk and then report right to us," Cecily said and Alicia agreed.

"We're a Christian family," Bethany said putting the food on the table and pulled out her Aunt Mary's rolls. "He's my son and I don't really approve of his drinking. But since it's with his Grandfathers and there's good reason, I'll not think anything of it. But we don't make a habit of getting him drunk."

"If only I were a fly on that tree over there by them now, we wouldn't have to resort to these extremes." Alicia said taking two of Mary's rolls onto a napkin. "I may not be a fly, but they look like they need a roll." Everyone at the table watched Alicia take the rolls over and neither Tucker nor Jessie looked up at her, they were lost in looking at one another and not eating.

"Ya'll might as well leave Tucker alone," Ethan said. He had sat silent for a long time and watched his son. "He's breaking his heart over that girl and she doesn't care that he is. He's never slowed down to notice anything, he's our wild boy. But he saw her and he stopped still. We can't help him in this, he has to find his own way." Ethan felt he was the one that was right, trying to help a girl dead set on not loving his son come to love him just wasn't going to work. He looked at Alicia and gave her a half grin. "Well," he said to his mother in law, "you made the Jerrold boy happy, he's long been sweet on our Ali and he's having a free lunch with his sweetheart."

Tucker had walked out of the church with Jessie feeling blessed, but once outside and settled on the blanket with the lunch he felt awful. Jessie wasn't looking at him, she wasn't speaking to him, and worst of all; she looked ready to cry. She was that upset with him for bidding on her lunch, Tucker thought and took a deep breath. He felt like he needed to excuse himself to punch a tree as his Grandpa Allen had taught him.

"I was trying to help you," Tucker said slowly and softly knowing his family was watching and listening. He also knew this was a hopeless situation. Jessie really didn't like him and she never would and all the time in the world wouldn't make her ever fall in love with him.

"I didn't ask for your help," Jessie said and two huge tears fell onto her hands folded in her lap.

"Goodness girl, you could at least act like you're a little grateful." Tucker faced the tree so his family wouldn't see the agony etched across his face.

"I'm going away tomorrow, Tucker. And I won't ever see you again," Jessie spoke slowly and softly seeing Tucker look at her like she had slapped him in the face with her words. "There's nothing to do now but say goodbye." She looked down at the food that she had made and wished she could tell him the truth, but this time she had to lie and she never wanted to lie. "It's best I go," she forced herself to try and sound glad and it came out sounding like a heartache. "I never really belonged here."

"Where are you going?" Tucker finally asked and saw Jessie shrug her shoulders. "You don't know?"

"I know, Tucker. I just don't want you to know." Tucker looked away from her and back at the tree. "It looks like Mama is getting what she wants completely," Jessie said and looked over at her sister with Taylor Blackburn. "She's getting a daughter married to a Blackburn," the sound of Jessie's voice was bitter as she stared at her sister and didn't see Tucker was looking hard at her again.

"What does your mother care about us Blackburns?" Tucker saw that Jessie was looking down at her hands again.

"Don't pay me any mind, Tucker. I'm not feeling well. I enjoyed seeing you this last time." Tucker watched her stand and brush at her skirt. "Goodbye." She said and Tucker watched her turn and leave, she walked away from him like he didn't matter to her in the least. And then he knew; he didn't matter to her in the least. Without thought he pulled back his fist and hit the mighty oak tree they had been sitting under with a force that shot up his arm in pain. He closed his eyes and didn't turn and look back at his family, he knew they were all watching him and he didn't want them to watch him. With all the dignity he could gather, and that was very little after the way Jessie had rejected him, Tucker walked away from the church and the picnic grounds wishing he had never met

Jessie or heard her name. "And what kind of name is Jessie for a girl? it's almost always a boy's name" he viciously asked himself. "Stupid, dumb name." When he turned at the bend in the road he looked off into the distance at the river and started running, he could cry in the river and no one would know, the river would wash away his tears and his sorrow and his humiliation. So like others in the past in his family, Tucker needed that old river and that was where he was running too.

Chapter Six

"I'm slowing down, Allen," Lang said as they sat out in the row boat on the river fishing. "I turned sixty six last week, how did I get this old?" Allen looked at the man he loved like a brother and smiled, Lang looked younger than his age and he knew that.

"You're slowing down because we are doing more fishing and less working at the mill. We're still young, Lang. Men today are living into their seventies. Old man Johnson is eighty eight."

"Comparing us to old man Johnson who is blind and senile and sits on his porch in a rocking chair all day," Lang laughed. "I'm not that slow yet." He looked at his cork bob and pulled in another fish. "Holly's sixty one and doesn't look like she's reached forty yet," Lang said after baiting his hook. "She's aged beautifully."

"So has Alicia, we have beautiful wives. Levi is missing a good trip, we've caught almost thirty six fish now."

"Levi stayed close to home because Tucker hasn't been seen since church yesterday." Lang looked back at Allen and wondered why he wasn't worried about his grandson when everyone else was worried to death over the young man.

"Tucker's around," Allen said and nodded to the bank on the other side of the river which Lang followed the nod and saw Tucker lying on the grassy bank and looked to be sleeping. "I found him last night. I told Levi to come with me today so I could ease his mind, but he wouldn't cause he said four of us can't fit in this boat. Now we don't have any room in this boat for the boy with all these fish we've caught. He's going to have to swim across the river to get home."

"You're going to make him swim in this current?" Lang asked in a serious voice and Allen laughed.

"No, he'd wind up in the Gulf if he tried. We have enough fish, let's go get Tucker and he can lay on the fish while we get him back to his mama and daddy." Allen rowed the boat to his grandson and poked him with the oar. "Hey," he called out to his look alike grandson that bore his name. "Tuck!" he saw Tucker moan and roll over.

"Grandpa, Uncle Lang, what are you two doing in my dream?" Lang saw the empty bottle beside Tucker and laughed.

"He's still drunk," Lang pulled on his arm and Allen kept poking at him with the oar.

"Get up you drunk," Allen ordered and Tucker sat up.

"Don't tell Mama and Daddy," he said seriously and rolled into the boat. "I feel sick."

"Don't you throw up on our fish," Allen ordered as he started rowing back to the other side of the river.

"Jessie left," Tucker said with his face in his hands. "I've been a complete fool over her. And now I need to figure out what I'm going to do with my life because all my plans were to be with Jessie forever."

"We both know you're not planning on settling down to the sawmill." Allen said sadly, but then he had always known that Tucker was different from the others that lived here. Tucker was going to wander away for a while, maybe forever, Allen knew.

"I think I'm going to join the Navy Grandpa. See some of the world," Tucker looked up at Allen with red rimmed eyes.

"Well, eighty percent of the world is water, I guess you'll see the world in the Navy," Allen said and Lang forced a laugh.

"Tucker, you're hurting from Jessie's rejection," Lang stated the obvious. "You need to give yourself two full weeks to think things through. You're also still half drunk. Give yourself two weeks before you do anything, son. It's vital you do this. We can't make life changing decisions when we're hurting or grieving or in pain." Tucker had his back to his Uncle Lang but he knew that he was right. He was hurting and feeling raw right now, it wasn't the best time to make a life altering decision.

"I'll take your advice Uncle Lang," Tucker said as Allen pulled up to shore and they pulled the boat onto the bank.

"Your Daddy and Mama are worried and your Grandpa Levi," Allen said seriously. "Go on home and we'll see you for dinner. Everyone is coming over for a fish fry." Allen saw Tucker running toward his house and looked at Lang. "You aren't any good at cleaning fish, and you with the skilled hands of a doctor. I've got the fish, you go on home to your Holly. We'll see you both for dinner." Lang patted his shoulder and thanked Allen not seeing Alicia coming toward them. Allen waved to his wife knowing there was time to take his wife for a swim in their private pool.

"Thomas looks good in his uniform," Bethany was saying to Sarah as they sat at the picnic table in her father's yard eating fried fish and cheese grits. "It's amazing how different our sons are and yet their all good friends."

Sarah looked back at her son Thomas and shook her head, "your son Tucker, my son Thomas and Charlotte and Shane's Taylor all look like Allen and Seth Blackburn. But they all act different. Thomas is just like his Uncle Shane, all serious and get the job done attitude." Bethany laughed and looked at Sarah nodding her head.

"Daddy calls Thomas the judge because he's so serious."

"Uncle Allen would give him a name like that," Sarah said as Charlotte came to sit with them. "And Taylor," she said looking at her nephew. "He's always wanted to preach."

"I wanted him to be a doctor like Daddy and Aaron," Charlotte said looking at her son, "and he told me he's a doctor in a way because he's saving souls." Bethany smiled and nodded that Taylor was right. "Then there's Shaun Allen. He has his whole life planned working at the mill and tending the trees and cattle just like his father and grandfather before him. He'll take care of this land. But our Tucker," Charlotte fell silent and looked at her full plate of food. "Tucker," she only said his name.

"He wants to join the Navy," Bethany said looking at Sarah and Charlotte, they were best friends, all almost the exact same age. Just as Holly, Cecily and Alicia were close because they were all almost the same age. When they had a problem with their boys, they turned to one another, they didn't stand alone with a problem, they all stood together.

"He promised Daddy today that he won't make any decision until he's no longer hurting over Jessie," Charlotte said in a relieved voice. "He'll follow through with what Daddy says; he's a good young man." Bethany looked at her son and saw him picking at his fish. Her wild boy that was always running toward a fight and that gave her no peace had grown up into a man that had fallen in love only to be rejected and she wanted her wild happy child back. "He'll be all right, Bethany," Charlotte reached for her hand and so did Sarah. "We'll all pray for him." Bethany nodded her head and forced a smile.

"He's a Blackburn, he'll get through this." she said and then frowned.

"What?" Charlotte asked and turned in time to see Heather drive up and stop in the side yard where her Uncle Allen had grass growing and didn't want anyone parking their car.

"The most difficult Blackburn in the world, and her Mama and Uncle Heath were the nicest people in the world." Sarah said seeing her Uncle Allen cringe upon seeing Heather and then he offered her some fish but she insisted on discussing the account books with him.

"We're having a party here Heather; either join us or leave because I'm not talking about the books until tomorrow." Allen turned back to his food and felt Alicia grasp his hand and squeeze, there was no use in getting upset with Heather. "I've also been doing some thinking," Allen said in a serious voice looking up at Heather. "I want you to give Tucker the accounting books now." Allen reached for the books and saw Heather shake her head. "I want Tucker to take over the financial side of our business, Heather. And if for some reason he can't, then Ethan and I will manage these books. You've had too much authority over our place here and you've not shared. All you do is criticize our whole operation and put down the cousins that run this place. You have your rights to the company and we'll pay you your share. But I've had enough of you." Allen held out his hand for the books and saw Heather breathing hard when she handed them to him and he was glad she knew nothing of the buried safe. "Have some fish if you'd like," he said not looking at her again.

Speaking to Heather this way had been one of the most difficult things Allen had done. He had been raised to respect women and treat them in a gentlemanly fashion. And with Heather he had spent years and years trying to accept her as just a difficult person, but he was done now. She was more than difficult and the death of her parents hadn't made her any kinder. Allen thought of his sweet little sister and how good she had always been to him and he was being hard on her only child.

Heather Ferrell narrowed her eyes and stared hard at her Uncle Allen, but he wasn't looking up at her, he was looking like he hated himself and wanted to walk away from her. And then Heather saw Alicia looking at her and she took a step back. She had always seen her Aunt Alicia as weak, almost stupid in her quiet, gentle way but right now, this look Alicia Blackburn was giving her was anything but weak, quiet or gentle. Her little Aunt Alicia was protecting her husband; she was letting Heather know with her look that if she did one thing to go against her Uncle Allen that she would take her down. After a moment Heather turned and left spinning her tires in the yard and tearing up Allen's newly planted St. Augustine grass.

"I don't care," he whispered with Levi and Lang giving him heartfelt looks.

"I'll do the account books, Grandpa. And make you proud of how well I do them too." Tucker took the books from his grandfather and patted him on the shoulder.

"Uncle Allen," Shane spoke and Allen looked up at him. "I just want you to know, Charlotte and I feel you're the best Uncle in the world." Allen smiled and saw Shaun bow to him adding,

"You've always had my highest regard. I came to you over Lester," Shaun laughed when Allen did knowing they had a secret that would always keep them close.

"You know how I feel about you," Ethan said and saw Aaron nodding his head with Jenny beside him. Allen looked up and saw everyone around him and they all lived here, they all were his family and he loved them, he would lay down his life for any one of them and he knew they would always be here for him and Alicia.

"I'm a blessed man," Allen spoke and felt his Alicia lean into him, "in so many ways, I have a loving family, friends, the love of my life," he looked down at Alicia, "children, grandchildren, nieces and nephews and son in laws. Nothing can harm us because we all have one another and we all have love. And one bad apple doesn't ruin the whole barrel." Allen thought of Heather and felt sorrow she was the way she was, she had been such a sweet baby and little girl. He would never know what went so wrong with her and that made him sad.

"Grandpa," Tucker came into Allen Blackburn's office late in the day on Wednesday and looked to make sure they were alone before closing the door. He saw his Grandfather motion for him to take a seat and he came to sit across from him with the accounting books for the mill, the trees, and the cattle.

"Heather's been stealing from us?" Allen said in a defeated voice. He had known, all these years he had known but had never said anything or tried to prove that she was. He couldn't handle deceit in his family or from a loved one.

"Yes, Grandpa and it's been going on for years. Uncle Heath suspected and he put back some of his own money that he had invested to try and make up for the loss. In fact, every year Uncle Heath gave back over half his earnings to cover what Heather was taking." Tucker saw his Grandfather cover his face with his hands and Tucker felt awful that he had told his grandfather.

"Since Heath died, how much has she taken?" Allen asked and Tucker hesitated to tell him. "I need to know," Allen said seriously.

"Over three thousand dollars in the last two years," Tucker said knowing that was a significant amount of money.

"Since Seth, Levi, Lang, Ethan, Shane and Shaun all own a part of the company I need to repay that amount." Allen said going to his desk. "Heath was giving back half his earnings to cover what she was doing to us, I need to make the past two years right." Tucker saw his Grandfather looking sad and tired and felt bad he'd had to tell him of what Heather was doing. He should have just kept it quiet.

"Grandpa Allen, no one needs to know," Tucker said as he came to him at his desk.

"I'll know son," Allen had reached into a box in his desk. "Don't worry, Tuck. I don't spend money much and I've managed to save almost all my personal earnings for the past ten years. This three thousand dollars is just pocket change." Tucker saw the strong arm box of money and nodded his head, his Grandfather was frugal. "I don't know what I'm saving for," Allen said as he stood up. "I guess I want to leave you all well off when I go. I want you all to know I worked hard all my life so you'd never want for anything."

"You know Grandpa," Tucker gave him a smile when Tucker hadn't felt like smiling for days, "you're leaving us the most valuable gift of all. You've taught us all how to love one another and how to show respect and to be kind at the same time. You've set an example we all want to follow. Money can't buy what you've taught us all. You and Grandma Alicia have given us the best."

"Well, early in the morning you are driving me to Tallahassee and we're putting this into the new account there for our business," Allen said as he put the money in an envelope. "Tuck," he called out to his Grandson before he left. "Let's keep this about Heather between you and I," Allen saw Tucker nod his head. "Do not alter the books hiding what she's done, but don't tell either. Not even your daddy. I'll make right what she's done tomorrow and we won't let her near the books again."

"I won't tell Grandpa and I'll make new books and give these to you to lock up so in case we ever need to tell anyone, we'll have them." Allen smiled and nodded his head. "I'll come for you about seven in the morning."

Allen sat on the upstairs porch listening to a whippoorwill cry out in the near distance of the night, his chair leaned back and his feet propped up on the ledge of the porch. He felt like he wanted his youth back, he wanted to make love to his wife all night long; he wanted to feel happy again. He felt bogged down with worries and wished he could just get away. And he didn't know what to do about Heather. A part of him wanted to have her prosecuted for her crime, but she was a woman and they would probably only slap her on the wrist and send her home. And she was filthy rich, all these years stealing from her own family and her father paying to cover up what she was doing. Why hadn't Heath come to him and told him? They could have faced her together. Heath had known and never told him and Allen felt almost betrayed and now Heath was dead and he would never know why Heath hadn't trusted him with what Heather was doing.

"Because she was his daughter," he heard his wife's voice say behind him. "Tucker didn't see me sitting in the chair facing the fireplace in your office today. I had been reading a book and was scooted down. So yes, I heard the whole conversation and I know you're out here wondering why one of the best friends you ever had in your life didn't tell you what was going on." Alicia came to stand in front of him. "I know you're hurting, Allen. I know how much you love our family. I remember you holding Heather the first day you brought me here, you adored that little baby. And she's a part of your sister." Allen pulled his wife close and put his face into her nightgown while she smoothed his hair.

"Alicia," Allen sobbed. "I failed her, I failed Heather. I always have tried to set a good example since I came home from Charleston and back to you. I was so humbled and thankful for what I have. You taught me so much. I keep thinking of the verse, 'with God all things are possible,' and our family has had God guiding us through some really bad times. Shaun and Shane and Ethan, God saw through that horrible war. And Thomas, God saw through that accident that he should have never recovered from and he was up talking before the end of the day. And Tucker running wild, God has kept my sweet grandchild safe for me. All our children and grandchildren have just been a gift from the God I adore. And the Tuckers coming into our lives, and the Taylors. So much good Alicia, so much to be thankful for, so much from the Glory of God and I'm breaking apart because Heather doesn't know God, and as a child of God, I know I have to forgive her. And I do. But I'm so hurt by what she did and that Heath didn't trust me so I might have helped her."

Alicia heard her husband fall silent; she had known he had a lot to say and a lot on his heart. He wasn't someone that took betrayal lightly. "Allen, we're going to let this go. You're going in the morning to the bank and replace the money Heather took. I want you to go by Michael's office and see how Hannah is doing;

her baby is due any day now. Take some time in the city, maybe see a movie with Tucker. And I'll be here waiting for you. Let this go, Allen, love Heather away and let's just be better Christians because of this."

"Should I tell Lang and Levi what Heather did? I wasn't going too, but I wouldn't want them to find out and know I kept this from them like Heath kept it from me." Alicia nodded her head and pulled him up from the chair.

"You can tell them at Sunday dinner," she said pulling him toward their room. "It's freezing out here, come and warm me up." She heard him give a soft laugh before she pulled him to the bed. "Remember that first time," she whispered. "Not our wedding night, but the first time here."

"I'll never forget," Allen breathed her name as he lay down on the bed with her. "My only regret about getting old, I cannot make love to you all night long."

"Ten minutes in your arms is as lovely as an eternity, Allen."

"I need to go by and see Michael," Allen said to Tucker as they left the bank and he looked down the street. "His office is on Gains Street beyond the Capital building. I'll walk down Monroe Street, it's not far. You want to drive the car over to his office?" Allen saw Tucker getting into his Nineteen Thirty Six Buick Victoria and he waved to him.

The weather was beautiful Allen thought as a cool breeze blew up the hill as he walked down. The street was cobblestone and then paved and then off in the distance it turned to red clay dirt. Monroe Street was lined with dogwood trees and they were all starting to bloom, it was a beautiful place to be and Allen was glad he had come. He passed a section of the city that was law offices and business knowing Michael's office was here and that's when he saw her sitting at a desk looking lost, alone and confused, he felt that way himself seeing her where she was, he had no idea she wasn't home with her mother and father.

"Jessie," Allen said her name too low for her to hear but she looked up and saw him and her eyes looked to be begging him for his help. He couldn't pass her by, that wasn't Allen Blackburn's way. If he saw someone he felt needed his help, he was there for them. He went into the office and up to her desk; she was too young to be here he thought, she was just a girl.

"Hello Mr. Blackburn," Jessie said and he saw her eyes filled with tears. "How is Tucker?" Allen sat down and she turned her head looking behind her at the closed door and then back to him with fear filled eyes.

"What are you doing here Jessie?" he asked and looked at the door behind her willing whoever she feared behind that door would come out.

"I work here now," she said softly. "I'm learning to be a paralegal for this law firm." She saw Allen Blackburn nod his head and look her over carefully.

"What are you not telling me?" Allen said in a gentle yet demanding tone.

"Please, don't ask me to say anything, I cannot. How's Tuck? I miss him." Her eyes were huge and pleading with Allen to not push her to tell him anything.

"He's here with me. Would you like to see him?" Allen saw Jessie shake her head hard and then the door opened.

"Who do we have here?" the man that came out from behind the door asked with a smile Allen couldn't like. He was fat and balding and when he glanced at Jessie, Allen didn't like the way the man looked at the very beautiful young girl.

"Allen Blackburn," he stood and held out his hand to the man not missing Jessie's look of terror as the man touched her arm. What is going on here? Allen wanted to ask but kept his silence.

"The Allen Blackburn," the man seemed impressed and Allen knew it was because the man knew how rich he was. "How can I be of assistance to you, sir?" Allen looked at Jessie's terrified face and winked at her trying to offer her assurance that he was aware something was wrong here and he would make things right for her.

"I need nothing from you. I was just passing by and saw Jessie in the window. She's very precious to me," Allen narrowed his eyes and smiled at the same time. "I miss seeing her at church on Sunday."

"I wasn't aware that you knew Allen Blackburn," the lawyer said to Jessie and she nodded her head and Allen knew she was nervous; he didn't like that she was frightened of the man she supposedly worked for.

"Actually," Allen spoke looking at Jessie, "she's practically engaged to my Grandson." Jessie pinched her lips together tightly and looked at Allen in near panic. "I hope you'll make it down to church on Sunday, Jessie." He said and shook the man's hand again before leaving the building. He went out and saw the lawyer's name above the door. 'Richard Ludlow' Allen read and turned the corner seeing Tucker by the car.

"Here I am Grandpa," Tucker called and waved.

"Get in that car and come get me now," Allen called back, his voice an order Tucker knew not to refuse and he raised an eyebrow wondering what was going on, as he hurried to do as his Grandfather said. "Drive to Rockhaven as fast as you can," Allen ordered.

"But what about checking on Hannah and Michael?" Tucker asked hitting the clay dirt road as fast as he dared to go.

"We're going back to Tallahassee today." Allen said and then sat quietly thinking of Jessie, of the look on her face, the fear. He knew that look; he knew that fear on a woman's face. He had seen it in the past and he would never forget what he had seen. If anyone knew how quickly a woman could become a victim, it was Allen Blackburn, and there were real evil men that made women a victim and that man Allen had just met was pure evil, he would bank on that as a fact.

Come Tame Someone Like Me

"Why are we going to Jessie's house?" Tucker asked as he kept glancing at his Grandfather, something was very wrong, his Grandfather never looked mad and he looked very mad right now.

"I'll tell you when I know," Allen said getting out of the car and going up the porch steps of Jessie's home with Tucker close behind him. He beat on the door and Jessie's mother came and pulled it open. "I need to speak to Chester," Allen said and Tucker wondered what his Grandfather wanted with Jessie's father.

"He's in the bed unwell," Jessie's mother said and Allen pushed past her.

"He better be in the bed unwell." Allen went down the hall looking into each room and finally found Chester Fairchild. "What have you done to Jessie?" Allen reached in the bed and pulled Chester up and out from under the covers he was lying under and heard Chester cry out.

"Be careful Allen," Chester cried out and Allen pushed him against the wall. He knew what Chester Fairchild was and he had an idea what Chester had done to Jessie, but he couldn't believe what he was thinking, Chester had to tell him because what he was thinking was too hard to imagine.

"Answer my question and then I'll be careful." Tucker stood in shock unsure what was happening in front of his eyes, his Grandpa had lost his mind.

"I was gambling again," Chester whined and Allen pushed him hard against the wall and he cried out in pain again. "I lost everything. Our home, all our money, everything," Chester cried out again and Allen tightened his hold on the man knowing he was right in what he was and had been thinking.

"You lost everything to that lawyer in Tallahassee, Richard Ludlow," Allen stated firmly while shoving Chester back against the wall. He saw Jessie's father nod his head.

"My wife shot me in the ass, that's how I got hurt. It was her," he pointed to his wife. "She went to that lawyer and asked how we could keep our home. He said he wanted Jessie to come work for him, give him Jessie and we could stay in the house and keep our farm. My wife gave Jessie to him."

"Oh my God!" Allen shoved Chester into the wall harder and growled in his face, "you gave that son of a bitch your daughter?"

"No, my wife did along with an IOU until Jessie's worked for him for one full year." Chester cried out as Allen dropped him onto the floor before turning to his wife.

"You know what that lawyer is doing to that girl, and she's not working for him the way you're portraying her to be working," Allen stated. Out of the corner of his eye he saw Chester's wife run for her rifle and Tucker grabbed it from her as she was aiming the gun at his Grandpa and the gun went off shooting the ceiling of the room they were in.

Allen watched Tucker empty the gun of all its shells and looked at him with pain filled eyes. "That man has been hurting Jessie?" Allen nodded his head and started for his car. "We have to go get Jessie."

"You can't," Chester's wife Betsy screamed out at Allen.

"We're going to get her," Allen growled in her face, this woman meant to shoot him because he was going to rescue her daughter from a man that was violating her. Allen heard Chester crying softly on the floor and felt no pity for the man; in fact he felt extreme hatred for what the man had done.

"If you take her away from him, we'll lose our home," Chester cried pathetically to Allen.

"Shut up," Allen Blackburn screamed and put his fist through the wall in the Fairchild hallway. "You love your home more than your own child! You make me sick, Chester. You gambled her away like she was nothing to you." Allen turned to Tucker saying, "Let's go get Jessie, now."

"I'm putting my fist through that lawyer's face." Tucker said throwing the rifle onto the front porch and the shells in the yard. "She shot her own husband and she was going to shoot you Grandpa," he said in disbelief. "And she gave her daughter as a slave to some man in payment of a debt." Tucker looked at his Grandfather.

"Jessie is more than a slave," Allen grieved. "That poor girl, she was terrified out of her mind. Let's go get her."

"Grandpa, has that man been doing to Jessie what I think he's been doing to her?" Allen was still and silent for a long time, his head was hurting remembering the look that little girl had given him. And with what Chester and Betsy had done, he felt ill and wanted to cry.

"I don't know for certain, Tucker. But she was scared out of her mind. Knowing what I know of how a woman behaves when a man is harming her that way, I'm afraid so." Allen thought back to Alicia, he had been so young, he hadn't known of anything like rape and molestation, he wished he had never known and he wished more that Alicia had never known. He then thought of Shaun's wife Sarah and he knew without doubt that Jessie was a victim. "Her parents gave her to that man, a sixteen year old child, to save their home. Their home had more value to them than their child."

Tucker sat silent driving as fast as he dared back to Tallahassee seeing that it was mid afternoon and soon business would be closing. "What if we don't make it before he locks up for the night Grandpa?" Tucker glanced over at his Grandpa and thought he looked younger than he had the day before when he had learned about Heather, he looked ready to go into battle, but Tucker knew that he had this handled. Tucker would take care of that lawyer and get Jessie home safe.

"If he's closed for the night, we'll find a place to stay and deal with this in the morning. But I hope we make it before he's closed up." Allen judged the distance from his memory and from his nephew's driving out to Rockhaven. "We'll make it before four.

We'll save that girl tonight," Allen said with hope that what he was saying would be correct, for Jessie's sake.

Richard Ludlow looked at Jessie Fairchild and grinned, he was very pleased with her, she was proving to do a good job in every way and she was also friends with one of the richest men in the whole state. Since Allen Blackburn had left she had confessed to knowing Levi Tucker and Lang Taylor as well and he wanted their business, just knowing them would raise his status in this community and in the state. He would become very important representing those three men and their business.

"So we're going to your church on Sunday and you're going to introduce me to all your friends," Jessie heard the man she referred to as the monster say to her. She knew she would do as he said, but she didn't want too. He owned her, she thought as she saw her mother's IOU in his hand, he had an IOU from her as well, but he kept it hidden from her. He held her mother's IOU out to her every day as he threatened her if she didn't do just as he said and she knew when she paid her parents debt she had her own debt to pay. "Come over here," he ordered and Jessie closed her eyes wanting to refuse him but knowing she couldn't. The monster pulled her close and pushed her face down onto his desk and she cried hard, tears rolled down her face and onto the papers on the desk as he held her down and used her while twisting her arm behind her back and grunting and groaning above her, her panties torn and her skirt lifted up to her waist. He was fat and disgusting and she couldn't stand the thought of him on her and the pain he made her feel. She didn't move, she did nothing but hold still and pray to God to save her fearing there was no God or angels that were able to come into this room right now and pull the monster off of her as he shoved hard and harder still into her while twisting her arm behind her back.

Tucker pulled up to the law office his Grandfather indicated to him and jumped out of the car leaving his grandfather behind as he ran into the building. The door opened, it wasn't locked, but he didn't see Jessie. And then he heard a horrible noise, the sounds of sobbing with a panting noise. And he saw her, her face was a picture of agony, wet with tears and she was held down with her arm behind her back and bent over the desk as the man violated her.

Allen entered the room as Tucker's fist smashed into the lawyer's face forcing him off of Jessie and she fell to the floor crying in pain and horror. He wondered how many times she had to stand up to this kind of abuse and violence and he wanted to go to her but he didn't, she was pulled inside of herself looking broken and scared. Instead he watched his grandson pummel the lawyer into the floor and made no move to stop him.

"Jessie," Tucker crawled to his sweetheart after the lawyer was still and silent and he tried to touch her, he wanted only to comfort her.

"Don't touch me Tucker. Don't look at me. Go away," Jessie screamed and covered her face with her hands and cried harder.

"Grandpa," Tucker said looking up at Allen and Allen bent down to Jessie.

"Jessie, let's go home. Not to your home, but to my home." Only sobs came from the girl on the floor. She was just a child, he thought, too young for this and he thought of his Alicia and how he had found her all those years ago beaten and abused by a man that was supposed to be her father and poor Sarah, Shaun's wife, taken against her will and beaten badly. Why were there men in this world that would hurt these delicate creatures we know as women? Allen wanted to ask God but knew he couldn't. He could only trust God and pray that evil was destroyed in this world and soon. Allen had the certain knowledge that Christ would return. "Jessie, you're my daughter now. Mine and Alicia's. We'll love you like you're our own daughter. You'll want for nothing. I swear. Come, go with Tucker and I."

For a long few moments, maybe five full moments Jessie stayed still and then she looked up at Allen. "He has my mother's IOU. If I leave him, something bad will happen, really bad. I can't leave him," Jessie insisted in tears and shaking.

"I'll pay him what your folks owe, Jessie." Allen held her eyes with his own and grieved for her.

"He had my mother's IOU in his hand," Jessie stood on shaking legs and reached into the lawyer's top desk drawer searching for her own IOU but unable to find it and crying all the more. She panicked that she couldn't find the one that she had signed and started crying harder because it wasn't in the desk and the monster on the floor was stirring, he would soon wake and she would never have another chance to be free.

"I've got this, Grandpa," Tucker said and saw Jessie's mother's IOU on the floor. He picked it up and tore the IOU into small pieces; then he put it in his mouth and swallowed it. "It's gone," he said and bent down to Jessie. "Now let me help you into the car." Tucker saw Jessie shake her head hard and knew she didn't want him to touch her. He wished she would stop crying, he would have done anything to make her stop crying so hard, her crying was killing him. "You're safe now," Tucker said while looking at his Grandpa. Jessie knew she still wasn't safe, she hadn't found the other IOU, the monster could still come after her or worse.

Slowly Jessie stood, pulling herself up by holding on to the desk and she cried out as she tried to straighten her arm. "He was holding it behind her back," Tucker said to Allen when they saw her arm was swollen and Jessie shook her head.

"He always did that when he," she looked down at the lawyer on the floor, "when he hurt me." She burst into tears and Tucker reached for her but she slapped at his hands and shoved him away. "Don't touch me," she cried in a cold and cruel voice and Tucker took a step back away from her.

The lawyer sat up causing Jessie to run to the doorway of his office and away from him, clinging to the doorway. "You can't leave," the lawyer said as he wiped his face. "I own you."

"Not anymore you don't," Allen Blackburn stepped up to the lawyer. "And you can bet the Bar Association of Florida will hear from me about you in the morning." Allen narrowed his eyes at the man before adding, "maybe you aren't aware, but I'm an attorney here in this state. I don't practice law beyond my business, but I keep my credentials in case I need to use them and I know people that when they hear what you've been up too, will take you down. You're done in this state."

Tucker watched as the lawyer got up searching his desk for the IOU and Tucker stepped toward him again seeing the coward run to a corner and cover his head. "You face little girls and hurt them, but not a grown man. The IOU it's gone. You lay one finger on her ever again and I'll tear you apart piece by piece." Tucker clenched and unclenched his fists and the lawyer stayed in the corner.

"We'll let the sheriff know what's gone on here," Allen said and followed Jessie to his car watching her get into the backseat and curl up in the fetal position. The lawyer watched them drive off, Tucker driving and Allen in the passenger seat with Jessie in the backseat.

"What are we going to do, Grandpa? She's hurt." Tucker glanced in the backseat and saw Jessie with her eyes closed but he knew she wasn't asleep, she didn't look restful.

"Stop at Aaron and Jenny's house. We'll have him check her over. Poor girl, she's been through a hell we cannot even fathom." Allen glanced in the backseat and saw Jessie staring off into space and he wondered if she were listening to them talk. "I meant what I said," Allen turned to see Jessie still staring at nothing. "You're my daughter now and Alicia's. Anyone hurts you in anyway; they go through us to do so. You're a Blackburn now and under full protection by any and all Blackburns."

Doctor Aaron Taylor, the son of Lang and Holly Taylor, was married to Allen's youngest daughter Jenny, they lived on the outskirts of Rockhaven, Florida. Aaron was who everyone turned too in a crisis in this area for medical attention so they were a well known family. Tucker banged on the front door of his Aunt Jenny's house and looked back at his Grandfather standing next to the car, Jessie hadn't moved from the backseat and Tucker was afraid for her, afraid of what he had seen that lawyer doing to her and aware that the lawyer had been doing that to her for days and he hadn't known, he hadn't saved her. He kept thinking of all the times he had been there when she was being teased and tossed around at school, all the times he had saved her and wanted only to keep her safe and now, to know that he had failed her, that he hadn't thought she was any danger at all, that she had left to be free of him as she told him she would never love him and he felt bad for her and for himself.

"What's wrong Tucker?" Aaron opened the door and asked. Tucker couldn't speak, he couldn't explain to his Uncle what was happening, all he could do was point to the car.

Allen had the back door open, it was almost dark out now and he knew they had to find some way to get Jessie out of the car so Aaron could look at her. A huge sense of relief came over him when he saw Aaron bending over into the car and then looking back up at Allen. "What's happened to her?" Aaron asked and Allen moved him to the back of the car and quietly explained looking at Tucker who was now standing with his mother's sister Jenny and he saw Jenny comforting his Grandson.

"We need my Dad," Aaron said. "I don't think we should touch her. Take her to your house, I'll follow and stop and get my Dad along the way. Just don't touch her; she seems to be in some state of shock." Allen nodded his head, if anyone knew that the mind could be affected by abuse, it was Allen Blackburn.

Aaron went and got his medical bag and kissed his wife before getting in the car to follow Tucker and Allen. Tucker kept looking in the backseat where Jessie was, it was completely dark out, darker than he had ever remembered. "Grandpa," Tucker said knowing he wasn't alone and thankful for his Grandfather's presence. "I don't want her hurt like this." He didn't sound like himself, Tucker thought as he spoke to his grandfather and they seem to hit every bump in the road.

"Tucker, let's concentrate on getting her home and some help, then you and I will sit down and talk. It's been a long day for you and a lot's happened." Allen put his hand on his Grandson's shoulder and was more than thankful when the house came into sight. He felt badly that just yesterday he was hurting over what Heather had been doing to their family for years and now this, yesterday seemed like nothing for him to have worried about. "Grandma's on the porch waiting for us," Allen said knowing Alicia was probably worried that they had been gone all day long.

Allen watched as Tucker stopped the car and then jumped out running to his Grandmother who he spoke to quickly and in low tones and she then followed him to the car seeing Allen get out on his side of the car. "How serious?" he heard Alicia ask and he was afraid in that moment what she might be remembering, he didn't want his Alicia to ever relive the horror she had suffered.

"Alicia, go inside. Lang and Aaron are behind us, we'll help Jessie." As he said this he saw his small wife shaking her head and climbing into the back seat of the car with Jessie. He heard Alicia telling Jessie she was safe now, no one would hurt her ever again and then Jessie was up and in Alicia's arms and crying, Alicia was rubbing her back and kept reassuring her she was safe.

Within five minutes Lang and Aaron had pulled up and Lang slowly approached the car to see Alicia had the girl in her arms. "Jessie," Lang said in his gentle way and Alicia moved trying to pull Jessie out of the car with her but the girl didn't move from inside the car. "Come into the house, please." Lang reached in a hand only and hoped that Jessie would take hold.

"I can't," she looked at Lang Taylor's hand and started crying harder. "I have to go back. That man has my IOU, he'll hurt my family if I don't go back to him. I have to go back." Lang looked at Allen from over the top of the car and saw Allen's head shake.

"Tucker ate the IOU, it's gone," Allen said seeing his Grandson still near the car but far enough away to give Jessie plenty of room to get out and go inside with Lang.

"Did you hear that Jessie?" Lang bent down to kneel by the car and saw the girl shake her head. "Our Tucker, he ate the IOU, it's gone. You're family is safe and you're safe now. Come into the house with us now." He again reached in his hand and Jessie at last took a hold and he assisted her out of the car.

Jessie Fairchild glanced around the yard lit by the headlights of the cars. She was at Riverbend, she saw Alicia Blackburn near her holding out a hand and taking her arm as she stumbled toward the house. Both Doctor Taylors, young and old were beside her and Allen Blackburn had moved to the porch with Tucker standing with his hand extended. She was stumbling, in tears, reaching out to Alicia Blackburn and then Allen as Lang Taylor held her hand and then she was in front of him, and the tears flooded her face. "Tucker," she said his name and he reached for her and swung her up into his strong secure arms.

"Show me what room you want her in, Grandma," Tucker said and went up the porch steps behind his Grandmother followed by the doctors. "You're safe now Jessie, you're safe," Tucker said several times before he reached the room and put her on the bed.

"Tucker, give Aaron and I time with her. Alicia, you need to stay," Lang said and closed the door blocking Tucker out.

Allen pushed Tucker aside and knocked on the door relieved to see Alicia on the other side. "I can't leave you in there knowing what you went through," Allen said to his wife and she came forward and gave him a hug before stepping back into the room.

"She needs me here, Allen. Remember how Greg helped me all those years ago? She needs me, Allen." Alicia saw her husband nod his head and she gave him a smile before closing the door.

"Grandpa?" Tucker said softly and Allen turned to him knowing the younger man was feeling a range of emotions. Allen knew Tucker was in love with Jessie and he knew that this was difficult for his grandson and he wanted to protect him, he wished Tucker and Jessie never knew anything like what he and Alicia had known, but now they did know.

"Let's go downstairs," Allen said and followed Tucker into the downstairs hall.

"Daddy, what's going on? Ethan and I saw the headlights on from the cars," Bethany was saying to her father in the hall as she and Ethan came into the house.

"Mama," Tucker said and went to his parents hugging his small mother close and Ethan, unaware of what was happening, hugged his son and his wife while looking at Allen.

"The little Fairchild girl," Allen said and looked up at the stairs. "Bethany, can you go up and make sure your mother's all right?"

"What's happened to Jessie," Bethany asked as she released Tucker and started for the stairs.

"Violated," Allen said softly and heard his daughter gasp.

"Mama," Bethany said softly as she knew her mother's history and rushed up the stairs.

Ethan followed Allen and Tucker into Allen's office and they all sat in the overstuffed chairs before the fireplace. "What happened?" Ethan asked his son when he saw Allen pouring them all a drink. Ethan knew Allen rarely drank so to see him pouring the glass full let him know whatever had taken place was bad and he accepted a drink from his father in law before Allen sat down next to Tucker.

"Tucker took me to town today because he found yesterday that Heather has been stealing from the company. I wanted to replace the money she took to make sure no one but me suffered the loss from what she had been doing, Ethan." Allen stopped and took a long drink seeing Ethan shaking his head.

"I'm not surprised Heather was doing that to us," and shook his head. "She was difficult to work with and often mean and cruel. We wanted to treat her like a lady so we didn't return her behavior, all of us Allen, we just put up with her."

"I put all the money she took in the last two years back into the company account," Allen assured his son in law. "I wanted to walk down to Michael's office and check on how Hannah was doing," Allen continued speaking of his brother Seth's youngest son and Lang's youngest daughter that were married and living in Tallahassee expecting another baby at any time now. "I passed by a lawyer office on Gains Street and saw Jessie in the front window at a desk. I went inside," Allen saw Tucker watching him closely as he told this to his father Ethan. "I knew right away something was wrong with Jessie. She was nervous and obviously scared. Then I met the lawyer and he seemed sleazy to me so I went out and told Tucker to drive to Jessie's parents house and along the way I knew, I knew in my gut something was bad wrong. Chester's always gambled, maybe that made me know I was really on the right track for something being horribly wrong, I don't know. But I was right, Ethan in what I was thinking, I just somehow knew. Chester lost everything to the lawyer gambling and the sleazy bastard let Chester and his wife keep everything in exchange for Jessie."

"What do you mean by, in exchange for Jessie?" Ethan asked Allen and saw his son leaning forward with his face in his hands.

"I had hoped she was just working there," Allen answered in a hoarse voice. "I had hoped it was only as a secretary or something along those lines." Allen fell silent and took a long drink seeing Tucker look up at his father.

"We went into the office, Dad," Tucker swallowed hard and looked to his Grandpa. "The lawyer had her on the desk, her arm twisted behind her back. He was hurting her bad. I've never seen someone with so much pain on their face. She was still dressed Dad," Tucker said and choked, his experience with women was not anything like what he had seen.

"I understand," Ethan said to his son putting a strong hand on his shoulders.

"Tucker beat the man up good," Allen said. "If I had been able too, I'd have beaten him into the floor, but I couldn't and Tucker did. We got Jessie out of there after Tucker tore up the IOU and ate it." He looked up and saw Lang standing in the doorway. "Jessie was more worried about her parents losing their home than anything else I think."

"She still is," Lang said as he came into the room and poured himself a drink. "She's so worried that her mother will hate her for not doing as she was told. What kind of mother would put their child in that situation?" Lang never drank, he never liked the stuff, but right now he was feeling too much and needed to do something to ease these emotions. He saw Aaron enter the room looking like he felt and handed his son his glass. "One won't hurt you Aaron," he said in his gentle doctor voice and saw Aaron take the drink and go sit down on the hearth of the fireplace.

"Jessie?" Tucker said looking from Lang to Aaron. "Jessie?" he said her name again.

"She's hurt," Aaron said looking at his father. "She has what's known as a spiral break of her arm, it happens when someone twists your arm like hers was. We've set it and it'll heal in time. She was forced to give herself to a man she didn't want in order to save her parents home, she wasn't prepared." Aaron stopped and drank all of the drink his father had given to him. "It makes me sick to see this kind of thing, and it's not talked about," Aaron looked at all the men in the room. "One in every three women will be abused this way sometime in their lives, by trusted family members, even husbands and fathers and worse, strangers with vile intent like what that man did to that sweet girl upstairs."

Lang saw Aaron fall silent in his frustration of the violent acts men do to small helpless women. "With the statistic showing how common this is, the fact is that right here in our family, with the number of women we have, four will have been violated as Jessie has been. And that's just the stats on this crime. We each in this room know a woman that has been raped and they can't tell, they can't talk about it for shame in what was done to them and because others blame them." Allen looked at Lang and nodded his head, they had this in common with their own wives and it was a bond between them that made their relationship stronger, it is also what had brought them closer as they both were living and dealing with fragile wives.

"She'll heal in time," Aaron said not looking at anyone and speaking more to himself. "She'll heal physically in time, but she'll carry the memory of this for a lifetime. And then the guilt, she thinks she deserved this, that there was no act against her, that she went willingly, which she did, but only to save her parents from ruin. She's a child still, she's just a kid. Who would do that to a kid?" Aaron stood and handed his empty glass to his father. "I'm going home to Jenny. There's nothing more we can do for her, time will have to heal her. But I'll be back in the morning to check on her. I need to go home to Jenny now." Lang walked his son to the door, he and he alone knew how deeply things affected Aaron, he was a good and fine man and Lang was proud of him, he always had been and he always would be.

"Aaron," Lang said while standing in the front doorway. "I just want you to know I know you feel things deeply and this today, well it's really hit you. And I'm proud of you. Very proud that my only son feels for others and has this compassion. You're the best son a father could have hoped for. You'll never know how your mother and I needed you. When you were born, you made things so much better in our lives."

"I love you too, Dad," Aaron walked into his father's arms. "You and Mom have been so good to us. And thank you for leaving the beach and moving here, we really do love it here, and all the Blackburns." Aaron smiled when pulling away from his father. "And I love one Blackburn girl I need to get home too. Night Dad!" he called as he bounced down the porch steps unaware his father stayed at the door watching him drive away.

"We weren't able to stop and check on Hannah today," Allen said as Lang came back into the room.

"Holly and I will take a drive into town in the next few days and check on her. I'm certain Michael is taking good care of her. I just wanted to be there to deliver her baby. I take pride in delivering as many Blackburns and Taylors as I can." Lang saw Tucker still sitting holding his face in his hands and felt for the younger man, everyone knew that their wild Tuck planned on a future with Jessie and that she rejected him. And now he brought her home like this. "Tucker," Lang said his name and saw him look up at him. "Can we talk private?" Lang met Allen's eyes and then Ethan before he went and closed the office door. "Your Grandfather knows, I trust your father," Lang said and went to sit down on the hearth facing Tucker.

"Is Jessie never going to be all right?" Tucker asked and Lang nodded his head.

"I wanted to tell you about my wife, Holly." Tucker sat forward almost certain that Doctor Taylor's wife was in the statistics of women violated. "She was young, younger than your Jessie," Lang started to speak and told Tucker everything about his Holly. "The thing is Tucker, when a woman survives something like that, she blames herself. Or she thinks she did something to deserve what was done to her. And she's left hurting inside where we can't bandage her." Tucker nodded his head and met Lang's eyes.

"But you and Aunt Holly are always kissing and hugging and so happy," Tucker heard his Grandfather laugh and defended his words. "It's the truth. You're that couple in our family and everyone knows it and says so. The deepest love is between Uncle Lang and Aunt Holly."

"I'm glad everyone sees us that way," Lang smiled. "It took a long time for me to reach Holly, to help her heal and know that what was done to her had nothing to do with the act of love. I spent a year treating her with only tender care and a long time after that just kissing and hugging. The healing for her was not easy. Nor was it easy for me. But now, yes you're right, we're that couple. I love my wife more than anything in this world, I love her more because of what she survived and she came through that nightmare and loved me. But she didn't love me right away; it was the worst time in my life." Lang looked away from Tucker; he was back, back to that little room that Holly lived in at his Uncle Sam's house. He had made love to his wife, he had reached her at long last but he had only reached her physically. "It's going to take a long time, Tucker. It took Holly almost eight years to recover from what was done to her and I wasn't there for the first six years. You're going to have to give Jessie a lot of time."

"We're keeping her, Lang," Allen spoke when Alicia came into the room. "Alicia and I are going to keep her for one of our own. She won't ever go back to her parents and run the risk of being gambled away." He saw his wife nodding her head. "She's our daughter now."

"Tucker," Alicia said softly when Allen fell silent. "She's asleep and your mother is going to sit with her for tonight, but I thought you could go sit with Jessie for a while, let your mother be with your father for a bit." She looked at Ethan and smiled, he was a good son in law and she loved him with all of her heart. The war had harmed him, changed him, but he was a good man and Alicia knew her daughter was devoted too. And Tucker, she looked at him, he needed to be with Jessie for a little while alone.

Tucker stood and rushed out of the room and up the stairs, Alicia could hear every foot step he made on the stairs in his hurry to be with his sweetheart and stepped into the hall looking up those stairs remembering a time that she had been frightened and alone and had run up those stairs only to lose her balance and fall.

"It was a long time ago now," Alicia said as Allen came and took her hand. "We've grown old," she said sadly. "And we love one another now more because of what we went through. Thank you for standing by me Allen," she turned into his arms and he like her, wished for their youth back.

"We should have kissed more," he said as he pulled her close.

"We kissed all the time but you're right, we never kissed enough." Lang stood in the doorway watching his best friend and his wife knowing their story as he knew his own.

"I'm heading home to my wife," Lang spoke and touched Allen's arm and then Alicia's. "Thank you for your help with Jessie," he said to Alicia. "And thank you for saving Jessie," he said to Allen and nodded to Bethany as she came down the stairs. "Night," Lang said to everyone knowing he had to walk home in the dark because he had ridden here with Aaron. "Allen, got a spare lantern? It's dark tonight." He saw Allen move to his study and come back with a lit lantern.

"Be safe my friend," Allen said as Lang went out the door and Allen turned back to Alicia. "Let's go to bed." He walked up the stairs with her not seeing Ethan and Bethany watching them as they disappeared around the corner at the top of the stairs. It had been a long day.

Chapter Seven

Tucker sat still and silent with his hands folded as though he were in prayer beside the bed that Jessie laid on. His mother had just left the room and he was thankful to be alone, he hadn't stopped to think much all day long and his mind had been racing since his Grandpa had ordered him to drive fast to Rockhaven and they had arrived at Jessie's parents home.

Tucker looked at Jessie small on the bed, she was lost in the covers and he felt so sorry for her, he felt anger that he hadn't known what was happening to her. Why hadn't she told him? He would have never let that man take her; he would have never let her parents give her away. She hadn't come to him; she hadn't trusted him to help her. All those years of keeping her safe from the school bullies and she hadn't even given him a hint.

He thought of the box social on Sunday, how silent she had been and not eating. She had known then that she was going to be 'sold' to that man for evil intent. He looked at her and wondered had she really known that? Or had she believed she was starting a new life working for some fancy lawyer and getting away from Rockhaven and him? She had said she would never love him. She had made it clear that he was the only one that felt anything in the relationship he was hoping to have with her.

Tucker grieved that she hadn't come to him, that she hadn't run away from that man and sought him out for help. She had stayed and let that man use her in the worst way a man could ever use a woman. And why? Why were there men out there that did this? Why were there men in the world that appeared good and upstanding and yet were abusing women at home? Tucker thought of his grandparents, Levi and Cecily Tucker were a very loving couple and kind and good to one another, they never fought though his Grandpa Levi had assured Tucker that he had been a bully for a time to Grandma Cecily, he had learned from his ways and mended them and was doing right by her. Tucker thought of other Grandparents, Allen and Alicia Blackburn and he knew that Grandpa Allen would die for Grandma and they were always gentle of one another. Then he thought of his parents, how his mother and father rarely fought and it was often his mother protecting his father because his Dad had never healed from the war.

Tucker was surrounded by goodness and love and kindness and care, he didn't understand pain and suffering and cruelties like this that Jessie knew tonight and he prayed to God he never would know anything like this again. He reached under the covers and found her hand and pulled it to his lips. He loved her; he had thought they would be together forever one day. Even when she had left, he had clung to the hope that he would find her and they would never part again, that being apart from him would make her miss him so much that she would know he was the only man meant for her. And now, after this, he knew she would never want any man for a long time. He thought of what Uncle Lang had told him in Grandpa's office, how it had taken Aunt Holly years to recover before Uncle Lang even knew her or approached her.

"Tuck," he heard her say his name and looked into her eyes, the pain was still there and he saw her fear as well.

"You're safe now Jessie, no one will ever hurt you again. You have my word."

"Everyone will know," she cried and looked away from him.

"I swear Jessie, no one will ever know." Tucker put her hand to his lips again and silently begged her not to cry anymore.

"He still has my IOU?" Jessie said in a broken voice. "I'll have to go back." Tucker sat up knowing he had eaten the IOU, she was safe now.

"No, sweetheart," he said in a soft voice. "I ate the IOU. I tore it up into little pieces and I ate it." Jessie nodded her head; she knew what he had done.

"That was the one he forced my mother to sign when she and my father," Tucker saw her swallow hard and take a deep breath, "when they gave me to him."

"Are you saying there was another IOU?" Tucker leaned forward onto the bed and saw her head nod and her eyes again met his.

"Yes," she said and looked into his pretty aqua eyes. She had been praying to God for an angel that would come and save her and Tucker and his Grandfather had come in and saved her. But she wasn't safe yet, Richard Ludlow still had her IOU. "He made me sign my own IOU, that I would," she looked away from Tucker and caught her words on a sob.

"It's alright Jessie, you can tell me anything. I want to make sure you're safe always." He saw her look back at him and she said in a rush of words,

"He made me sign my own IOU stating that I would allow him my body to use any way he chose for one full year," and then she was crying harder than before and Tucker stood up and left her bedside and Grandpa Allen had a huge hole in the wall of his guest room. "You hate me," she sobbed and Tucker came to her shaking his head and his fist.

"I hate the bastard that hurt you," Tucker said touching her hair. "I'm going to that lawyer's office and I'm finding that IOU, Jessie. I should have killed that man today. If I had been thinking right, I would have." Jessie watched Tucker reach for his coat on the back of the chair. "Grandpa and Grandma want you for their own daughter, in case you didn't hear them tell you so tonight. You'll be safe forever with them and my parents will help you all they can. So no worrying about your future Jessie, you're safe now."

"Where are you going?" Jessie pleaded from the bed as Tucker opened the bedroom door.

"I'm going to get that IOU you signed, sweetheart. And no one will ever know what happened to you or what your disgusting parents did to you. You're a Blackburn now; Grandpa Allen made you one today. Go to sleep, I'll be back before too long."

Jessie watched Tucker leave the room and saw the wall where he had put his fist into the wood and the hole he had left behind. She rolled onto her side and cried. Cried because she had gone along with everything and told no one and now others might find out and she couldn't stand the thought of that happening. And Tucker, he might not find her IOU, she might never be safe ever, she had signed away to a monster her own body and she was afraid for her sister if she ever told why she had done that.

"Don't cry, Jessie," Bethany said as she came into the room. She and Ethan had seen Tucker leave and she didn't want to leave the girl alone. Ethan was sleeping in the room next door tonight and she was going to stay here with Jessie. "You're safe now," Bethany reassured her and climbed into the bed pulling the girl into her arms. "What?" she asked Jessie knowing the girl wasn't able to speak, she was sobbing too hard but Bethany followed Jessie's pointing finger and saw the hole. "Just like Daddy," Bethany said softly to herself knowing her Tucker had put that hole in the wall. For a minute she wondered where he had gone too but knew he was her wild child, he was probably running around the woods in the dark releasing his pent up energy.

Tucker drove his Grandfather's car slowly over the dirt roads toward Tallahassee, there was no reason to hurry now, he knew the lawyer's office was closed and he would knock down the door and find Jessie's IOU and be gone within a short time. He kept trying to understand why Jessie hadn't told him what was happening to her. Why had she just left and gone off with that man to give him her body? Why hadn't she just let him know she was gambled away? Jessie knew that he would have made her safe. She hadn't told him and this ate away at his gut, his heart and his mind. And the price her silence had forced her to pay, Tucker thought. She was hurt now and might never get over what was done to her.

Tucker drove closer to Tallahassee thinking that for over a year now he had been planning his future according to his relationship with Jessie and they never really had a relationship. She was too young and now at sixteen she was ruined and would want no man all because of some bastard with no morals or values or standards. He wanted to be like his Grandpa Allen, he wanted an education. He was smart and he knew he was. It was time to change his future, Tucker thought now. He would go away to college and leave Jessie behind, he would be gone for a few years and when he came back he could be like Uncle Lang and work at reaching Jessie, teaching her what good men were to women and erase the bad man from her memory. And Jessie would be safe, she was now a Blackburn under the protection of his Grandfather.

Could he really leave this river? Tucker wondered. He had been born here, he only knew this place with his family and he knew, he was surrounded by his family and protected in the cocoon of their love. His Grandparents weren't getting any younger and they might not be here when he got back from school, he lost his breath thinking of life without his Grandparents. He was loved unconditionally by so many; they were all spread out on that river where he loved to live. But it was time for him to grow up, Tucker knew in his heart. Thomas was a deputy now and Taylor was a Minister and fixing to start preaching at their church. Shaun Allen was taking over the sawmill with his father Ethan and his cousins Shane and Shaun. Heather was gone and other than doing the books, there was no place for Tucker. He needed to make his own way, find what he wanted out of life and when the time was right, he would come back and win Jessie's love and help her heal.

Tucker pulled his Grandfather's car up to the lawyer's office just as the sun was starting to rise. The day was beautiful for late February, the wind cool but not cold and the trees were starting to bud on Monroe street in front of the Capital building. Spring would be here soon, the birds were already singing in the trees. This month had been unseasonably warm, Tucker thought and hoped his family wouldn't suffer a long summer.

Tucker went to the office door prepared to force it open but he looked and saw that it was already open and with a frown he went inside. The dawn light was streaming through the window and he saw him, the lawyer that had violated Jessie the day before, dead on the floor, a gunshot hole right in the center of his forehead. Tucker felt no grief for the man and stepped over his dead body knowing he had to find Jessie's IOU and get out of here as fast as he could.

Five minutes passed like five hours as Tucker tore open all the drawers of the lawyer's desk looking for the paper Jessie had signed. He had found a flashlight in one drawer and was using it now to search hard and fast dumping papers onto the floor as he searched. And then he saw what he was looking for and it wasn't in a drawer, it was on the desk, pinned to a calendar in plain sight. He reached for the paper and didn't tear this one up or eat it as he had Jessie's parents IOU, this one he put in his pocket as he stepped over the dead lawyer's body and went to his Grandpa Allen's car. He wanted to cry, he didn't know why; he wasn't the kind of man to ever cry, Tucker thought as he swung back onto the old highway out of town. It took him less than an hour to reach Woodville and then turn on the Natural Bridge Road toward home. The mid morning sun shining when he went through Rockhaven and he waved to Tom Cartledge who was out sweeping the walkway in front of his general store. He had been awake now for twenty six hours and he knew he wouldn't sleep until he talked to his Grandpa; he needed his Grandpa Allen more now than he ever had.

Levi Tucker sat at the breakfast table with his wife Cecily, Allen was watching them close as Lang and Holly came into the room holding hands and sat down still holding hands. "I can't find Tucker," Allen said seriously. "My car is missing too. Bethany said he left in the middle of the night after putting a hole in the bedroom wall upstairs."

"He'll be here soon," Lang said with confidence. "He'll never stay away from Jessie that long." He smiled at Alicia when she came in with a platter full of scrambled eggs followed by Bethany with bacon and ham.

"Mary brought rolls over yesterday," Alicia said and nodded for Ethan to put them on the table from the sideboard. "Tucker is out running somewhere. Everyone knows how he holds everything inside and then runs it out on the banks of the river."

"Jessie is at last asleep," Bethany said as she sat down next to Ethan and they all took hands and Allen blessed the food.

"In time, she'll heal," Lang said putting bacon on his plate and ham on Holly's. "God bless and keep her," he said leaning into his Holly and she hugged him close.

"Your love made me forget," Holly said to the man she adored, a man that helped her find herself when she was more than lost. "All these years with you, almost forty one years of happily ever after," she breathed against him, "and we'll have heaven after this. In heaven will know even more joy, Lang."

Allen looked at his best friend aware that everyone else at the table was as well. "Have you written your story down like you told us all to do years ago?" he asked Lang and saw Lang nod his head and reach for his fork.

"I certainly did," Lang said with a smile. "And I intend for Tucker to read our story when he has time. And then it'll go into your library for our future family to find and know that love can make everything wrong perfectly right, when you never give up on one another."

"Amen to that," Levi said looking at Cecily. "We wrote our story down as well, together," he saw his wife smiling up at him and leaning into him. "Ours was a love story with some bad moments, but love saved us and a little boy with his mama's eyes." Levi looked at Ethan and winked seeing his son's smile and he hurt inside for his child. What might Ethan have been like if not for the Great War, that war had harmed his soul.

"Well, you boys have beaten me," Allen said. "I have a lot written down, but I have a ways to go. Alicia and my story isn't finished. I doubt that it ever will be done." He felt his wife's hand slip into his and saw her smile at him, her curly wild hair streaked with gray but now she wore it loose and long, the days of wearing her hair up had passed.

Tucker came into the room and grabbed a plate from the sideboard not realizing that the sighs that filled the room were in relief for him. "I need to talk," he said and put eggs, bacon and ham on his plate along with two rolls. "Jessie signed her own personal IOU and we didn't get it yesterday, Grandpa," he looked at Allen and took a bite of the roll and shoved in some eggs, he hadn't eaten since breakfast yesterday morning and Grandma Alicia made the best breakfast ever. "Once Jessie told me of the IOU," he swallowed hard and drank from the milk glass in front of his father, lifting it in a gesture of thanks.

"You went to Tallahassee in the night and got that IOU?" Bethany knew now what her son had done but had to ask to be certain.

"Yeah, Mama. Give me a minute, I'll tell you everything, I'm just starved down." He swallowed another fork full of eggs. "I got to the man's office and the door was open," Tucker looked at his Grandpa Allen. "He was dead inside, shot in the forehead." Tucker heard his mother's gasp and his grandmothers as he ate another fork full of eggs. "I went through all the drawers and finally found the IOU on top of the desk right where anyone could see it. I don't want to tell what it says." He stood and took it to his Grandpa Allen seeing his Grandpa Levi leaning over to look. "I don't want you ladies to see this," he said looking at the women at the table.

"Dear God in heaven," Allen prayed and bowed his head but not before meeting Levi's eyes and seeing his were horror filled as well. The paper read that Jessie promised the man the use of her body, any way he wanted to use her body, for one full year and if she refused him even one time, another month would be tacked onto her debt. "I need to keep this Tucker. The man was murdered and we don't know who did it or if they saw this on his desk. Go finish eating."

Allen watched his grandson sit back down and continue to eat, he tried to eat himself but his mind was moving fast. Had anyone been on the street yesterday and seen them leaving Richard Ludlow's office? Tucker had beaten the man to up pretty badly, if anyone knew that Tucker had done that, might they think he killed the man? Allen shook his head and worried, the lawyer was dead, the lawyer that was raping that little girl upstairs. And Tucker and he had been to his office.

Alicia watched Allen stand and pace the breakfast room for a full few minutes and she knew he was worried. He kept looking at Tucker and shaking his head and he held onto that IOU. She wished he would tell her what he was thinking. She wished in that moment she could read his mind.

"We can't let anyone find out what was done to that girl," Allen spoke to everyone in the room. "People will blame her first and more so since she went agreeably with that man."

"Why do you think she did, Grandpa?" Tucker asked in a voice of agony. "She could have told me at the box social, I would have helped her. I would have come to you and Grandpa Levi and Daddy for the money to pay that lawyer for her daddy's gambling debt. But instead, she went with him and signed that paper." Tucker pointed to the IOU his grandfather held.

"I don't know the answer to these questions, Tucker. I know that little girl upstairs is awful young and she doesn't think like an adult. Your grandma told me that you said that Jessie told you that she makes everyone hate her," Allen saw Tucker nod his head. "She's a young girl and she was put in a horrible situation, God bless her she probably had no idea what to do and did what she was told by her mother."

"If her mother told her to do this, that is your answer Tucker. Children often obey their parents even when they feel what they're asked to do is wrong." Cecily looked at Levi and remembered her own situation. "Once I was young and I had a choice to reach out to Grandpa to help me when in trouble. But I was so ashamed Tucker, I didn't want him to know." Tucker saw his grandmother look at his Grandfather; it was as though they were alone in the room. "I should have told you," she cried softly and Tucker, though he didn't understand Jessie's reason for not telling him knew that she had made a mistake like his Grandmother had years ago and should be forgiven.

"I should have let you tell me," Levi said leaning his forehead onto Cecily's. "Every single day for over forty years I've tried to atone for my behavior toward you."

Allen watched Levi pull Cecily into his arms and put his hand on Alicia's shoulder looking down at her. "I've tried to atone to you as well," he said softly to his wife and she laid her cheek on his hand which was resting on her shoulder.

Tucker watched everyone in the room and wished he had a love like this with Jessie. His mother was leaning on his father eating her breakfast and his father had an arm wrapped around her. Uncle Lang and Aunt Holly looked lost in one another, and his grandparents were as they always were, showing their unconditional love and devotion to one another.

"I'm worried," Allen broke the spell that surrounded the dining room with his words and all eyes turned toward him. "Yesterday we left that lawyer's office with the lawyer beaten up by Tucker. And now today that lawyer is dead and I don't know who might have seen us leave and know we had something to do with him being beaten up. Nothing may come of this fear, and I'm aware of that. But say someone did see us and accuses one of us of killing the lawyer?"

"You certainly think more than I do, Allen," Levi said. "I never would have thought of this."

"It's not just that, Levi. Someone might find out what was done to Jessie. We might have some trouble ahead. I know we Blackburns, Taylors and Tuckers keep to ourselves but this might be more about that lawyer being dead than us keeping quiet." He remembered Lester, the man that had hurt Sarah years ago and he knew; anything could happen.

"What's worse," Tucker said finishing off his bacon, "is last night I told Jessie I should have killed the lawyer yesterday and now I go there and he's dead. She might think I did kill him, but I didn't. I don't even have a gun other than the one I hunt with."

"Wait," Allen looked hard at his grandson. "You told Jessie you should have killed that lawyer and then you left her here last night to get this," he held out the IOU, "and you found the lawyer dead?"

"Yes," Tucker said and swallowed down the last of his father's glass of milk.

"What are you thinking, Allen?" Ethan asked and looked from Allen to Tucker.

"I always plan for the worst," Allen said again pacing the room. "If you plan for the worst and it doesn't happen then all is well. But you have to be one step ahead at all times." He looked again at Tucker. "Did anyone see you enter or leave that lawyer's office today?" Tucker sat for a long moment and thought, he saw the dogwood trees with buds forming and thought of the wind and how nice it was, not too cold, but he hadn't looked around for anyone when he entered the office.

"It was around seven this morning Grandpa, I wasn't looking for anyone else." Tucker saw the worried look on his Grandpa's face. "I was there for a while tearing open all the drawers looking for the IOU, I just didn't pay attention to my surroundings."

Allen thought of Shaun and Sarah and years ago what he had advised them and he knew now he had to be more serious with Tucker. "You say nothing to no one, Tucker about being there. Listen to me, if someone saw you and tells the Sheriff, or if they saw you and Jessie and I leaving yesterday and tells the sheriff, the law could come here trying to connect us to this man's death. We might be the first ones they look at for his murder. So as of right now, you only speak to me, I'm your attorney."

Tucker nodded his head and then saw his Grandpa look up at the ceiling. "And we have another problem," he said still looking up at his ceiling. "Jessie. If you told her you should have killed that man and she testifies to that fact, you're going to be the first and probably only suspect they'll have." Allen looked back down at Tucker and then Bethany who had gone pale.

"Daddy, they hang men for murder in Florida," his daughter cried out and Ethan stood up knocking his chair over.

"Allen, we have to keep my son safe," Ethan said in a voice filled with pleading.

"I need to talk to Jessie," Allen said and left the room unaware everyone in the room had followed him. He stopped on the stairs and looked back and knew, they would all go into the girl's room, she would be supported and so would Tucker.

Jessie Fairchild was sitting up with the pillows behind her and looking out the double doors that lead to the porch, she could see the river beyond and felt safe, no one would harm her now, Tucker had saved her and he had told her now she was a Blackburn under the protection of his family. The knock sounded only seconds before Alicia Blackburn entered the room and Jessie thought she was beautiful with her long curly hair and huge clear eyes. She knew Alicia was in her fifties but she hardly looked to be that old, she still had a girlish look about her.

"We need to talk with you Jessie," Alicia said and made sure Jessie was covered before she nodded to the others to come in.

Jessie was shocked by everyone coming around her bed. She saw Allen Blackburn and Levi and Cecily Tucker and Lang and Holly Taylor followed by Ethan and Bethany Tucker and she wondered what was going on. And then Tucker came in and she relaxed, Tucker wouldn't let anything happen to her.

"Jessie," Allen spoke and she met his eyes. "I want to be your attorney," he said seriously, too seriously.

"I didn't do anything wrong," Jessie cried and Alicia sat on the edge of the bed taking her hand seeing both Holly and Cecily sit on the other side and reach for her.

"No one said you did," Alicia assured her. "Just listen to my husband."

"Yesterday, Tucker and I went into that lawyer's office and Tucker beat the man up, with good reason, he was defending you." Allen stopped speaking and looked at Lang trying to find the right words that Jessie could understand.

"Jessie," Lang spoke and she looked at him. "We don't want anyone to find out what was done to you." Lang saw Jessie nodding her head and tears falling onto her cheeks.

"Everyone will blame me," she cried out and Alicia patted her hand.

"We're going to all see that no one beyond this room finds out," Lang said firmly thinking of Aaron and knowing his son would never tell anyone what had been done to harm this girl. "We'll all fight to keep you safe." Lang saw Jessie stop crying and look a little more calm than she had been only seconds ago and he turned the conversation back to Allen.

"Last night Tucker went back to get this," Allen held out Jessie's IOU and she nearly fell apart again. "It's all right, we assure you, no one will know of this. We'll fight for you, you have my word." Allen saw Jessie calm down again though not as much as she had before. "Tucker found the lawyer this morning in his office when he went for your IOU. He was dead Jessie." There was no reaction to these words, it was as though Jessie didn't care, no relief was shown, no anger or hurt or fear. Jessie's face was blank and expressionless.

"I was here," Jessie said. "I didn't kill him." Allen nodded and looked around the room.

"But you know that Tucker beat the lawyer up, and you know why."

"I won't tell anyone," she said in a very calm voice.

"We don't know but someone might have seen us leaving there yesterday. Someone might think that Tucker killed that lawyer." Allen watched Jessie's face and saw her look hopeful at Tucker.

"Did you kill him?" she saw Tucker shake his head.

"He was shot in the head, my only gun is the one I use for hunting and it's at my folk's house," Tucker said stepping further into the room so Jessie could see him.

"I wish you had killed him," she said softly still looking at Tucker.

"Me too," Tucker responded.

"This is why you need an attorney, Jessie. And you as well Tucker. If anyone saw us or Tucker, he could become a suspect in that man's death. Jessie, you would have to testify to what Tucker said of wanting to kill the man, it would make him look more guilty," Allen stopped talking when he saw Levi and Ethan both looking at him hard.

"Why are you thinking like this, Allen?" Ethan asked and Allen turned toward him but before he could answer Levi spoke.

"You're acting like this is going to happen, Allen. You're preparing us for something that probably won't even occur. That man will be found dead and the Sheriff will think he was murdered for money or in a robbery of his office or something. Everyone knows we don't need money."

"You're probably right Levi, but I have to protect our grandson and Jessie, I can't have this hope that no one saw us yesterday or saw Tucker this morning. In a few weeks you can laugh at me for being paranoid, I don't care. But today, better we prepare for the worst and expect the best." Allen turned back to Jessie. "There's a thing called spousal privilege," Allen said looking from Jessie to Tucker. "A wife cannot testify against her husband or give information that might incriminate her husband," Allen spoke to Jessie. "The same applies to you Tucker. You cannot tell what was done to Jessie if you are married to her because it may make her look guilty of killing that lawyer."

"We're not married," Jessie said in a serious voice.

"You need to be," Allen said looking from Jessie to Tucker. "Only for right now, when all of this blows over," he looked at Levi and said seriously, "and I hope it all blows over, then we'll have the marriage annulled. You'll only be married in name, Jessie," he said softly to reassure her she was safe.

"I won't touch you, Jessie. I swear I won't hurt you," Tucker said holding Jessie's eyes and she believed him.

"And as your attorney," Allen spoke gently to them both hoping Levi was right and he was overreacting. "I'm advising you both to say nothing of any of this to an officer of the law unless I'm with you or Seth's son Michael is present. We are representing you now. I'm going to ride into town and meet with Michael this afternoon."

"Will you tell him what I did?" Jessie asked with tears forming in her eyes and saw Allen nod his head.

"He will be bound by an oath he took to never tell anyone what he knows, Jessie," Allen said holding her eyes. "I told you yesterday when Tucker and I found you that you would be my own now, my own daughter. Just like Bethany, I'll die to protect you. You have my word. And Tucker is my grandson and just like me, he'll not let any harm come to you. No one beyond our family, now your family, will know the truth of how that man hurt you."

"You'll live here with us," Alicia added. "You'll carry Tucker's name but you'll be here with us and safe."

"I respect what Allen is preparing us for," Levi said to everyone in the room. "But there is only a very slim chance Tucker will be accused of anything to do with that man. Like I said, it'll be handled as a robbery and no one ever be caught. And the man is where he needs to be."

"Dead," Ethan said firmly. "I just want my son safe. What Allen is doing seems to be as he said, paranoid, but I trust him. I trust Allen Blackburn with my life and my sons, he won't steer us wrong, he never has. And it won't hurt anyone to have an attorney representing them and married in name only for a time. The marriage can easily be annulled in time."

"I'm not hopeful like you fellows," Lang spoke to Levi and Ethan. "I think Allen's very wise to put this plan into play, and we all better brace for a storm ahead. The goal is to keep Jessie safe and to keep Tucker safe."

"Jessie, do you feel up to a little trip?" Allen asked and Jessie sat up in the bed straighter.

"I'm hurting, but yes, I can go out."

"Tucker, your grandmother and I will drive you to the train station in Woodville. The Doo Diddlie leaves for the city of St. Marks at eleven this morning and comes back at four this afternoon. Your cousin Taylor is down there at the Methodist church and Wakulla County issues licenses in the church with no wait period. Get to Taylor and get married and then come back to Woodville.

You'll probably beat your Grandmother and I as we're going to Tallahassee to meet with Michael. So just wait for us at the station." Allen saw Tucker listening closely to him and Jessie as well. "We need to leave here in the next thirty minutes." Allen watched as everyone started leaving the room and saw Jessie's torn blouse hanging on the back of the chair, he touched his wife's arm and she saw what he saw.

"I'll get her one of mine and we'll make it work," Alicia said to her husband and hurried from the room intent on finding something to fit the very petite Jessie.

"Here," Allen handed his grandson a stack of bills. "I already paid for your tickets they're in there as well." He saw Tucker counting the money he had handed him and then look up at him with shocked beautiful aqua eyes so like Alicia's eyes. "You earned that, son. You worked hard on those books and you came to me with your findings and helped me fix the situation. I have spoken to the others about what Heather was doing, so it's not a secret. And I'll pay you a monthly wage from now on for doing the books." Allen hugged his grandson seeing his wife standing with Jessie on the station platform.

"I love you Grandpa," Tucker said in a serious voice and looked into the grass green eyes that were the window to his Grandfather's soul.

"I'll be honest with you Tucker," Allen said looking again at Jessie. "I hope this marriage turns into a love match for you and you know the joy that your grandmother and I have and your parents. I'm going to be praying hard for that."

"I thought all last night about my future Grandpa," he heard the whistle of the Doo Diddlie train and rushed to Jessie's side. "I'll talk to you about that when I get back. Love you Grandma," Tucker turned to his grandmother and kissed her cheek then waved to his Grandfather who waved back before he helped Jessie on the train.

Jessie looked out the window of the train and thought of what she was doing here, and with Tucker sitting across from her looking like he needed a nap. The trees flashed by in the window as the train moved quickly to the city of St. Marks. It was really a small village and she'd only been there a handful of times, but she knew that Taylor Blackburn, Shane and Charlotte's son was working with the Pastor there before he took over the church in Rockhaven. She looked down at her skirt and tried to smooth out the wrinkles and then down at Alicia Blackburn's blouse that she wore, it was pretty but she didn't fill it out and they had pinned it closed.

Tucker looked up and saw tears on Jessie's face and sat forward taking her hand and she let him. "What's the matter?" he asked her and she shook her head and almost laughed.

"My blouse was torn; this is your Grandmother's blouse. And my skirt is all wrinkled. This isn't how I had dreamed of marrying."

"Not what I had thought of this day either," Tucker said with a half smile and knew he was marrying the girl of his dreams. "I just want you safe, Jessie. That's all that matters to me." Tucker looked at her, she was so young, so fragile looking, she wasn't ready to get married to anyone, she needed to grow up. It made him more determined to do what he knew he must, what he had thought of last night. He had his plan made and set in motion and the next few weeks would determine how soon he could make his move to making his life the way he wanted it to be.

"I feel sick," she said and lifted her splinted arm up, it was hurting her and making her head spin.

"Take some deep breaths," Tucker advised sounding like his mother when she spoke to him when he wasn't well. He moved to the vacant seat beside her and waited to be certain she was all right that he did so. After a few moments he put his arm around her and she actually leaned into him. "We're going to get through this together Jessie, you and me and our family. Take a rest until we get to the station in St. Marks." She relaxed beside him and Tucker found himself dozing off as well.

"Sir," the lady across the aisle from Tucker touched his shoulder and woke him up. "Are you getting off here?" she asked and he nodded his head telling Jessie to wake up.

"Thank you," he said to the lady and stood helping Jessie to her feet. "The church isn't far," Tucker said and took a hold of Jessie's good hand and walked beside her, she was just up to his chest and he knew he was a good foot taller than she was, he didn't want her to run to keep up with him so he shortened his stride.

"I'm sorry I caused you and your family all this trouble, Tucker." Jessie walked faster knowing her pace was slow compared to his.

"You're worth so much to me, Jessie. You'll never be trouble and my Grandparents need you as much as you need them. They love the house full of people, they'll help you heal and find your laughter."

"You sound like you won't be around," Jessie said in a weak voice that Tucker heard a hint of fear in and felt good that in some way she wanted him.

"I'll be around." He said absently as he saw a small dress shop just a few yards off of the train station. "I didn't know they had that store here," he said and pulled Jessie behind him forgetting to shorten stride for her comfort. A bell rang when Tucker opened the door and saw a young girl behind the counter and an older woman sitting in a rocking chair. "Hello," he said and saw all the premade clothes in the shop, they had a store twice this size in Tallahassee.

"Do you need a dress?" the woman in the rocking chair asked Jessie and Tucker pulled her forward as Jessie was hiding behind him.

"Do you have any readymade in her size?" Tucker asked and the woman looked at Jessie for a long moment.

"I believe that I do," she said and got up from the chair. "You don't need to hang around do you?" The older woman asked Tucker and he smiled shaking his head.

"I'll go find Taylor and be back for you within the hour," Tucker said looking down into Jessie's light blue eyes and saw her nod her head.

Jessie watched Tucker leave her in the dress shop and the woman took her to a back room where she tried on three dresses and then couldn't decide which one to take to wear. She waited for Tucker to come back and help her decide impatiently and worried if he might get arrested on account of her. He had saved her and he might go to jail for the rest of his life. And then Jessie felt a cold fear consume her, what if Tucker were to hang? She sat down hard on a chair in the dressing room and fought not to cry and felt like sobbing herself blind. She would tell the Sheriff everything if that were to happen. She wouldn't let Tucker get hurt. The bell above the door sounded and Jessie felt she could breathe again when she saw him, when she saw Tucker.

"Taylor is waiting on us," he said to Jessie and saw her still in the clothes he brought her in. "You couldn't find anything to wear?" he asked looking at the older woman in the store.

"She found three dresses but wanted you to choose." Tucker laughed and without thought hugged Jessie.

"Silly girl, I don't know anything about a dress. Which did you like?" Jessie stood still as a stone while Tucker held her in his arms and when he pushed her away and looked into her eyes she couldn't think.

"I like them all," Jessie said in a voice of confusion, she felt like she was lost and would never be found. She was allowing Tucker to hug her, yesterday that monster had hurt her and the day before and they were talking about a dress and she was marrying Tucker to keep him from hanging and the truth of what she had done to save her parents home and more from being made public.

"We'll take all three dresses," Tucker said to the store owner. "And she'll wear the pink one because pink will look beautiful on her." He gave Jessie a gentle push toward the dressing room and she went to change her clothes as though she were in a daze.

Taylor Blackburn, the son of Shane Blackburn and his wife Charlotte Taylor, grandson of Lang and Holly Taylor and Seth and Mary Blackburn married his cousin Allen Roston Tucker to Jessie Ann Fairchild in the St. Marks Methodist Church on a Thursday afternoon, the bride in pink and the groom in jeans and a white shirt with a tie and coat. Taylor felt that Jessie wasn't showing much emotion and Tucker was looking far too serious, much like their cousin Thomas and he wondered why this rush to marry, but he didn't ask because Tucker had told him that their Grandpa Allen wanted him to marry them as soon as possible. Taylor then watched as they hurried to catch the Doo Diddlie train home, poor little Jessie couldn't keep up with Tucker and the train was in the station, Taylor saw Tucker pick Jessie up into his arms and run with her holding on to him and he laughed. So like Tucker, he had always been running everywhere, he was known as the wild child in their family and Taylor counted Tucker as one of his very best friends in the whole world.

Things seemed more unreal to Jessie as Tucker lifted her up into his arms and ran to the train. They would be in Woodville soon and she hoped that she would come out of this haze she felt she was living in. She wondered about the Sheriff, had he dismissed the murder of the lawyer as a robbery or was he coming after them? She was too afraid to think and prayed that soon she and Tucker would know what was going to happen to them.

Tucker settled Jessie onto the train and took the seat across from her so he could see her face. She was looking so lost and alone, he didn't like the look she had on her face. "Jessie, stop looking so frightened," he said in the gentle tone he had heard Grandma Alicia use a million times. "You're not alone now. I'm going to provide for you and you won't have to worry about me ever hurting you in any way." He saw her eyes look at him, really look at him and he smiled.

"I don't understand," she said in a confused tone. "We're married in name only," she added.

"Yes, we are," Tucker said taking her hand. "And it'll stay that way for as long as you say. But while we are married, I'm going to provide for you, you won't want for anything." He saw her nod her head and then look ready to cry again.

"I was going to go to work in an office or library," she said near tears. "I was never going to marry ever." She threw her face in her hands and started crying and Tucker moved to sit beside her and pulled her back into his arms.

"Sweetheart, this is name only, nothing more. You can work wherever you want and do whatever you want. Grandpa will need help with the accounting books for the estate; you can certainly step in there if you want." Tucker held her close as a father would his child. "This is all going to work out, we just need time."

"I hope you're right Tucker," Jessie laid in his arms feeling comforted, she remembered all the times he had saved her from the bullies in the schoolyard. She was safe with him, like an angel he had flown in and saved her from that bad man and she was safe now, she was safe because of him.

Tucker saw his Grandparents on the train platform along with his cousin Michael and he was concerned because all three of them looked worried. "Are you married?" Allen rushed to his grandson and took the marriage license from him that he held out.

"Legally she's mine Grandpa and I know you and Grandma will watch over her for me, but I want to make sure she has everything she needs."

"Tucker," his cousin Michael came to stand in front of him. "Three people went to the Sheriff and told him that they saw you leaving Richard Ludlow's office this morning. They thought you were sneaking around robbing the place and they went in after you left and found the attorney dead."

"Oh no!" Jessie cried out and Tucker caught her as she fainted and lifted her into his arms.

"Uncle Allen has told me everything," he looked at Jessie who appeared small in Tucker's arms. "I think this will go better if you come with me now and turn yourself in." Tucker saw his Grandma Alicia leaning and knew he couldn't catch her as well. He was relieved to see his Grandpa Allen grab hold of her and support her.

"I'll go turn myself in, but first let me get Jessie home and settled," Tucker said and started for the car. "Don't worry Grandma Alicia; I didn't kill that man so everything will be just fine. It might sometimes though." Tucker put Jessie in the car and he reached to help his grandmother in and saw she was crying. "We're the Blackburns," he said looking at her and his cousin Michael and then his Grandpa. "We battle our way home to the river, I've not had to go to battle to get back to my river, not like you Grandpa when you were forced to be away from Grandma and my Daddy and Shane and Shaun when they went to fight in the Great War. I think now this is my time and I'll get home quick as I can. I promise."

"We'll get you through this," Allen said. "If I have to bring a gun to the courthouse and break you out, son. We'll get through this. We're the Blackburns." Allen got into the car with Alicia on the front seat beside him and Michael beside her. Tucker and Jessie sat in the backseat.

The ride home was hard on Tucker; he knew he probably wasn't coming home for a while. He wasn't really afraid, he trusted his Grandfather and he trusted Michael. They would see him safe and Grandma would take care of Jessie. He saw his parents and Aunt Holly and Uncle Lang on the porch, his Grandpa Levi and Grandma Cecily were on the steps. He saw Allen open his door and give them all a grim look and then heard his mother scream no and turn into his father's arms as the rest of them looked at him with concern. Grandpa Levi pulled him out of the backseat and assured him he would find a way to get him out of that jail, even if he had to pay all he had and give up all he owned. Tucker could say nothing; he could just hope everything would work out fast so he could get on with his life providing for Jessie.

Jessie felt like she was coming awake from a far off place and wondered if she might be dead and ascending into heaven. Then she saw his face above her as he carried her cradled in his arms into the house. She could hear his mother crying and his grandmother Alicia assuring everyone that this would all be over with soon. "Tucker," she said his name as he laid her on the bed. "I won't let them hang you," she cried and he touched her cheek.

"I won't hang, Jessie. This is just a bump in the road we have to get over sweetheart. You do like Grandpa Allen says and say nothing to no one of what happened. We'll have this behind us in no time." Tucker looked down into her face thinking again that she looked like a little fairy with her shoulder length hair and her turned up nose and clear blue eyes. She was beautiful, he thought and without realizing what he was doing he lowered his head and put his lips to Jessie's.

She wasn't expecting the tenderness of this kiss; she wasn't expecting a kiss at all until it happened. One second he was assuring her everything was going to work out and the next his lips were on her lips and he was holding her close. Someone moaned and she knew it was him and after only a minute he raised his head and looked down at her. "No matter what happens, keep quiet. Do like Grandpa told us and I'll be home soon. And Jessie, I do love you. I know you don't love me, and that's fine, I'll love you right now enough for us both."

"I'm scared," Jessie cried and Tucker wiped her face.

"Me too," he said and kissed her head before he stood from the bed. "I'll be back, maybe not right away, but I'll be back." He turned in the doorway and saw his family in the hall. "I'm ready to go," he said to his cousin Michael and felt his mother slam into him and his father right after her. "Don't cry Mama, I did the right thing you know. I did what Grandpa Allen would have done. I'm protecting someone and all I ever wanted to be when I was little was a hero. Take care of Jessie for me," he said this to everyone in the hall and looked to see Aunt Mary and Uncle Seth at the end of the hall looking at him with love and he smiled. Shane and Shaun were on the stairs and Sarah and Charlotte, they were all here, even Jenny and Aaron. "I bet I won't have this many people at my funeral," he teased. "And if worse comes to worse, Aunt Mary, you can make me a huge roll with a gun in it and I'll bust myself out of jail."

"You know I will, Tucker!" Mary said and everyone laughed a tense laugh.

"Love you Grandmas," he kissed Alicia and then Cecily. "Grandpa Allen, Grandpa Levi, will you come with me?" he saw them both nod and took a deep breath. "All right, let's go." He turned and everyone turned with him and started down the stairs. "Sounds like a herd of cattle coming down the stairs," he tried to tease again and then he was being hugged and touched by everyone and told he was loved and he smiled and got into the car with his Grandfathers one on either side of him. "No, Dad," he spoke to Ethan when he tried to squeeze in the car. "Stay with my Mama, she needs you. And look at all the women crying," he pointed to the porch. "You would think they were ready to hang me and there's not even been a trial." Ethan backed out of the car and went to Bethany, his son was right, she was falling apart and was now doing so in his arms with her mother next to him looking ready to join her daughter.

"Alicia," Allen called to his wife. "I'll make this all right," he saw his wife nod her head and wave. Allen lifted his hand from the window and Michael drove the car out of the driveway, no one saw Jessie looking out the window from upstairs watching her hero drive away.

"Mr. Tucker," the Sheriff said as he came into the room Tucker sat in with his Grandfather on one side and his cousin Michael on the other side. "I have to tell you Mr. Blackburn," he looked at Allen and Tucker saw his Grandfather grab a deep breath. "That new State Attorney is worried our good ole boy network will see your grandson free of a murder he committed. I happen to know for a fact that Richard Ludlow had many enemies and to jump the gun and say your grandson did this is premature. But like I said, that new State Attorney is policing us. He wants to call for a grand jury indictment and a speedy trial. I'm of a mind to investigate this thing through and through first. But in the mean time, your Grandson will have to stay in the county jail."

Allen looked at Tucker and knew to put his wild Grandchild; the one that ran free on the banks of their river into a jail cell was going to be hard. He half expected Tucker to be upset, but instead, the young man surprised him by being calm. "We are entitled to full disclosure of everything you have on this case," Allen said in a firm voice to the Sheriff. "I already have a private investigative firm called in to get started on this." He saw the Sheriff smile and nod his head.

"As you're Allen Blackburn, I knew you wouldn't let any grass grow beneath your feet. You'll have this case solved before trial. I know that young man didn't kill anyone and you know why I know?" Allen shook his head never moving his eyes from the Sheriff, "because Richard Ludlow was the most hated man I know. I can name three people right now that had the means and the motive. Your Grandson being in his office at the crack of dawn is concerning, but I have an idea of what it was about." Tucker looked at his Grandfather when the Sheriff's eyes fell on him. "The new little gal, and I mean little, she couldn't have been fifteen, he had working in his office, and I use the word working in multiple ways.

I'm glad she's safe now son and I'm glad you saw her safe. You have my word I'll work hard alongside your Grandfather's private investigators to get you out of here and home to your family and that river your family loves so much." Tucker sighed in relief, the Sheriff knew he was legally married to Jessie and he couldn't question her in relation to this case about him and Grandpa Allen had told her to say nothing and answer no questions.

"You don't want to ask my client any questions?" Michael asked in disbelief.

"I told you already, I know this boy didn't kill Ludlow and if he did, well the man might have needed killing." The Sheriff stood up and started for the door. "You gentlemen may talk in private for as long as you like, let my deputy know when you're ready to leave. Mr. Tucker will have a cell to himself." The Sheriff left the room and Tucker looked up to see Thomas coming in the door in his uniform and his eye patch on.

"Thomas," Tucker said and went to shake his cousin's hand. "You Mama and Daddy were at the house and saw me off."

"You sound like they saw you off on a trip, Tuck," Thomas said in a serious voice that didn't bother Tucker because Thomas was always serious. "How can I help, Uncle Allen, Uncle Michael?" Thomas asked and Michael touched his shoulder.

"You can't help in this Thomas," Michael looked at Allen and they both looked at Tucker. "Tucker, listen to me, you cannot discuss this case with Thomas at all, not one word about what's happening here. He works for the County Sheriff and everything you say to him, by law he must report to the Sheriff." Michael saw Tucker nod his head in understanding.

"I have to take him to his cell," Thomas said and saw his Uncle Allen look ready to pass out. Tucker was his grandson, his first born grandson and they were alike in many ways. Thomas didn't want to see his Uncle hurt in any way, he loved Uncle Allen because he knew Uncle Allen loved him, he was family. "I'll make sure he's safe," Thomas said and Tucker asked him how he knew that Taylor was sweet on Elise and Thomas told him it was because he was sweet on her himself and when he told Taylor that he had seen the hurt in his eyes.

"We're the four Musketeers Tucker, you me, Taylor and Shaun Allen. And Taylor was always the good guy, he deserved the girl." Tucker smiled knowing his cousin Thomas was a good man and he would be looked out for while in this jail.

"Love you Grandpa, take care of my girl." Tucker hugged Allen quick and shook Michael's hand. "I hope Hannah has the baby soon," he said before he followed Thomas out of the room, Allen was impressed that Tucker wasn't upset over the handcuffs. "Hey Grandpa, when you come back this way, can you stop and get me some books at the library on Engineering? Our President just passed a bill in Congress by the National Advisory Committee for Engineering Defense Training, I think that's the direction I want to go in with my life. I want to be educated like you." He smiled and Allen felt better that Tucker was focusing on his future.

Levi Tucker hadn't been allowed back where the attorneys were allowed to go and he decided to walk down to Gains Street where the lawyer's office was and look around. It was pitch black outside and he wished he had a light when he saw a light shining from inside the lawyer's office. He moved up to the window carefully and looked inside knowing whoever was in there wouldn't see him unless he shined the light on him because it was so dark outside. Standing still and quiet, Levi looked and saw the person in the office was a girl, she couldn't have been much older than Jessie he thought. She was crying and tearing through the drawers of the desk and Levi knew, she was looking for what Tucker had coming looking for the night before, an IOU.

Levi followed the girl when she left the office, her light showing him the way and he saw her get into a car and he suddenly knew why the girl was familiar because Levi knew that car. He took a deep breath and headed in the dark back the way he came relieved when the moon came out from behind the dark clouds that were letting him know it would soon rain. He saw Allen standing by the car talking with Michael, Seth and Mary's youngest son that was also a lawyer and he knew he wouldn't trouble Allen with what he had seen, Allen was looking worn down with worry over Tucker. Levi knew he would do some sleuthing on his own for a while.

"I was wondering where you went," Allen said as Michael got in the backseat and Levi in the front.

"I went down to that lawyer's office," Levi said as Allen started the car.

"In this dark? Without a flashlight?" Michael asked and saw his Uncle Allen pull up in front of his house while Levi nodded. "All the lights are on," Michael said and jumped out of the car. "Hang on, I may be a Daddy again and you can let the folks at home know what I have now." Allen watched Michael disappear in the house and waited with Levi in silence for more than ten minutes.

"Do you think he forgot all about us?" Levi finally asked and Allen forced a laugh and got out of the car, looking back in he caught Levi's eyes.

"I was just thinking of how Tucker is spending his wedding night," Allen said and went to the door calling out for Michael.

"Hannah gave me another boy, Uncle Allen. Can you let all the Taylors know and my Mama and Daddy?" Allen nodded when he saw Michael peek around the corner of the hall. "We'll get together in two days and start on getting Tucker free."

"Sure thing, Michael," Allen called back in a tired voice and when he turned around he saw Levi sitting at the steering wheel. "I guess you're driving," Allen said and got in on the other side of the car.

"It's a long drive home, Allen. Get some rest, tomorrow we'll start fresh." Allen leaned back against the seat and closed his eyes letting the motion of the car soothe him. He heard Levi whistling an old soft tune and relaxed even more, he wasn't sure when he fell asleep, but he needed the sleep.

"Where are we?" Allen asked as the car rolled to a stop with the lights off in the darkest of night. "What are you doing Levi?"

"Be quiet, Allen," Levi whispered. "Our voices travel in the darkness." Allen watched Levi get out of the car with his flashlight and walk away; all he could do was wait for his friend to come back.

"What are we doing?" Allen whispered as Levi pushed the car down the road in the darkness before he started the engine. Allen was impressed, Levi was older than him and had just pushed this car away from the house they were at, he'd also coasted in. "All right, Levi. What's up? Why are we sneaking around in the dark?"

"I need to do some more looking around," Levi said. "I'm not sure about what I saw tonight or even if it might help Tucker, but I need to keep this to myself for right now, Allen."

"Then you shouldn't have involved me by bringing me along," Allen said and saw Levi pull up to Seth's house and the whole place was dark. "And now you want me to wake up my brother and tell him he's a Grandpa again?" Allen saw Levi's head nod and the man had a smile right before he blew the car horn. "I guess we'll repeat this up river at Lang and Holly's place," Allen said seeing Seth poke his head out of an upstairs window.

"News from Michael and Hannah?" Seth called down seeing his brother and Levi standing by the car in his yard, the headlights were all the light there was as it was a dark cloudy night.

"Another boy for the Blackburn Taylor clan!" Allen yelled up and Seth waved right when Mary stuck her head out the window.

"Is Hannah doing all right?" Mary called down.

"They're fine. I'm going back to town tomorrow to see Tucker if you want to ride in with me."

"We do, we'll be up in the morning."

"Now," Allen turned to Levi as they started down road. "What are you up too?"

"Let's get to Lang and Holly and me home, then we'll talk over breakfast, Allen. It's late." Allen knew Levi was right, it was late and it would be later still before he got home.

Levi Tucker was up before the sun and dressed only to become frustrated when his car wouldn't start, but he knew, he hadn't driven in over a week and the battery was probably dead. He knew he had to go look and make sure he was certain of what he had seen last night, he had tried to do so in the dark on the way home but Allen woke up asking too many questions he wasn't ready to answer.

"Where are you off to on foot so early in the morning?" Lang Taylor drove alongside of Levi and asked, Holly had rolled down the window. Levi perked up, help had arrived.

"Can you give me a lift?" he asked and Holly scooted over after opening the door so he could get in. She smiled and snuggled up to her husband and saw him smiling down into her eyes.

"This is right where you need to be," Lang said to Holly not noticing Levi Tucker looking at them with a smile.

"You two are always love birds." He laughed as Lang started the car moving.

"So where are you headed, Levi?" Lang asked while snuggling closer to his wife.

"Last night I saw a girl in that lawyer's office. It was dark and she had a flashlight and was going through the desk. She was crying her eyes out and I knew, that lawyer has an IOU on her like the one he has on our little Jessie. The girl looked familiar, I couldn't place her though but I followed her and she got into a car. I didn't see the driver, but I feel certain I would know that car when I see it again, it was familiar to me. Turn here Lang," he had Lang turn down a road off of the Old Plank Road and Lang knew the house when they drove up to it as Jessie's home. "Back out before they see us," Levi ordered when the girl he had seen last night came out onto the porch and looked right at their car.

"Too late, she's seen us," Lang said and Holly shook her head.

"Let me out, Levi," she pushed on him and he opened the door and got out so that Holly could. "Hi Elise," she called out and walked up to the porch of the house.

"Mrs. Taylor," the girl called back, Holly had been one of her Sunday school teachers two years ago and she really liked her a lot, Elise thought. "How can I help you?"

"I came to get some of Jessie's things," Holly said and Lang knew he had a smart wife, he saw Levi was impressed by Holly's quick thinking as well.

"You know where my sister is?" Elise asked and came down the steps of the porch with a concerned look on her face.

"Yes, she's at Riverbend with the Blackburns." Holly saw the look of panic on Elise's face as she looked back at her house then to Holly again.

"I need to see her," Elise said in an anxious voice. "I have to work the whole week over at the Cromer house taking care of the children because Mrs. Cromer is laid up with the new baby she's expecting. Your son doesn't want her up and around. Do you know when Jessie might be coming home"

"She's not," Holly said in a gentle voice and wondered how safe Elise was in this house with her father that gambled her sister away. "Tucker and Jessie married yesterday." Holly saw the shock on Elise's face and then the joy.

"Good, she's safe now." Elise came closer to Holly. "Don't go in there and get her things, Mrs. Taylor. Please, run now before Mama wakes and finds you all out here talking to me. Just forget that Jessie ever lived here. I'll come see her as soon as I can and try and bring some of her things."

"Elise, if you need anything, please, let me know. I'll help you anyway I can," Elise started pushing Holly toward her car.

"Just go now, please." Holly got into the car and Levi followed her when she took his hand and pulled on him.

"Drive Lang," Holly said firmly and her husband backed up the car until the house and Elise were out of sight. "Something is very wrong in that house. Elise told me not to come in for Jessie's things, she told me not to come back and that she would come see Jessie as soon as she can."

"We have to get into that lawyer's office," Levi said. "Cecily is going to wonder where I've gone, but if you two are going to see that new baby, I need to go and search that office."

"Don't you think the Sheriff's department will have deputies there?" Lang asked as he started toward Tallahassee.

"If there are deputies there Lang, then I guess I'll get to see a new baby," Levi smiled wishing he had left a note telling Cecily where he was.

Chapter Eight

"I have lost my husband," Cecily came into the kitchen at Riverbend and spoke to Alicia, Bethany, Sarah and Charlotte as they were fixing breakfast. "The car is still in the yard, his work boots are by the back door, and his heavy coat that he wears hunting is hanging on the hall tree with his gun leaning in the corner. I've looked everywhere for him and he's not to be found." She sat down at the kitchen table waiting to see if one of the women might know where he is.

"Shane!" Charlotte called out for her husband and he peeked around the corner. "Have you seen Levi this morning?"

"I haven't been looking for him," Shane said in a teasing manner.

"This is serious, he's missing." Charlotte looked at her husband and he saw she wasn't playing around.

"Uncle Allen, have you seen Uncle Levi?" Shane called out and within a few minutes all the men that were in the dining room appeared in the kitchen.

"It's only seven in the morning, last I saw Levi was around midnight," Allen said looking at Cecily's worried face. "He was distracted last night about Tucker and he said he had something he had to look into."

"Wherever he is, he's on foot because the car is in the yard," Cecily said and then looked at the men. "What if he fell in the river," her voice was full of panic and everyone turned to look at her now as worried as she was.

"Shane, Shaun, run down to your Uncle Levi's house and see if there's foot prints leading any direction. We have all this sand here, and you boys are good at trailing." Allen watched his two nephews run out the door and the running turned into a race as they always were competitive and Shaun was out to win. "Don't worry yet, Cecily," Allen said in a reassuring tone. "Honestly, Levi was very distracted over something he refused to talk to me about last night that involved Tucker. He'll show up soon."

"While the boys are out looking for tracks, we have another problem," Alicia said and sat down at the table next to Cecily taking her hand. "Upstairs," Alicia pointed to the ceiling. "Jessie, she's done nothing but cry since Tucker turned himself in yesterday."

Sarah turned from the kitchen sink and put some toast, eggs and bacon on a plate with a cup of milk. "I'll go up and talk to her," she said to everyone in the room. "If only we could find Uncle Levi," she put a hand on Cecily's shoulder and felt her pat her fingers before she took to the stairs.

Jessie lay in the bed looking out at the river. She had cried herself to sleep and she woke up crying. She couldn't stay here and take advantage of these kind people and she would never go back to her home ever again. And to add to everything being a complete mess in her life, she was now married to Tucker and he was in jail because of her. She had to go to the Sheriff, regardless of what Allen Blackburn had told her, she had to go to the Sheriff and confess everything. She just didn't know how she would get there and she knew with her arm broken, she wasn't up to walking twenty six miles.

The sun was up and she could hear the noise downstairs, she had to go down and face this family of Tucker's and let them know she didn't fit in and thank them for their help, but as soon as she was able, she would find a new place to stay. Careful of her arm, Jessie left the bed and went to look out the window; the river beyond in the early spring was beautiful, she could hear the waterbirds calling and see the geese flying over the house.

"Oh, you're up," Sarah said as she came into the room with a tray of food and put it on the bedside table. "How do you feel, Jessie?" she asked and came to stand next to her looking out at the river.

"I can't stay here," Jessie confessed. "And I can't go home." Sarah took hold of her hand and held it tight. "I have to go to town; I have to tell the Sheriff everything. I know Mr. Blackburn told me not too, but I have too."

"Come, sit on the porch with me," Sarah said pulling Jessie onto the porch, she saw her husband Shaun coming toward the house closely followed by Shane and hoped that they had found Uncle Levi. She then laughed as she saw Shaun Allen run between the twins yelling his head off. "We're all a little crazy here," Sarah said turning to Jessie.

"I can't leave Tucker sitting in jail," Jessie cried and put her face in her hands.

"Do what my Uncle Allen tells you, Jessie," Sarah said in a serious voice. "Years ago, I was hurt, kind of like you were. Uncle Allen took care of us, no one knows but this family what I went through and now you. I kept quiet just like Uncle Allen told me too. Listen to him, Tucker will be home soon. Uncle Allen fixes everything, trust him because you can Jessie."

"I don't feel right staying here," Jessie said and stood up going back into the room followed by Sarah to touch one of the new dresses Tucker had bought for her. "We aren't in love, you know. We only married so I can't say anything against Tucker and he can't say anything against me. This whole thing is just pretend."

She sounded so young, Sarah thought and then knew that Jessie had just turned sixteen, she was young and she was very pretty with her blond hair that was cut to brush her shoulders and her up turned nose and slanted eyes. "Jessie, you're not going anywhere. Uncle Allen says you're a Blackburn now, so here is where you stay. You'll get use to us all in time, we can be a bit overwhelming but we'll love you and make sure you're safe and in time happy as well."

Sarah saw that the breakfast she had brought up was cold and she reached for one of the new dresses that Tucker had bought for Jessie yesterday. "Let's get you dressed and down to breakfast, this food I brought is cold." Jessie knew that it was useless to protest, Sarah wouldn't listen to a word she said and no one else here would either.

Levi Tucker walked into the lawyer's office, the place wasn't locked and there were no Sheriff Officers around, the building was deserted. He had waved Lang and Holly on knowing they would come back for him in a few hours and he quietly went to work. He saw that the front room of the lawyer's office was easy to see into with the large plate glass window looking out onto the street, the back room had no window and Levi decided that if he had an IOU on someone, he wouldn't hide it in the front office where everyone that passed by could see into, he would have something like that in his back office.

Levi could see where Tucker had torn all the drawers apart and everything off the desk in his mad dash of a hunt to find Jessie's IOU, the place really looked like a robbery had taken place. Levi sat down in the chair and tried to think where a man, an evil man with harmful intent, would put other IOUs in this office. And these IOUs weren't being used right now; Ludlow had been using Jessie's IOU right now. If a man had two IOUs you could bet there were more. He got up and wandered around the room looking behind a painting of a ship on the far wall, looking for some sort of place to put a safe, maybe in the floor and he checked for a loose floorboard but found none. He was getting frustrated in his search and knew he just didn't have an evil mind to figure this out, he should have told Allen last night since that man had a way of figuring everything out.

"Levi sat back down in the chair and leaned back thinking it was a comfortable chair, a bad man like Ludlow shouldn't have been so comfortable and he put his hands under the chair to feel how it worked that made it lean back as it did and he felt something. Getting up out of the chair he crawled on the floor and looked up and saw inside a spring latch of the chair was a small note pad and he leaned the chair back with his hand and reached up to pull out the pad just as he heard voices coming into the office.

"Oh God," Levi groaned and crawled up under Ludlow's desk wishing he wasn't as tall as he was, something he had never wished for in his life, he liked being tall or high up as Cecily would tease him. The voices came near and Levi held his breath wishing whoever was here would go away. He was too old to be on the floor like this and was feeling all of sixty six years. He should have told Allen about this last night, Allen was sixty four, he could still crawl around on the floor, he didn't have a bad back.

"He's not here," Holly said to Lang as she looked around the office.

"I wonder where he went. We need to get home, it's almost noon and I bet his wife is worried to death over him."

"Oh for heaven sake," Levi called out from under the desk. "Lang, come help me up." Lang and Holly went into the back office and Lang reached down a hand to his friend.

"What are you doing under the desk?" Lang asked and Levi gave him a look of exasperation.

"I thought you were the Sheriffs deputies," Levi said as they all walked to the door and out to the car. "You both scared the life out of me for a minute there." Levi got in next to Holly who was scooted over to Lang in the front seat.

"Should we go see Tucker?" Lang asked and Levi shook his head.

"Find a place to park and let's look at this," he held out the note pad and started to look without Lang.

"What is that?" Lang pulled over under an oak tree and leaned in to see what Levi had.

"A book of IOUs," Levi said. "All on women around the county he won as part of a gambling debt."

"I had no idea we had a gambling problem in this county," Lang said looking at all the names. "Don't look Holly, some of these ladies are from our church and he's written ugly things about them and what he did to them on the IOUs." Holly heard her husband's words, she knew that he would do everything in his power to protect her but she couldn't help but look.

"Lang," she reached out to Levi's hand and made him stop on one of the pages. "Oh Lang," she grieved and looked at her husband.

"So the bastard didn't just have Jessie, he had Elise as well," Lang said in sorrow for the girl.

"Oh no," Levi said as he turned the next page and Lang read what was written there while shielding his wife's eyes. "We need to take this to Michael right now," Lang said and then looked up to see Allen's car coming down the highway. He leaned on his horn and saw Allen turn his car to where they were under the tree. "Stay in the car Holly girl," Lang said before kissing her hard on the mouth and getting out to go to Allen with Levi beating him to Allen's car.

"Everyone is up in arms at my house, Levi. They can't find you." Allen nodded to Lang as he got out of his car.

"That's because I'm here," Levi said seriously. "Look, I saw Jessie's sister here last night in the dark; she was crying and looking for something. I saw her get into a car, I wasn't sure it was Elise until I saw her in the light of day this morning and the car parked in her yard. So I came into town and went to that lawyer's office."

"You went into his office? There weren't any deputies there?" Allen asked in amazement.

"Place was deserted so I started looking around, it doesn't matter now where I found this, but it's a book of IOUs and it's on women in the county Allen, some we even know and he writes what they owe him and how they'll pay. They're all part of payment to their father or husband's gambling debt." Allen looked at the book of IOUs Levi held out. "We found one on Elise," he showed Allen and then he showed him the next one.

"Oh no," Allen breathed while he looked closely at the IOU and then the note. "We all thought Maggie had moved to Wakulla County and married. That bastard killed the girl."

"And her father helped bury her in the backyard and within hours gave his daughter Elise to him. The man cared more about his farm and money than he did his children."

"What do we do with this Allen?" Lang asked looking back to be certain his wife was safe in the car and not hearing any of this.

"I don't know," Allen said looking at Holly as well and knowing Lang was keeping her safe.

"Take Levi home, Lang. I'll take this and go to Michael and we'll try and think of what's the right thing to do now. This opens up a can of worms and exposes good innocent women of this county, most only girls that have been a victim and will be a victim again when this is made public." Allen put the book in his shirt pocket and went to his car. "By the way Levi, you're in a lot of trouble. Your wife is certain you either fell into the river or you're suffering from senility and have wandered off."

"I should have left a note," Levi muttered and got in the car next to Holly. They watched Allen drive off in the direction of Michael's home before Lang pulled out onto the Woodville Highway. "This still doesn't get Tucker free," Levi said with his disappointment in his voice. "I don't know that showing that book to the Sheriff will help or not. It just gives motive for Tucker to kill the man."

"Couldn't we say it was self defense?" Holly asked. "He saved so many women from being harmed." Lang took his wife's hand and knew that she was affected by the names she had seen in that book of IOUs.

"Holly girl, you're talking like you think Tucker killed that man. He doesn't even own a gun like the one used on that lawyer. Tucker might fight, but he wouldn't do murder," Lang squeezed her hand and Holly knew her husband was right, Tucker was like Allen, he got frustrated but he wouldn't ever really hurt anyone.

"I just want him out of jail and home where he belongs," Levi said firmly and both Lang and Holly agreed with him.

Allen sat on the sofa in his nephew's home holding the new baby and looking at Mary chase after two little ones that were only three and five years old. Michael had the IOU book from the lawyer's office and was going through the notes along with his father Seth. "I guess you know this doesn't help Tucker," Michael turned to Allen and spoke as he looked down at the innocent newborn. "In fact, this gives Tucker reason to have killed the man. But, this about Maggie being killed by the lawyer in a violent act, well it might redirect the district attorney from looking at Tucker and look instead at Jessie's parents."

"Her father couldn't have shot Ludlow, he's laid up shot in the backside by his wife probably for losing the farm like he did. Betsy Fairchild did try to shoot me when I went out there and found out about this whole IOU mess." Allen lifted the baby onto his shoulder and patted his back. "Betsy Fairchild is a much stronger suspect than Tucker, more so once the Sheriff finds the body in the backyard of her home and this note and knowing what was done to Elise and Jessie."

"Let's wait a couple of days Uncle Allen, and think this thing through," Michael said. "There has to be a better way to get Tucker out of jail without ruining the reputation of all these women in the county." Allen agreed and handed the newborn to Mary after seeing she was never going to catch the other two.

"I'm going to see Tucker, take him some books on engineering and then I'm going home." Allen took the IOU book from Michael and put it back in his pocket. "I'll talk to you in a couple of days. That's a pretty baby boy you have there, Michael." Allen slapped his brother on the shoulder and smiled calling him Grandpa and then he kissed Mary and called her Grandma. "I guess you'll be too busy helping with the babies to make rolls for our Sunday dinner on the grounds at church," Allen said and saw Mary shake her head.

"I'll stay up late to get my rolls done. We'll need a bunch now that our family has grown so much. I need to hand down my secret recipes to one of the girls." Allen hugged her quick and walked out the door intent on seeing Tucker.

"Levi Tucker," Cecily said in a near hysterical voice and then burst into tears when he came through the front door of Riverbend with Lang and Holly. "Where have you been?"

"Lang and Holly needed me to go to town with them," Levi said trying to look innocent.

"Levi!" Holly and Lang said at the same time and saw him turn to look at them still trying to appear innocent.

"You two don't have to go home with her," Levi said in a serious voice. "But I do need to explain to her," Levi moved toward his wife speaking in low tones and put his arms around her taking her out onto the porch.

"So where was Uncle Levi?" Shaun Allen asked and Holly and Lang looked at one another.

"I think we'll let Allen explain when he gets home," Lang said and looked to see Jessie sitting alone in a corner of the drawing room looking out at the river. He wondered if she knew about her sister Maggie and thought she couldn't know or she would have told Allen. "Let's go sit with Jessie," Lang said to Holly but Shaun Allen stopped him.

"You should know that she's taken it into her head that she's a burden here and needs to go away. But she knows she has nowhere to go. Poor girl." Shaun Allen looked at Jessie and shook his head. "And Tucker's not here to help her and she won't let anyone else reach out to her, not even my mom." Holly touched Lang's arm and he knew she wanted to go sit with Jessie without him.

Lang saw his beautiful wife sit down next to Jessie and take her hand; the two women sat on the sofa for only a few moments and then went out onto the porch together. Lang saw them walking toward the river a few moments later and he worried if what had happened to Holly might happen to Jessie. Only a handful of people knew the truth including Holly's brother and he had died last year of a heart attack. Lang thought now how innocent Holly had been and how innocent Jessie is, what happened to her wasn't her fault. He hoped that Holly could reach her and make her see that as the facts.

"How's Jessie?" Tucker said as he took the books from his Grandfather.

"She's not good. She's closed up inside of herself as you can imagine she would be. But don't worry about her, we have a house full of women that will take care of her and keep her safe and men as well. She's our family now." Allen reached for Tucker's hand and patted it. "How's the jail cell?"

"Uncomfortable," Tucker said wanting to be back outside on his river chasing after squirrels or swimming in the river. "The Sheriff came in today and tried to talk to me casual, not about the murder. But I didn't talk to him. I basically ignored him." Allen nodded his head. "I'll read these books now."

"What do you want with these books?" Allen touched them and asked and Tucker leaned back in his chair glad to have changed the subject.

"The Government passed a program that if you could pass certain tests and subjects related to engineering that you could skip college classes and get a degree sooner. They're desperate for engineers and I've got nothing better to do. This will help me forget my running free on the river and rafting down to the bay." He saw his grandfather was impressed and he smiled at the older man. "I was really smart in school, Grandpa." Allen knew that about Tucker, he had a great deal of potential.

"A college degree would be a wonderful thing," Allen said worrying that his grandson would leave home and not come back. "I don't want you to leave our river."

"Grandpa, if I do, you have my word I'll come back. I'll always come home to you and Mama and Daddy and the whole family." He saw his Grandfather lean back in the chair and nod his head.

"Levi, Lang and I aren't getting any younger. We're all in our sixties. The younger ones have taken our place running the estate, but the only ones from your generation are you and Shaun Allen. My son will need you someday, Tucker. He's a good son and I love him, but I worry about him. He's got an innocence about him, like his mother even though he looks just like I did when I was his age. I worry too much in my old age," Allen laughed at himself. "No matter what you do or where you go Tuck, you'll take this river and land with you; it's a part of who you are. And you'll take a part of me with you. Remember that when you're taking your college courses, you're never alone, I'm with you."

"I'm so blessed to have you for my Grandfather," Tucker said seriously before Allen looked to make sure they were alone in the room and no one could hear them.

"Your Grandpa Levi found this today in that lawyer's office," Allen showed it to Tucker. "I talked to Michael and it shows just how evil that Ludlow was, but sadly it also gives you motive to have killed the man." Allen stopped at the page that showed what was written about Jessie's sister Maggie. "Before we expose all these women to the Sheriff, we're going to see if we can't give the Sheriff another direction to look in. Trust me, we need a week to figure this out, but so you know Tucker, we're working hard to figure this out."

"So Grandpa Levi found this," Tucker said while handing it back to his Grandpa Allen and saw the older man put it in his pocket. "I know you'll get me out of here as soon as you can, Grandpa. And I'll get started studying. Can you do me a favor and tell Jessie I'm doing really good and for her to just hang in there for a little while."

"I hope you two can grow up together, Tucker. I hope you two will get past this time and make me great by having a house full of children." Allen stood and saw the deputy come to the door, it wasn't Thomas today and he wished it was, he felt Thomas would make sure Tucker was safe.

"See you tomorrow," Tucker said and watched Allen leave the room. He had wanted to tell his Grandfather to tell Jessie that he loved her, but he knew Jessie wouldn't want to hear those words from him and certainly not his Grandpa Allen. Jessie had other plans for her life just as he did and he knew the time was coming for him to let her go and move on with his life, she was only his for a moment in time and only in name only.

Holly Taylor had spent the afternoon with Jessie trying to comfort her and get her to talk, the girl had done little talking and wouldn't be comforted. Holly understood her feelings and didn't push her; Jessie had to deal with what had happened to her in her own way. Holly was also aware that Jessie blamed herself but from what Lang had taught her, that was normal. When they came back from walking along the river, Holly passed Jessie off to her husband with the excuse that Lang needed to check her arm.

"It's going to be weeks before we can take this splint off, Jessie." Lang had made sure it was tight enough with the swelling going down. "Try not to use this arm or the fingers, get someone to help you; goodness knows there's a lot of people here that will help you."

"Doctor Taylor," Jessie leaned into him and whispered and he knew what she was going to ask him.

"Jessie, listen to me, you can't worry about that right now. You need to just give that to God for right now. No matter what, this family will love and support you."

"I can't have that monster's baby," Jessie cried and Lang knew that was what was eating away at the poor girl. What a nightmare to have to live through, first being taken as she was, then abused and hurt and to have it end up with a baby inside of her. He looked at his wife and saw Holly sitting in a chair lost in thought and he wondered if she were thinking of what was done to her before he found her. He hoped not, Lang never wanted Holly to hurt ever again, he wanted to keep her safe always, he loved her more than he loved himself or anyone else.

"We'll pray and get through this Jessie, no matter what; we'll help you through this." Lang saw Allen enter the room and wondered what Michael had advised. Allen looked at him and shook his head and Lang knew they were still right where they were, no way to get Tucker out of jail and no idea who the real killer was. The private investigative team Allen had hired would be here in a week; Lang hoped they could help get Tucker out of jail fast.

"We need to talk to Jessie," Allen said and Lang helped her up from the chair.

Allen motioned for Alicia to come with him, "You and Holly as well Lang. Where are Levi and Cecily?" He asked and saw them on the porch and he saw that Levi had turned his way when he said his name and Allen motioned for them to come inside.

Jessie went with the older family members leaving the younger ones together in the drawing room; she was nervous and afraid of what they wanted with her as Allen closed his office door and the door leading to the porch. "Have a seat Jessie," he said using

Alicia's gentle voice and was relieved to see Jessie sit down on the sofa next to his wife. "What I need to talk to you about is not going to be easy," Allen started speaking and sat down in a chair across from her. He saw Lang in the chair on one side of him with Holly sitting on the arm and Levi on the other side with Cecily on his lap.

"I know," Jessie hung her head. "I have to do what's right, Mr. Blackburn. I'm going to the Sheriff and I'm telling him everything and getting Tucker out of jail."

"Jessie, if you tell the Sheriff everything, Tucker will hang. You'll be giving Tucker a reason for having killed Ludlow. What I need is for you to tell us everything. Why did you go with Ludlow? You knew Tucker would have saved you if you were in trouble. It's all right to tell us, we are on your side and we want to protect you. It's time to open up and tell us everything Jessie." Allen saw her eyes looking into his and he could see her pain and that she was suffering. He honestly didn't want to reveal what was done to her to anyone, but there were other stronger suspects out there besides Tucker.

"It's the peck order, Mr. Blackburn."

"You're my granddaughter by marriage now and his," he pointed to Levi. "If someone in our family is a lot of years older than you, then they're called Uncle or Aunt. So starting now, I'm Grandpa Allen and that's Grandma Alicia," Alicia squeezed Jessie's hand and smiled. "They're Grandpa Levi and Grandma Cecily and this is Uncle Lang and Aunt Holly." He gave her a grin and added, "and you're Jessie." He saw her nod her head and wished he could put her at ease even more.

"You were saying something about the peck order," Lang prompted Jessie and she looked at him and nodded her head seeing him holding Holly's hand.

"Yes, sir." Jessie sat back on the sofa and knew it was time to explain everything. "I'm that chicken in the chicken yard that all the other chickens peck to death because I'm weak. But I'm really not weak, I'm just sweet." She saw every head nod around her and felt comforted. "My mother came to me a few weeks back and told me that she had found a job for me in Tallahassee, I wanted to go to Tallahassee and try to start a new life. I told Tucker I was never getting married, I was going to live alone and work hard, maybe in the library or someplace like that because eventually I do something to the people I love and they hate me and like that chicken, they try and peck me to death. And I never want to make Tucker hate me; he's the only real friend I've ever had in my whole life." She felt Alicia hug her close and knew the woman had been more than kind to her; she had been like a real Grandmother.

"So your mother got you this job with Ludlow, and you just went, no questions asked?" Levi pushed the conversation on to the subject of looking for another suspect in the murder of Ludlow other than his grandson Tucker.

"Yes, and at first I was happy, I could leave here and no one would remember me because I'm just not well liked and I could start over again, maybe reinvent myself." She saw Allen nod his head and felt he really understood her. "But," her voice low and her eyes downcast, Jessie continued, "when we arrived at Mr. Ludlow's house," she shook her head hard, "no, not Mr. Ludlow, calling him that shows a sign of respect and I don't have that for him," Jessie looked up at Levi first and then Lang and then Allen. "When we arrived at that monster's house my mother told me that I had to do everything the monster said for me to do without question. She said that he had Maggie, that my sister Maggie isn't in Wakulla county living and working, that the monster had her and he would kill her if I didn't do like he said." She started to cry and Alicia pulled her close. "I don't want Maggie dead," Jessie turned her face into Alicia's shoulder and heard the older woman offering her comfort and care.

"We now know why she went along with everything so willingly," Lang looked at Allen and Levi then up at Holly. "Holly girl, why don't you join the others in the drawing room?" He didn't see the look Holly gave to Alicia and Cecily. They all belonged here, Holly thought, these three women that each in their own way had suffered a horrible time before knowing joy, they needed to show this young girl that she was loved and supported and would get through this time together. Yes, hearing what Jessie was revealing was bringing back her own past, but she was safe now and she had been safe for the forty two years she had been married to Lang.

"I'm fine Lang," Holly said smiling down into his purple eyes, eyes that were right this minute looking only at her. "I love you," she said just above a whisper and he pulled her down onto his lap and held her close.

"You did what you had to do," Cecily said softly to Jessie. "Sometimes we have to do hard and difficult things we would never think to do in order to protect ourselves or someone else." She felt Levi's hand touch her shoulder and she leaned closer to him.

"But I never saw Maggie at the monster's house. If he had her, I couldn't find her. And then you came into the office and I just knew you wouldn't peck me to death. You reminded me of Tucker of how he was always saving me. Tuck looks a lot like you," Jessie said to Allen and he reached out and took her hand glad that she was starting to trust him.

"No one in this house or in this area will ever peck at you, Jessie. You'll always be safe." He looked at his wife who still held Jessie close and wished this girl hadn't been put in the situation she had been put in.

"Elise might be able to tell you more," Jessie said looking at all the men in the room. "She's older and she was upset when I left. We didn't get to talk; my mother wouldn't leave us alone."

"Your father told Tucker and me that he lost you gambling. He never said anything about Maggie," Allen continued trying to get all the information he could from Jessie and saw her head nod.

"My father gambles, that's true," Jessie said. "He's part of a group of men that come out to our house sometimes and they gamble in the kitchen at the table all night long. That's where I first met the monster," Jessie closed her eyes remembering how that man had looked at her when she went into the kitchen for a drink of water, even then he looked like a monster. "My mother told me that the monster had Maggie and I had to do everything he said or he would kill Maggie. That's why I went with him and why I stayed. Maggie is my sister, she would have done anything to save me."

"Jessie, can you go back into the drawing room with the others? We need to talk over what you've told us and decide what to do. But just know we're going to do all we can to keep you safe." Allen stood and helped Jessie up using her good arm to help her off of the sofa. "Don't worry," he said as he walked her to his office door and saw her out and down the hall, he didn't move until she turned into the drawing room doorway and he heard Bethany talking to her.

"We need to talk to Elise," Lang said when Allen turned back into the room and he nodded his head.

"According to that book of IOUs Maggie is dead and that girl just allowed a monster to hurt her repeatedly for no reason," Levi said in a harsh anger filled voice. "Poor girl, God bless her."

"Why would Chester say he lost her gambling when her mother told her that she had to go with Ludlow to save Maggie? Her mother and father have two different stories and her father was shot in the backside by his wife supposedly for gambling Jessie away." Allen put his head in his hands and tried to think. "Usually I'm good at putting the pieces together in things like this, but not right now. I need to talk to Chester but that crazy wife of his nearly shot me last time we were there. Tucker saved me."

"Thomas," Alicia said sitting forward. "I know you said he would have to report everything to the Sheriff that he hears, but if he can get you past Betsy to see Chester in private," Alicia's voice trailed off as Allen looked up at her smiling.

"You're brilliant," he said to his wife and saw her blush. "Now to figure out how do we get to Elise and see what she knows."

"She's working with the Cromer's every day this week," Holly offered. "Lang and I could drive over there tomorrow afternoon and ask her to come with us to see Jessie."

"You're brilliant too, Holly." Lang smiled at her and looked at Cecily and she shook her head with a laugh.

"I'll find Thomas in the morning and go see Chester and have him tell me all he knows," Allen said mapping out their plan in his mind. "You and Lang will get Elise tomorrow afternoon and bring her here and we'll talk with her. I wonder if she knows her sister Maggie is dead and buried in the backyard."

"I went through the IOU book, Allen," Lang spoke and looked at all three women in the room. "I don't want to talk about this in front of our girls," he said and saw all the women look at him with a look that said they weren't leaving.

"Speak up Lang," Cecily said firmly. "We know this situation is horrible and we want to help. The more information we have, the more we can help."

Lang looked from Allen to Cecily and back to Allen before he took a deep breath and told what he had found. "If you look at the IOUs and the women we know Ludlow won while gambling, they are young. I knew some of the names and asked Holly and Alicia how old the girls were earlier and they're ten and eleven." Lang saw Allen sit up and gasp at his words. "Yes, many of the women in that book are as young as Jessie or younger."

A knock sounded at the door and Bethany peeked into the room. "Daddy, Thomas is here and you said no talking about Tucker's case when he's around." Allen stood up and went to his daughter.

"We're done in here," he glanced back at those in the room. "We all know what we're going to do," he said and saw all the heads in the room nod. The plans were made, now to just see where this would lead and Allen still worried how it would get Tucker out of jail. They had to find the real killer, that was the direction he was going in.

Allen went right to Thomas who was with his father Shaun and his Uncle Shane standing in the doorway almost on the porch. "Uncle Allen," Thomas said as he stopped beside him. "I just saw Tucker, he's studying away. He told me this has been the hardest thing he's ever had to do in his life. He wasn't meant to be caged up. But he said he's planning and preparing for his future."

"I'm hoping to have him out soon," Allen said looking at Shane and Shaun who both asked that he hurry, they missed Tucker working alongside of them. "I need you to do something with me tomorrow," Allen took a deep breath hoping he was right in involving his nephew in this, but he knew no other way to safely visit Chester. If only he were younger, he thought. Back in the days of his young adulthood he would have barreled into Chester's home and taken hold of his wife while he talked to Chester and she would have no time to get a gun and try to shoot him as she had the other day.

"I'll be free around two and out this way," Thomas said and Allen was relieved, this time tomorrow he would have answers that might set his grandson free.

"I need you to go with me to Chester Fairchild's house. I need to talk to Chester and when I went the other day with Tucker, his wife tried to shoot me." Thomas' face filled with shock wondering why anyone would want to shoot his Uncle. "I have to ask you to let me see Chester alone, Thomas. I can't involve you in what I'm doing, but I need you to protect me."

"Uncle Allen," Thomas said in a very serious voice. "Tucker is my cousin and one of my best friends in this whole world. We grew up together, we're almost like brothers. I know I work for the Sheriff, but I want to assure you, my family comes first. I hear anything that might make Tucker look guilty, I won't tell anyone ever, you have my word." Allen looked into Thomas' grass green eyes so like his own. All these boys looked like him, they were all a huge part of him. Shaun and Shane were like his own sons and always had been, he loved them with all his heart and now the boys that were Tucker's age, Thomas, Shaun and Sarah's son, Taylor, Shane and Charlotte's son, his own Shaun Allen and his grandson Tucker, they were his legacy.

"I trust you Thomas," Allen spoke looking at Shaun and Shane when he did. "You boys are a gift to me. The girls as well. But my boys," he knew all three were going to hug him when they did.

"We've had some good times," Shaun said patting his Uncle's back. "Like Uncle Heath use to say, we all grew up together in different ways."

"Heath," Allen said his friend's name and felt like he could cry for the loss of his dear friend and brother in law. "How did I get this old," he wondered out loud.

"You're still in good shape for an old man," Shane teased him and saw Lang coming toward them. "And him, he's two years older than you and he can still row like mad against the current and up river." Lang smiled at his son in law seeing Levi and Ethan coming to join them.

"There was a manatee in the river," Lang said looking at Shane. "We were out fishing and saw the thing; it just begged to be touched. So I rowed after the thing and then it just stayed with us, while the boat drifted back toward home, the manatee never left the side of the boat until we rowed for shore."

"I've not seen many sea cows in the river," Allen looked down at the river he loved. "Lots of alligators," he winked at Shaun and saw his nephew give a short laugh.

"After all this with Tucker is resolved," Ethan spoke standing next to his father, "Let's all plan a day on the river. A picnic, and fishing; all our family together. Michael and Hannah can come from town and Aaron and Jenny. All of us together."

"And Mary's rolls," Allen said softly remembering all the times they had all been together on the river and in the churchyard. Family, that's what life was all about. What he was leaving behind on this earth was his children, his nieces and nephews and grandchildren. The future generations were what would be his wealth. And the river, Allen thought.

"I know what you're thinking," Lang said to Allen when Alicia and Holly joined them on the porch.

"You're like my own brother Lang, what do you think I'm thinking?" Allen turned and looked at Lang looking out at the river.

"That we've done well," he nodded his head toward Charlotte and Shane. "All three of my children married into the Blackburn family and us all." He looked at Levi and Cecily and Alicia and then saw the others coming out onto the porch, this house was always full. "The love here is endless. The love here is our family. And that's what I think you're thinking." Lang patted Allen's shoulder and looked at Levi. "I'm glad our children brought us together, we were meant to be brothers."

Holly hugged her husband tight and he looked down at her and smiled into her beautiful brown eyes. "Remember when I first saw you all those years ago? And you wouldn't look at me. Then that first glance, that first peek you gave to me wearing that hideous hat and I saw how beautiful you were and I lost my heart. I never dreamed we'd be spending our old age on a river surrounded by such unconditional love." Lang saw Jessie standing alone looking lost and afraid and he looked from her to Holly knowing his wife would do as he was silently asking her to do.

Jessie felt a hand take her own and looked up at Holly Taylor and followed Holly as she pulled her into the crowd that was known as the Blackburn clan. "You're one of us now, and for always," Holly said hugging Jessie close.

"We love you, Jessie," Alicia added.

"I'm honored to have you for my grandchild," Cecily gave Jessie a smile with these words.

Allen looked at all those around him and thought that not so long ago he was riding a horse and lifting Alicia out of a buggy and she had on long skirts and her hair up. Now, skirts were shorter, there were more cars than horses on the road and women wore their hair down. Times had changed so much in his lifetime, it was as though he was living in a different world compared to the one he was born into. He turned and saw Lang had pulled his Holly into his arms and was deeply kissing her. The couple loved like none others he had ever known, he thought as he saw Lang take Holly's hand and go for the front door knowing they were going home to be together.

"Now, together," Allen said as he saw Lang Taylor run down the front porch steps and thought the man still acted like he was twenty instead of sixty six. "We need to focus on getting Tucker out of jail and home where he belongs."

Tucker lay on the cot in his jail cell and looked at the ceiling, but he wasn't seeing the ceiling. Tucker was seeing his river. He was seeing Jessie running ahead of him jumping on a fallen oak tree and then turning to wave at him. She had been only thirteen and he had been eighteen. He had built a raft and they had gotten on the thing and caught in the current, she had been afraid as they had no paddle and he assured her he would keep her safe. They were three miles down the river from home that day before he managed to get the raft out of the current and to shore. It took him another half hour to find a thick enough stick to pull the raft back up the river. He and Jessie became friends that day, she had told him she needed a friend because everyone hated her, he had laughed then knowing no one hated her, you couldn't hate Jessie.

Tucker rolled over on his side and thought of what Jessie had told him about everyone hating her, he hadn't taken her seriously but here in this cage as he was referring to this jail cell, he had time to reflect on things and think. The girls in school Jessie's age often picked on her for being small, the boys often would pick her up and toss her back and forth or they would form a circle and push her back and forth, never letting her hit the ground, but they were rough. She just didn't grow like everyone else, Tucker thought of Jessie. She was the same size as the girls at the age of ten and twelve and even thirteen but then she just stopped growing. And then Tucker blushed, there was one place Jessie hadn't stopped growing and he thought of her rounded breast and rolled back onto his back. Jessie was shaped better than any girl he had ever known or seen in his life. Yes, she was small but not everywhere. He smiled thinking how different things would be if she loved him back, but she was only his friend and only wanted to be his friend and after what that lawyer had done to her, he knew he had to give her time to grow up and to heal.

Tucker thought of what Uncle Lang had told him, he knew when he got out of this jail what he was going to do and how he would win his Jessie's love. He smiled thinking of how Grandpa Allen called his Grandma Alicia his Alicia and he was thinking of Jessie in the same way now. She was his and he would one day win her love, she was meant to belong with him, they were meant to grow old together. She would see that and know that someday. Tucker loved Jessie, he loved her with all of his heart and he would never love anyone but her forever.

Chapter Nine

Allen met Thomas out by his car and saw his nephew was in full uniform and he wasn't alone, Ethan, Shane and Shaun and Shaun Allen were with him. "Mrs. Fairchild won't bother you with all of us with you," Allen heard his son in law Ethan say and looked to see Bethany on the porch, Sarah and Charlotte with her and all looking concerned.

"Don't worry, girls!" Shaun called out to the women, "Thomas will protect us." Shaun patted his son's back and saw Thomas was going to drive them to the Fairchild farm.

"Thomas is blind in one eye," Charlotte said softly and felt her mother hug her from behind, and turned to smile at Holly.

"Thomas has learned to be more watchful because of that blind eye," Cecily spoke standing next to Bethany. "Those boys came home from the war, they were Marines and heroes. They'll be fine in this."

"Let's start dinner," Alicia said and turned to see Lang and Levi behind them.

"First," Lang spoke and saw Levi nod his head in agreement, the man knew what Lang was going to say. "Let's all bow our heads and pray."

"And hold hands," Levi added taking his wife's hand while Lang led them in prayer asking for the Lord's protection today and every day.

Tucker sat up when the door to the cell area opened and saw his cousin Michael coming toward him. "I have good news," Michael said as the deputy opened the door. "Grab your stuff, I'm taking you home." Tucker reached for his things and didn't ask questions while he hurried from the cell, he knew Michael would tell him when he got out of here.

Home, Tucker thought, Jessie, he thought more as he rushed to keep up with Michael who was opening the car door for him. "The air smells so good out here," Tucker said knowing he had only been locked up for a few days and couldn't imagine what it was like to be locked up forever. "Everything is green. Spring came while I was in there." Tucker jumped into the car and silently inside begged Michael to hurry and get him home.

"I have to stop and get Hannah, she wants to take the children and stay with her mother for a few days," Michael said as he pulled into his driveway and within minutes Hannah, Michael's wife and the daughter of Lang and Holly Taylor was getting into the car with her three small children.

"Can you tell me how you got me out?" Tucker asked taking one of the children onto his lap and playing patty cake with the little one.

"The Sheriff came to me today and said they had evidence that Ludlow was involved in a gambling ring and made some fellows mad and he has no motive for you to have killed Ludlow. He didn't have enough evidence beyond the witness' to hold you and the county doctor told the Sheriff this morning that he believed Ludlow's was dead around midnight, you were seen in the early morning hours leaving his office. The Sheriff said no way you spent the night with a dead man." Michael saw his cousin breathe a huge sigh of relief.

"So Grandpa was right when he told Jessie and me not to talk," Tucker leaned back in the seat and hugged the child on his lap. He was free and going home to his Mama and Daddy and family.

"Best advice came from Uncle Allen," Michael said seriously. "When I was trying to decide what to do with my life," he turned and saw Tucker listening. "My dad, your Uncle Seth told me to be like his brother. He said there was no one else in the world he admired more than his brother. And that's why I became an attorney."

"I'm going to do my very best to be just like Grandpa," Tucker said and looked back in the backseat at Hannah. "And your father as well, Hannah. I love Uncle Lang so much."

Allen got out of the car with Thomas in front of him and they headed up the steps with Shane, Shaun, Shaun Allen and Ethan behind them. Betsy Fairchild came out onto the porch and blocked the door but within a few moments realized that she wasn't going to keep them out of her house and her gun was inside.

"Elise is at the Cromer house?" Allen asked Betsy and saw her surprised look that he knew where her daughter might be.

"How do you know that?" Betsy asked in a low harsh voice and Allen knew that soon Lang and Holly would have Elise at his house and she would help piece this mess together.

Allen walked to Chester's room with the rest of the men and they stood around the bed seeing Chester didn't look good at all. "We should have brought Lang," he said to the others.

"I think Betsy let my wound get infected," Chester said in a low voice and Allen sat on the bed beside him. "I'm not telling you anything," he said firmly looking at Allen and then seeing his wife in the bedroom doorway. He nodded to his wife and Allen saw Betsy turn and leave. "Wait," Chester said and took several long deep breaths. He heard the front screen door slam and then looked back at Allen.

"She trusts you enough to leave you alone with us," Allen said looking into Chester's eyes.

"She's killed me," Chester said and took another long slow deep breath. "What do you know that's brought you here?"

"I know Ludlow killed your Maggie," Allen saw the shock and horror that came over Chester's face and saw him shaking his head in denial. "She's buried in your backyard, how could you not know? Ludlow wrote on the IOU that you helped him."

"I didn't help him," Chester cried and put his hand over his eyes. "She did," he cried more and Allen looked at Thomas. "Ludlow has a gambling ring going around the county, when he wins and he often does, then he doesn't have us sign for money, he has us sign for our girls. To keep everyone quiet, Ludlow came to my wife and told her if she helped him, he would give her a cut of his winnings. He paid my wife for those girls because they trusted her and she took them to him." Chester cried harder and Allen could only wait on the man to talk and tell all he knew. "Betsy encouraged me to gamble, and I lost as usual. And she signed the IOU to Ludlow giving him our littlest girl Jessie. I think he might have already been using Elise and now you tell me my Maggie is dead. Betsy had our daughter killed," he grieved.

"Lang and Holly probably have Elise by now," Thomas said to his Uncle. "We know now that Betsy Fairchild was Ludlow's partner and helping him get those little girls." Allen nodded his head looking down at Chester knowing his love of cards had cost him his daughter and probably his own life.

"I'll send Doctor Aaron Taylor out to you later, Chester. Right now we're going home to get Elise and take her to the Sheriff to tell all she knows and Jessie as well. I didn't want this coming out, I wanted to protect Jessie. But this thing is way bigger than I knew and Betsy needs to be in jail."

Thomas led the way out of the room and all the men piled into the car. "My God," Ethan said as Allen told them everything on the drive home. "The women were young?"

"Yes, small like Jessie and Elise, some even eleven years old."

"Babies," Shaun said and thought of Betsy Fairchild convincing those little girls to allow that man to touch them and not tell.

"She made Jessie believe that her sister was being held against her will and would only be safe if she did what Ludlow wanted," Allen said. "Who knows what Betsy threatened the other children with? Young girls don't have the same way of thinking as we men do so we really can't understand. Maybe she threatened to hurt them or their families or have Ludlow hurt them. I hate like hell that we have to tell what's been happening and it'll become public. I sure wish we could keep it to ourselves."

"Someone needs to protect the girls," Shane said as he looked out the window, the world looked different to him now; there was an innocence that he had that was now lost with the knowledge they now had.

"Maybe we can find some way yet to keep from telling," Shaun said and looked at his brother knowing this would never stay a secret.

"Poor Jessie, she'll have to live with this the rest of her life. She's already been targeted all her life because she stopped growing years ago. Now this, she'll be ruined," Shaun Allen grieved and his father turned and looked at his son, Allen was proud Shaun Allen felt for the girl, it showed the fine man he had grown into.

"Let's just get home and get Elise and Jessie to the Sheriff," Allen said and everyone in the car fell silent, he knew they were all like him and lost in disbelief and horror. And poor Maggie Fairchild, murdered and buried by her own mother in the backyard of the house she had all her life called home.

Holly Taylor waved to Elise when they saw her walking on the road toward home and smiled as they pulled up to her. "Elise, can you please come with us to see Jessie for a bit?" Holly saw Elise look down the road toward her home with an undecided look on her face. "She really needs to see you," Holly pleaded and Lang got out of the car and came to Elise.

"You know what was done to your little sister," he said in his gentle voice. "She needs you Elise," he took her hand and led her to his wife. "We all do." He saw her head nod and Holly got into the car followed by Elise and Lang walked back around after closing the door to drive to Riverbend.

Michael helped Hannah out of their car and took the baby while she took their daughter and Tucker had their son. The house was full of people and he wondered how they knew he was bringing Tucker home today. Hannah opened the front door and everyone in the drawing room turned and saw her and then saw Tucker and his mother screamed his name.

Tucker handed the child he held to Sarah and rushed to Bethany holding his mother close. "I'm all right Mama, I'm pretty sure this is over for our family." He looked back at Michael who was smiling at him and nodding. "Why is everyone here?" he asked seeing even his Aunt Jenny and Uncle Aaron were on the sofa. The Blackburns and the Taylors and the Tuckers, he smiled glad he had come home to his family. He scanned the room for Jessie and saw her sitting in a corner. "I gotta talk to my wife," he said to his mother in a low voice and after quickly hugging his Grandmothers and Grandpa Levi he went and took Jessie's good hand.

"Tucker," she said his name and he pulled her toward the door.

"Let's talk in the yard," he said knowing what he meant to say to her and wanting her to know how safe he was going to make her.

Jessie went onto the porch just as Lang pulled up in the yard and she saw her sister. "Elise!" she cried out and ran to meet her sister as Lang helped Holly out of the car and Tucker came to stand with his Aunt and Uncle by the girls.

Betsy Fairchild narrowed her eyes as she walked across the yard toward her daughters. Elise knew everything and if she didn't shut the girl up, soon everyone else would know what she had been doing as well. Betsy trusted Chester to say nothing, she had long been the leader in their home and he was use to doing as she ordered him to do. But her girls, she had to threaten them to get them to do the simplest thing and even then it was a battle. She had been forced to bury Maggie because Maggie refused to be with her business partner Ludlow in the way he wanted her. But that was at an end. Her means of getting rich died when that Allen Blackburn got involved and she had been forced to shoot Ludlow between the eyes because he had planned to take her farm away and sale the place. She couldn't lose everything, not after all these years of building her life up to becoming rich.

Lang saw Betsy Fairchild first and pulled Elise between he and Holly. He went cold when he saw the rifle Betsy held. With what Elise had just told he and Holly and Tucker about Betsy, Lang knew the woman was more than dangerous. It had been Betsy that was helping Ludlow harm all the girls in the county and it had been Betsy that Ludlow was paying to get the girls to come to him and not tell on him. "My mother killed Maggie because she fought Ludlow," Elise said softly not hearing Jessie cry out and Tucker pull Jessie close to comfort her in part and because her mother was coming closer and the look on her face reminded Tucker of a rabid dog.

"We thought Ludlow killed Maggie," Lang said in a sharp whisper.

"No," Elise looked at her mother coming closer. "It was my mother."

Holly pulled Elise behind her when she saw Tucker shielding Jessie and Lang stepped in front of his wife. No one would hurt these girls, he thought and his eyes looked into Holly's.

"She won't touch her," Holly said to Lang looking at Betsy while holding Elise behind her.

"I love you Holly girl." Lang turned back around and faced Betsy. "We know everything Betsy," Lang held tight to Holly's hand and she held tight to his. "Go home and leave these girls alone. They're staying here with us."

"They'll tell on me," Betsy screamed and Lang stepped closer to Holly swallowing hard and almost breathing a sigh of relief when he saw Allen's car coming down the road.

Tucker screamed when the gun went off and Lang fell into Holly. "No!" he yelled and let go of Jessie running toward her mother. The gun went off again and again before he tackled her to the ground. Jessie was screaming when Shaun Allen jumped out of the car and grabbed her, pulling her back toward the house. Shane, Shaun and Ethan all ran to help Tucker as he fought with Betsy over the rifle and it went off again and Betsy went still while Tucker stood up.

Allen looked to see his Grandson stand up and ran to Lang and Holly screaming help over and over. "Oh God, oh dear God." Allen prayed as he pulled Holly off of Lang and saw blood covering her breast and he screamed again for help seeing all of his family rushing from the house and hearing Holly and Lang's son Aaron screaming with him.

"Mama!" Hannah yelled followed by Charlotte who was pushing everyone out of their way to get to their parents.

Lang saw Allen above him holding Holly in his arms and crying. "I never had a brother, Allen. Until you." He gasped out. "Give me my wife," he pleaded and Allen laid Holly back on Lang's chest. "Holly girl," he said as he hugged her knowing she was leaving him. "I'm coming, Holly girl," he breathed seeing his son Aaron's face above him and his son tears mixing with his own. "Amy," he said softly and reached up to touch Aaron's face. "Oh Amy, Mama and Daddy are here. We always loved you." Allen heard a gurgling sound as Lang fought to breath and he reached over and closed Holly's eyes, she was now forever asleep in Jesus. "I'm coming, Holly," Lang said in a choked voice and coughed up blood. "Holly girl, I'm here," and he said no more words.

"Dad!" Aaron fell onto his father sobbing; his sisters were hugging one another and crying as hard as he was. Allen looked up at Tucker and wondered for a second why he wasn't in jail and then saw Betsy on the ground also dead.

Allen couldn't stand; he rocked forward and realized he was crying almost hysterically. He hadn't cried like this but one other time in his life. He saw Alicia reaching for him but he still couldn't stand. Then he saw his wife crumpling to the ground, he saw Tucker catch her before she hit and realized that Levi was on his knees holding Cecily and Mary had her faced turned into Seth's chest. These women, of the same generation had a deep bond and they had just lost one of their sisters. As he and Levi had just lost a brother. And there were children here without their parents.

"Lang was so good," Allen cried out talking to everyone. "Holly was his angel. How in the hell are we going to go on without them? Oh God, oh God help us."

Chapter Ten

Taylor Blackburn had at last come home to settle into his new life and to Pastor the Shady Grove Church. For years he had been preparing to Minister to this community; and his first task was to bury his Grandparents. He looked out at all the people in the churchyard and knew there was no way they would all fit inside this church. He saw his cousins Thomas and Shaun Allen standing near to Tucker who was beside Jessie and Eddie was bouncing around them and he thought of all the years they had spent together out on the river growing up. He closed his eyes and saw his Granddaddy Lang baiting his hook because he was afraid to touch the worm, his Granddaddy Lang carrying Thomas who had lost his eye in an accident down by the river. Grandma Holly brushing his hair and telling him how much like a Blackburn he looked but he had her brown eyes. His Grandparents parented all of them, they were gentle and loving people. He could close his eyes now and he did and see his Granddaddy Lang jumping over the creek, holding on to his hat so it wouldn't fall off as he ran to Grandma Holly. They were in love for all of their marriage; they were the perfect couple and loved by everyone around them.

Shane stood holding Charlotte close and waiting for everyone to try and fit into the church. Charlotte was crying still, she hadn't stopped for days and he didn't blame her. He remembered pulling

Holly out of the ocean and going back in for Lang, they had been so happy as a family and he didn't understand how this happened. He knew Uncle Allen was going to speak; not just his nephew Taylor. Shane looked up at Taylor on the porch steps and thought how he had been named for the Taylor's and the Blackburn. He defined this family; if only he had some of the Tucker blood he would tie them all together. But then Shane knew, they had all been tied together for years with and without blood.

"I wanted to come to you and tell you thank you Shane," Allen Blackburn walked up to his favorite nephew knowing he shouldn't have favorites, but Shane was meant to be that one that was special to him. He hugged Charlotte and held her while he shook Shane's hand with Shane staring at him with a questioning look. "If not for you, we wouldn't have had all these years with Lang and Holly. If not for you and Charlotte falling in love, my daughter Jenny wouldn't have Aaron and Michael wouldn't have Hannah."

Shane had never realized that it was him, his war injuries and recovery that had brought Dr. Lang Taylor and his wife and three children to Riverbend. He could remember the day they came here, the day he had been reunited with his family, the day Lang Taylor had become Allen Blackburn's best friend. "They were the most special people," Shane said and could say no more as Allen handed Charlotte back to him. He watched as his Uncle went to Aaron and shook his hand and then hugged Lang's only son and he cried as hard as his wife. Jenny, his Uncle Allen's daughter was Aaron's wife and she was crying as hard as Aaron was, as he was.

Allen looked at Seth standing with his son Michael and Michael holding his wife Hannah, and he went to them taking hold of Hannah as he had Charlotte. "Your father told me of his sister, Hannah," Allen said to her and felt her cry harder. "He said she came back to him in the form of you." Allen saw Michael reaching for his wife and handed her back to him. All three of Lang and Holly's children were now Blackburns and they now belonged to him to watch over and protect. If only he had protected Lang and Holly.

"I read their story," Alicia said as her husband came to stand next to her. "We need to finish writing ours as Lang told us too," she said leaning into him.

"I already have more than half of it down on paper," Allen kissed the top of her head. "We'll work on it more often, Alicia. I promise."

"Don't forget to write about all the holes you put in the hallway wall," she said gently and he held her closer.

"Tucker put the biggest one there," Allen said looking back at his grandson who was still looking upset over what had happened. "It happened so fast," Allen said to no one but Alicia heard him. One minute they were driving to the house, Betsy had the gun, he saw Lang step in front of Elise and then in front of Holly. He could still see Holly taking tight hold of Lang's hand, they said something to one another and then the blast of the rifle and it hit Lang in the chest, he had fallen into Holly and Holly had screamed and grabbed him when the rifle went off again and Allen saw Holly fall into Lang and another loud blast and Holly landed on Lang. She had been shot in the breast and the neck, she had bled out in seconds while Lang fought to live, but he was saying goodbye, he wouldn't have wanted to live without Holly.

"Lang and Holly named the story they wrote of their lives, A Return of Innocence," Alicia said to her husband when she heard him moan. "They wrote it together on a typewriter and it looks nice and neat. They also typed up for Levi and Cecily their story, both works are on your desk. I was wondering if we could have someone copy them and bind them." Allen was looking down at her; she had taken him away from his thoughts and his memories.

"So Levi and Cecily are done as well," he stated and looked at them standing near Mary and Seth. "What did they name their story?" Allen looked at Alicia determine to focus on her and put this horrible agony aside for a moment.

"No Sound the Silence Makes," Alicia touched her husband's cheek gently thinking of their life together. "And our story, if you give me what you've written I'll type it up for us." He nodded his head and asked her to name their story and she assured him she would when it was finished.

"We have to focus on our story Alicia," he said too seriously. "None of us are promised the next minute." She hugged him and knew she would get busy tonight after he was asleep.

Only family were allowed in the church, blood relation or marriage which meant that the Blackburns, Taylors and Tuckers filled every pew. Taylor looked out at his family and knew he had to speak. He had to say the words of comfort they all wanted to hear. The windows were open so that everyone in the churchyard could hear. Taylor looked at his mother Charlotte and his father Shane and he knew he was going to cry and not be able to speak. He swallowed hard and looked at his Uncle Allen who saw his situation.

"Lang and Holly Taylor were my Grandparents," Taylor said before the tears started to fall and he kept looking at his Uncle Allen with a plea in his eyes for help.

"Allen," Alicia pulled on her husband's arm. "Allen, Taylor needs you. Taylor needs your help." Allen looked down at Alicia and then back to Taylor and stood.

"The finest man I ever knew," Allen said as he stood up and started down the church aisle and took Taylor in a hug before turning to their family. "First Corinthians chapter fifteen verses fifty four through fifty seven." Allen saw many opening their bibles and turned to Taylor, this was for him to say with Allen supporting him, it was what Lang and Holly wanted said at their death. "Taylor," he said in a low voice, "you need to say the words son."

Taylor stepped forward and looked at his Mama and Daddy while holding his bible close. "This mortal shall have put on immortality, then shall be brought to pass the saying that is written, death is swallowed up in victory. Oh death, where is thy sting? O grave, where is thy victory? The sting of death is sin; and the strength of sin is the law. But thanks be to God, which giveth us the victory through our Lord Jesus Christ."

Allen looked out at all the faces he knew so well and spoke of Lang, his tears were not alone. As he spoke of Holly he told of the great love this couple held for one another, they were the love story in the family and their love had spanned nearly forty years. Holly had only been sixty three, too young Allen thought. Lang had been a young sixty eight and Allen thought of him chasing that manatee and rowing against the current with his son in law Shane. Allen had been forced to stop speaking several times to catch his breath and looking down into the open coffin that held Lang and his wife Holly. Allen had ordered it special built to hold them both side by side and Charlotte had placed her mother's hand where it was holding her father's. They looked so peaceful, Allen thought. "They died as they lived," Allen said these last words. "They were heroes always helping and protecting others. And they died protecting another."

Allen left Taylor alone at the pulpit and went back to his wife. Within a few moments everyone was standing and walking up to the beautiful coffin paying their last respects to this loving couple that set an example we should all follow.

Tucker saw his Grandfather and wanted to make everything right for him, but he knew he couldn't. He couldn't help anyone. He kept reliving that moment the gun went off, why hadn't he realized that crazy old woman was going to shoot Uncle Lang? and then Aunt Holly. He grieved over Holly's death. Had he not run toward Betsy might she have not shot and hit Holly? He would never know now, it was too late. And it had happened so fast. Tucker looked at Jessie sitting next to Elise, they were both broken beyond words, not for their crazy mother but for Lang and Holly.

Had the couple not been protecting Elise they wouldn't have died. Elise had told the family Holly's last words to Lang were that her mother wouldn't hurt her.

Tucker knew Jessie and Elise wanted to go away from here, Jessie had asked him to annul their marriage but he had refused, he said they needed time to heal. And Elsie, she was like Jessie, she had nowhere to go. Chester Fairchild had died peacefully in his bed the afternoon that Lang and Holly had been murdered. There was no funeral for him, and the girls refused to go back to the house and the sheriff's officers had found Maggie, she was now in the cemetery next to the church. Those two girls had a lot of healing to do and Tucker knew his Grandparents would keep them until they were well and strong and Jessie until Tucker was no longer her husband.

Tucker went forward and with most of the men in his family, they closed the oversized coffin that held Holly and Lang Taylor and took them out to the wagon in the churchyard. Tucker was shocked to see how many people were following the wagon to the Blackburn Cemetery out on Riverbend. He and his cousins had dug the grave themselves and were ready to lower the coffin when they arrived. "I want a love like that someday," Tucker said to Thomas not knowing where Jessie had gone, she was small and lost in the crowd.

"Me as well," Thomas said looking at his Uncle Allen and Aunt Alicia, "or like their love," and Tucker nodded looking at Grandpa Levi holding Grandma Cecily. "Yeah, them too," Thomas agreed looking at his mother Sarah and Father Shaun Blackburn. "My parents, I want what they have." Thomas looked at Elise and sighed. "I think we will have that kind of love someday Tuck, it runs in our family."

Tucker watched as the coffin was lowered into the ground and the boys covered it, their shovels hitting as they lay to rest the sweetest couple ever. Tucker saw his Grandfather stumble and almost fall, his Grandma Alicia so tiny trying to hold him up and calling out his name. Aaron, just having buried his parents rushed to Allen and supported him while he struggled to breath.

"I need Seth," Allen cried out and his brother came to him supporting him on one side while Aaron held him up on the other. "Levi," Allen pleaded for him and stood up straight reaching for his friend. "Help me home fellows." He said looking at Shane and Shaun and Ethan and Michael who all moved to walk with him. "Tuck, Taylor, Thomas, Shaun Allen, Aaron" he called out and his boys and they fell in beside him. "Lang," he called out as they walked home looking at his boys knowing one of them was missing and would be missed forever. "Yea, I have a goodly heritage." Allen looked at his family and fought to breath. He loved all of his family more than his own life and he loved them more now.

Alicia watched her husband walking home and looked at Cecily and Mary, they were together in that second with Sarah, Charlotte, Bethany, Jenny, Hannah and Jessie and Elise. Someone said Holly's name as Allen had said Lang's name, no one was sure which of them said her name, maybe they all had. "I love you Mama," Hannah said and Charlotte pulled her close. "And Daddy. Always our Daddy."

The silence in the house was far too loud, Allen thought as he wrote his and Alicia's story in long hand sitting on the porch. Alicia had been banging away on the typewriter all morning and now she was laying down napping and he was alone. Everyone had gone home hours after the funeral and the house felt dead, his house was always alive with noise. And now three days later only he and Alicia were here with Elise and Jessie. Both of the girls were withdrawn and he saw they were hurting, but he hadn't felt strong enough to support them and so he hadn't reached out to them. He knew he needed too, they needed to know what their future was.

Allen walked into the house and searched out the girls, they weren't upstairs, the bedroom they shared the door was standing open and was empty. He then searched every room downstairs finally going into the kitchen and seeing them at the table just staring into empty cups of coffee. "Hello," he said and sat down across from them. "We need to talk," he said seeing both girls lean back in their chairs and look at him. From the look on their faces Allen knew they needed to talk and he needed to listen.

"Mr. Blackburn," Elise started and he let her be formal with the use of his name. "Jessie and I thank you for all you've done for us. But we don't belong here sir." Allen saw her look down at her hands clasped in front of her. "We know we have nowhere to go,"

"Yes, you have somewhere to go." Allen saw his nephew Thomas standing in the kitchen doorway, his hat in his hands. He saw Elise turn to Thomas and look confused as he took a step toward her. "Excuse me for interrupting Uncle Allen," Thomas said politely then looked back at Elise. "You and me have been doing a kind of dance all our lives, girl." Thomas was standing now only feet away from Elise. "I never thought I was good enough for you because of my eye," he swallowed hard and hoped Elise would say something to him, but she was silent. "I know you like Taylor more than me."

"No, no I don't," Elise jumped up from her chair and turned facing Thomas. "I mean I like Taylor and all but, but it's you I love Thomas." Allen sat up straighter when he saw Thomas pull Elise into his arms and kiss almost as well as Lang use to kiss Holly and he kissed his Alicia.

"Holly cow," Allen said when Thomas pulled away from Elise and she was looking up at him.

"You want me? Even after that Ludlow," Thomas kissed Elise again and to hush her words and Allen was again impressed by Thomas, but then Thomas was Shaun and Sarah's only child, he had grown up with parents that loved one another deeply.

"I want you to come live with my parents until we can get married," Thomas said firmly giving Elise no room for questioning his desire. "And I want a big church wedding. There's been too many elopements in my family. I want you covered in flowers and a veil and music. I want the whole world to see I'm marrying the most beautiful girl in the whole state."

Allen saw Jessie looking at him and knew he was still in for a talk. Thomas looked at him and then at Jessie and said to the girl, "you aren't going anywhere either Jessie. Tucker has plans for your life and for his so you need to settle in here and wait." Thomas then looked over at Allen, "Uncle Allen, Tuck is coming to talk with you about his plans; I think Uncle Ethan and Aunt Bethany are coming as well. He said something about bringing some of Aunt Mary's rolls and his mama making dinner. So prepare for company." Thomas still had an arm around Elise and looked down at Jessie. "I'm taking her to my parents house now, it's just down the road and our door is always open to you, just come on in." he ruffled her hair and pulled Elise by the hand.

"My things," she said and Allen heard them both go upstairs.

"Well that was a surprise," Allen said to Jessie and saw Alicia come into the kitchen yawning. "Hey sleepy girl. Thomas just said that Bethany, Ethan and Tucker are coming up and bringing dinner."

"What was Thomas doing holding Elise's hand and going upstairs?" Alicia asked and looked out to find Thomas at the top of the stairs kissing Elise. "I thought Elise liked Taylor." She heard her husband laugh and turned back to meet his grass green eyes.

"She does like Taylor," Allen said giving Jessie a wink and wishing the girl would smile, she was far too serious. "She is in love with Thomas."

"I wish Shaun Allen would find a girl," Alicia said and sat down next to Jessie.

"I have found a girl," Shaun Allen said as he came up behind his mother and gave her a kiss. "You're my best girl Mama," he teased and she shook her head with a smile. "Ethan said to tell you

Bethany is bringing dinner up and Jessie," he pulled her hair and she looked up at him, "Tucker is waiting on the river facing porch for you." Shaun Allen grabbed a muffin from the bread box and his parents watched him run out knowing he was going back to the sawmill.

"Well," Alicia said giving Jessie a gentle nudge. "Tucker is waiting."

"Alicia," Allen looked at his wife and she reached for his hand. "I'm tired. Do you want to take another nap before the children get here?" He saw her face soften, the smile come to her lips and her head nod. "Are Thomas and Elise still at the top of the stairs," he saw Alicia peek down the hall and nod her head. "Let's go get them to move."

"I love you forever, Allen," Alicia said as he took her hand knowing the loss of Lang and Holly was still a raw unhealed wound.

"Forever, Alicia. Forever."

Tucker turned and saw Jessie leaning in the doorway, she was so small and he hoped that she might grow some more to better fit him while he was away. Away, he thought and knew tonight he would tell his parents his plan. And Jessie. "Come walk with me," Tucker said and reached back his hand to take her hand, her other arm was still in the splint Uncle Lang had put on. "It's a pretty day," he said as they got down to the river bank, the wreck of their old raft was lying on the shore and he smiled remembering the day they had gotten caught in the current.

"Tucker, I think it's time you had our marriage annulled and let me set you free." Tucker didn't look at Jessie; he looked out at the river flowing by them.

"Jessie," he said slowly, his eyes never moving from the river. "You're young yet, real young. And I know you need time to grow up and find yourself. I do as well. I'm not going to annul this marriage or allow you to do so until I get home."

"Where are you going?" she asked hoping he would look at her and he didn't.

"I want to tell everyone at dinner tonight," Tucker kept looking out at his river and saw an alligator on the other side slip into the water, a snake slid by on the current and he knew he would miss this place with all of his heart. He was also still being haunted by his Uncle Lang and Aunt Holly's death, had he caused Holly to get shot by racing toward Betsy? Might she have not shot a second and third time had he just stood and held his place? He would never know. And he would hurt forever. "I'll be gone awhile, Jessie. But I'm coming back, and I hope you'll wait for me." Tucker turned away from his river and looked down into Jessie's eyes. "I want you to promise to wait for me to come back and to give me a chance as your husband when I do come home."

"I can't stay married to you, Tucker." Jessie looked down at the ground. "I'm soiled. I'm ruined. I'm not fit for any man."

"Hush Jessie," Tucker put his hand over her mouth. "Those words aren't true. You are innocent and sweet and good and kind and I'm coming home to you someday. You'll be older and I'll be wiser and we'll see if we're meant to be together then. If we're not, then I'll annul the marriage. But right now, Jessie, I need your promise to wait for me."

Jessie looked up at Tucker, it was as though she were seeing him for the first time, he seemed changed, he seemed more grown up and more sure of himself. "How long will you be gone?" she asked and he smiled down at her.

"About four years, sweetheart. Enough time for you to grow up," he teased and saw her almost smile.

"I'm sixteen now, Tucker," Jessie tried to stand as tall as she could but with him six foot four inches and her only five feet two inches she was still little compared to him. "I might not get any bigger than I am right now."

"We'll see," Tucker said leading her to the bank and sitting down pulling her down beside him. "I'm going to probably die missing this place," he said and felt Jessie lean her head on his shoulder like she use to do when he saved her from the bullies or they were playing down here at the river. "I've known you all my life," he put an arm around her. "You're as close a friend to me as Shaun Allen and Thomas and Tayer."

"You've always been my best friend as well, Tucker."

"Take care of my Grandparents and parents while I'm gone, Jessie. I'm afraid I'll lose one of them and not be here to say goodbye. My Grandpa Allen, he'll watch over everyone, but he's getting old now and with Uncle Lang dying, he seems almost lost." Tucker looked down at Jessie and into her clear blue eyes. "I could forget everything, Jessie. I could forget the hurt and the horror and the sorrow and get lost in your blue eyes if you'd let me." Jessie reached up and touched his cheek and took a deep breath and he knew he had to have her.

"Oh," Jessie breathed as Tucker covered her mouth with his own. "Oh," she breathed into his mouth and he laid her back on the bank and kissed her more.

"I need you Jessie, I need you so badly," he kissed her cheek and her eye lids and down her neck and she was letting him. "I've loved you all my life it seems. You've always been my sweetheart. Please, wait for me to come home to you, please."

Jessie nodded her head and reached up to pull his lips back down to hers and he forced her mouth open with his tongue and slid inside causing her to lose her breath. She touched his soft thick hair and leaned her head back as he kissed her neck and told her how he loved her. "I don't know," she started to cry and Tucker lifted up and looked into her eyes.

"You don't know if you'll wait for me? " he asked and she shook her head.

"I only talked to Doctor Taylor about it and now he's gone," she covered her eyes with her good hand as Tucker brushed her tears aside.

"I know," Tucker said tenderly. "You don't know if Ludlow left a baby inside you." Tucker lay on the river bank in the grass with the girl he loved remembering Uncle Lang's words. He had also read the book that Uncle Lang and Aunt Holly had written, A Return of Innocence and he knew their story and how Uncle Lang had saved Aunt Holly. One day, curled up in bed with Jessie, he would read it to her.

"I won't know for weeks," Jessie looked at the fluffy white clouds floating overhead, the sky was a beautiful blue and she felt her heart was heavy.

"Jessie," Tucker lay down beside her. "If you do have a baby inside of you sweetheart, then it'll become a Tucker and a Blackburn because you're my wife. And it'll be part of the Taylor bunch as well because it'll grow up out here on this river. Don't fret about this. I didn't understand at first." He rolled over and looked down into her eyes that were the color of the sky. "I didn't know you went to Ludlow to save your sister Maggie."

"But I didn't save her," Jessie cried. "She was already dead. Everything I did to help her was for nothing." She turned her face away and he kissed her cheek.

"Jessie, that's what heroes do, they go into a blazing building to save someone and the building is empty, but they went in to make sure and they're a hero forever. You will always be my hero Jessie, as little as you are, I know you'll save me and I'll save you right back. I love you Jessie, with every single beat of my heart, I love you." Tucker pulled her close and she let him, he was nearly lying on top of her. "Just let me kiss you," he said as he lowered his mouth knowing that he was leaving her and leaving here more boy than man and when he came home, he would be man enough to earn her love.

"Alicia," Allen called his wife and when she didn't come to him he ran and grabbed her hand "Come look," he laughed and Alicia thought she had never seen her husband like this, he was tickled all over, he was almost dancing. "Look," he pointed down toward the river and Alicia squinted her eyes to see.

On the bank in the gleaming sunlight Alicia saw her Grandson Tucker lying on top of Jessie Fairchild kissing her. "There's something about that old river than makes lovers have to kiss there," Alicia said and turned away from the tender scene. "Remember all the times we kissed there Allen?" She saw her husband chase her and she giggled and ran to the bed. "You're too old to catch me now," she laughed and jumped up onto the bed feeling like a child with her playful husband.

Allen jumped up onto the bed and grabbed a hold of his wife pulling her close. "There won't ever come a day Alicia, that I'll be too old to catch you. I love you as much today as I did thirty eight years ago. When we die and go to heaven, which I hope I do," he gave her a grin and they sat down together on the bed, "I'll love you and chase you always. You're my whole world." He laid her back on their bed and looked down into her eyes. "Think I can kiss you like Tucker is kissing Jessie?"

"You'll do better, we've had years of practice," Alicia said and pulled him down to her, this was where she was meant to be, in his arms, in the arms of her family, her husband and her best friend.

Bethany sat at the table next to her husband Ethan and looked at her in laws Cecily and Levi Tucker across from her and her Daddy Allen Blackburn and mother Alicia at each end and her handsome son Tucker next to Levi and Jessie next to her. The family was far from complete, but this is who Tucker had wanted her to invite over and she knew he had something to tell them tonight.

Half the food was gone from the plates when Tucker put his fork down and sat up straight looking at his mother. She was as beautiful today as she had been when he was a little boy and he adored her. She was just like Grandma Alicia and his father looked just like his Grandpa Levi, and he, Tucker looked like his Grandpa Allen, and he was like his Grandpa Allen in many ways. He didn't want to leave them, he thought as he looked at Jessie but he knew he had to go, he had to make his own place in the world for a time as Grandpa Allen had done when he went off to school and got his law degree. He was a man now and it was time to act like a man.

"Congress just passed a bill," Tucker started to say when everyone fell silent, "our President FDR signed it into law that any man that could pass the testing of physics and mathematics could skip taking those college courses and earn his honorary degree in engineering." Everyone at the table was now looking at him, his father was impressed he could see and his Grandpa Allen was nodding his head.

"What's physics?" his Grandmother Alicia asked and his eyes met hers as he smiled.

"It has to do with matter and its motion, Grandma. It's about energy." Tucker didn't know how to explain this to his Grandmother in simple terms and looked to his Grandpa Allen.

"It's something we don't ever think about Alicia," Allen said simply. "It has to do with atoms and movement and is above my education."

"Thanks for explaining that for me Grandpa," Tucker said in a sarcastic way and heard his Grandpa Allen laughing. "So today I went to the college and took the tests and I did well. I'll have to take some college courses to get a degree."

"I'm so proud of you Tucker," he heard his mother say and his Grandpa Levi patted his back saying,

"Thank God you didn't take after me, I'm still trying to learn to read," his wife slapped his shoulder and he kissed her quick.

"I went to the recruiter's office after the testing and I signed up for the United States Navy. They'll sponsor me while I get my degree and I can start working as an uncertified engineer right away."

"Navy?" he heard his parents say at the same time and saw everyone around the table looking shocked and Grandma Alicia looked ready to cry."

"How long will you be gone, Tucker?" Allen asked and he turned to see his Grandpa Allen was calm and cool and accepting of his leaving.

"I enlisted for three years," he said looking at Jessie. He had told her his plan down at the river today and asked her to wait until he came home and she agreed. "I'm asking all of you to take care of my wife for me while I'm away," Tucker kept looking at Jessie. "I'll be all right Mama, don't start crying."

"There's a war happening in this world," he heard his father say and he nodded his head, he knew his father wasn't all right with the word war or even the thought of war.

"It's a long way from us, Dad. Please, don't worry about me. I promise I'll come home safe in a few years." He saw Shaun Allen come in dressed in his Sunday best and knew he had a date with a girl in Jefferson county and saw Grandpa Allen hand him his keys.

"Tucker, I'll miss you," Shaun Allen said leaning down to kiss his mother. "Maybe I'll join you." He smiled at his father and winked.

"Maybe you won't," his mother said and slapped his hand.

Tucker wasn't expecting his grandmothers to both burst into tears at the same time and then his mother started crying. Things weren't suppose to be like this, he thought and looked at his father not seeing Shaun Allen hurry from the room of crying women. He had told his cousins and their wives this morning and they had all been proud of him, as long as they didn't go to war. And Tucker feared in his heart that they were going to get dragged into this war and he would have to join the military then anyway. This way he could get his degree, he could go in as an enlisted and work his way up while getting his degree and when he came home, he would have a skill no one could take away from him and an education.

"I'm proud of you Tucker," Allen said and knew this was going to happen, tears or no tears. He prayed there would be no time for crying as he remembered another war his boys were in and how they all came home hurt and changed. He looked at Ethan, tall like his father and a handsome man, but he had dreams still that haunted him. He would jump at the slightest noise; he would run and hide if you chopped wood and didn't warn him you were going to do so.

Allen closed his eyes and saw his boys climbing up to his second story porch to wrap it in screen, Lang in his fifties and pulling himself up first and so proud of what he could do as an old man. Tucker climbing up and even Taylor. All of his boys. He looked at Levi and felt alone and old and wished that Lang were here now to counsel him over his Tucker going into the Navy.

"I'll be all right Grandpa, it's only three years." Tucker reached for Allen's hand and their eyes met and held, he could see Tucker's promise to come home safe in his eyes and Tucker saw his Grandpa Allen's promise to live until he came back so they had more time together.

"I'll be here," Allen said and Tucker forced a smile for the women who had now stopped crying.

"With all the family here, you won't miss me," Tucker made light or tried too of the situation.

"Just come back to me," his mother pleaded and he promised her he would.

"Take care of Jessie for me," Tucker looked at everyone at the table. "Make sure she's all right until I come home." Everyone nodded and smiled at Jessie who sat small and still at the table, she knew right then in that moment that she loved Tucker, she might not be in love with him. But she loved him, he was her best friend.

Jessie pulled her nightgown on and climbed into the bed that was her bed at Riverbend. Grandpa Allen had teased her tonight over her name being Jessie Tucker and she had laughed back that at least it wasn't Tucker Tucker and her Tuck told her his name was Allen Roston Tucker and she was Mrs. Allen Roston Tucker. She had no idea he had another name besides Tucker. She pulled down her bed and turned out the light, she had already been hugged goodnight by both Allen and Alicia and she knew tomorrow they would all be going into Woodville to the train station to see Tucker off so she had to be up early in the morning.

Tucker opened the river door of his Grandpa's house and slipped inside, he knew the house like the back of his hand and went right to the staircase and up to Jessie's room knowing which room she was in. He eased the door open and saw her on the bed and not wanting to frighten her and make her scream and walked to the bed and bent down putting his hand lightly over her mouth.

"Jessie girl," he said her name as Uncle Lang had said Holly's name and felt a sorrow come over him, a sorrow he had never known as he again saw Uncle Lang fall onto Aunt Holly and heard the gun blast that had taken Aunt Holly's life.

Jessie heard him say her name and gasped but his hand was over her mouth. "Don't yell," he pleaded and she nodded her head. "I just wanted to be with you one more time before I leave." He pulled off his shoes and socks and climbed onto the bed pulling her into his arms. "Are you all right with this?" he asked and felt Jessie nod her head. She actually snuggled into him and he smiled kissing the top of her head and was glad that she had allowed him this.

"I'll miss you Tucker," she said right before he rolled her over and looked down at her.

"I want to kiss you all night long," he said and Jessie nodded her head, he had given her so much, the least she could do was allow him to kiss her and hold her. He wouldn't do more; he knew he couldn't because if he did, they wouldn't be able to get an annulment.

Tucker kissed her, he ran his tongue over her lips slowly for what felt like forever, and then he put his tongue inside of her mouth and played with her tongue. He wasn't hurting her, Jessie thought as she felt his tongue enter her ear and she gasped harshly and clung to him. "More," she pleaded in a whisper and felt him giving her more, going on and on he played with her ear and then down the side of her neck, he was making her feel like she had never felt and when he lifted up over her he pleaded with her to let him just kiss her more and she nodded her head.

Somehow her nightgown was up and over her head and on the floor and Jessie didn't know how that had happened. Tucker was kissing her in places she had never known anyone to kiss and he touched both of her breasts, holding them in his hands. "You're so beautiful," he almost cried. "You're so small and yet here, oh my God," he took one of her breasts in her mouth and she almost cried out in the feelings that shot through her. He stayed there for an hour, his mouth on her breasts and she pleaded with him to not stop, he felt so right there, he belonged with her.

"Tucker," she said his name over and over as he kissed her and then she felt him leaving her breast and he came back to her lips.

"I'm not hurting you?" he asked and she gasped out that he wasn't. He went back to her body, trailing kisses as he moved lower onto the bed and spread her legs. She went tense and he came back up to her. "I need to give this to you, Jessie." He kissed her gently on the lips. "Please, let me do this for you before I leave you."

She couldn't deny him, Jessie had thought. He had given her so much and he hadn't hurt her tonight, he made her fell alive and anxious and burning inside. He made her forget what happened to her and he made her want to hold him and kiss him as he was holding and kissing her. This wasn't like what happened to her, she thought. This was her best friend Tucker.

He moved back down her body, his mouth back on her breasts until she was moaning and then lower still where he gently spread her legs apart and came between them, his mouth gently touching her. "Oh my God," Tucker heard Jessie gasp out in a breathless whisper and he moved his mouth closer to her knowing what to do because of a book his cousin Shane had given to him last year. She was crying, a good crying and gasping and he felt her tense, it was as though she were climbing a mountain and the higher she went the better his touch became. And then he felt her shaking, felt her stiff and ridged in his mouth. Slowly he came back up her body and pulled her into his arms and she lay there shivering and contented.

"What did you do to me?" she pleaded to know and he smiled as he held her close.

"It's called making love," he answered simply.

"Does this mean the marriage can't be annulled?" she asked in a small voice and he shook his head.

"Do you want that Jessie?" he asked and held his breath.

"I don't know," she said honestly. "I don't know what we'll be like in three years" She felt his hand touching her breast and tensed up again wondering if he would make her feel like he just had again.

"I thought you were a little girl," he said before coming back over her. "But these," he held her well rounded firm breasts in his hands, "you're a woman," he said and kissed her again.

"Tucker, I'm not good enough for you," her words stopped him for playing with her breasts.

"We're meant for one another," he insisted and she shook her head.

"We have three years before we have to decide if we'll stay married. Please, wait until you come back and we have time to get to know one another and then decide what we both want and both need." Tucker nodded his head, that was the reason he was leaving, to give her time.

"I just want to hold you before I go," he said and went back to kissing her body and hearing her sigh, the way he made her feel, he knew she wouldn't want their marriage annulled, he had already seduced her completely and he hadn't even left yet.

"Do you want me to?" Jessie asked as she could feel him hard and solid against her leg. She was not unaware of men. He knew what she was asking and he told her no, this night was for her and her alone, his parting gift so she would hopefully miss him forever.

Dawn came in through the porch doors and Tucker sat up on the bed putting on his shoes. Jessie lay asleep in the bed, he had worn her out. There was still time before they had to leave for the train for her to sleep a few hours, he was packed and all ready to go.

Tucker came out of Jessie's bedroom and saw his Grandpa Levi, his Grandpa Allen and his father in the hall with fishing poles and tackle boxes. Shaun Allen was coming down the hall and he saw Shane and Shaun in the stairwell with Taylor and Thomas. "Where did you come from?" Thomas asked in surprise and Allen gave him a pat on the back.

"That's Jessie's room," Allen said softly as they all went downstairs. "No annulment now," Allen said and Tucker stopped him in the hall.

"Grandpa, we didn't," he shook his head seeing everyone was listening even his Grandmothers Alicia and Cecily who had somehow appeared at the bottom of the stairs and he was thankful his mother wasn't here. "We just slept," Tucker said in an assuring voice and Allen shook his head and looked him deep in the eyes.

"This is how this works Tucker. You can get an annulment if you've not slept together according to the Florida law. But you have more than ten people in this room that saw you come out of your wife's room at dawn and looking wrinkled and slept with. No annulment now, son." Tucker swallowed hard and looked up the stairs to be sure Jessie wasn't there listening to this.

"Look Grandpa, I want Jessie to have the freedom to choose me for herself when I get home," he turned to everyone in the room. "That girl has had things forced on her for too long and she's been hurt. I won't be something more shoved down her throat. No one, no one is to tell her we can't get an annulment." Tucker saw everyone nodding their head and several looks of admiration.

"No one will tell her," Bethany came up behind her son. "You have all of our words. As Blackburn's, you can trust us always."

Tucker looked again up the stairs and was relieved; he would allow her the choice to stay with him because he would make her want nothing more than to stay with him. "I love her, Mama," he said softly and his mother grabbed hold of him and squeezed tight.

"She'll love you too," his Grandpa Allen said.

"Just promise me," Tucker turned to Allen and Levi, "that you'll not die until you're really old." He knew his Grandpa Levi was sixty six and his Grandpa Allen was sixty four, they weren't young. Both men nodded and smiled at him.

"Are we going fishing or not?" Seth said from the doorway. "It's almost six in the morning and we'll only get about two hours in since we have to get Tucker to the train by noon."

"We're coming, Daddy," Shane and Shaun said at the same time and hurried out the door racing for the boats not seeing Shaun Allen and Taylor were already ahead of them.

"Levi, want to race?" Allen asked and Levi shook his head.

"I'll get there just as fast walking as I will running." Levi opened the door and held it open for Allen and almost fell over when Tucker raced out telling Thomas he would beat him.

"Yea, I have a goodly heritage," Allen said and winked at Alicia. The river was calling to them all, all of them had the river running through them, that old river was their families blood.

PART THREE

TUCKER'S WORLD AT WAR

Chapter Eleven

October 1941
Boot Camp San Diego, California

Everyone was now calling him Allen and he wasn't responding because his name was Tucker, but the Chief Petty Officer completely ignored him when he tried to explain he was Allen Tucker and called Tucker and had ordered everyone to call him by his given name. Every time anyone called him Allen he turned around expecting to see his Grandpa.

Boot camp had been a nightmare, the men were harassed and kept awake for long hours, they had cut all of his hair off and he didn't realize how vain he was about his hair until he had none. When it started to grow back some he kept the sides in a buzz cut. Somehow Tucker had survived being a boot, but he wasn't sure how and he was waiting for his test results to see what his rank would become, right now he was a seaman that had survived six weeks of boot camp and was now in special training in Hawaii and had been for more than four months. As soon as he was done with his training and he had his new rank, he was due to board the USS Northampton; she was a heavy cruiser with eight inch guns and he knew he would be in the Pacific Ocean working as an Engineer aboard the Nora, he smiled at the nickname of the ship thinking he should be able to use his nickname while serving on her.

Tucker lay in his bunk hoping today he would know what his new rank would be. He had done very well in studies and was finishing his courses early, he also was getting specialized training and was excited to be doing something so different than he had ever dreamed. He wrote home once a week and he told his Grandpa about California, it was very different from Florida and he was homesick in the worst way. Sometimes he wrote to his Uncle Lang and Aunt Holly, he kept thinking maybe they weren't dead, maybe they were at home waiting for him. It was hard to grieve when you were far from home and homesick as he was. Every week he would write to Jessie, he never complained to her as he did his Grandpa Allen. He was careful in all he wrote to her to let her know how he was doing and what he was doing. He had one of his buddies go with him and take his photo sitting on a huge ship anchor that he sent home to her and to his Mama. Jessie never wrote him back but he didn't mind, he knew she had things to go through. He kept thinking of the story Uncle Lang and Aunt Holly had left behind of their lives and he knew time would help Jessie more than anything else would.

"Hey Allen," he looked up and saw a Chief Petty Officer in his doorway waving an envelope. "Word is you're getting an appointment as a non-commissioned officer," Tucker sat up and made eye contact with the officer and knew he was teasing him; the Petty Officers always were messing with the seaman. "You're getting better," he laughed and Tucker almost growled at the man, he was tired of this treatment, he was beginning to understand Jessie's chicken and the peck order, he was being pecked to death. "Do you want this or not."

Tucker looked at the Petty Officer and thought, 'hell yeah I want my appointment,' but he said nothing and waited, this was how the game played out. And then out of nowhere another Petty officer appeared and came in to shake his hand. "Congratulations sir," and saluted him before handing him his new insignia. He had done so well in his studies and courses he was now a Chief Warrant Officer second class and an uncertified engineer and he knew he had hopes of becoming certified before he had to report to his ship. Tucker almost laughed and he almost cried at the same time while the Petty Officer that had been teasing him told him to take a few minutes and write home to his mother. Tucker had smiled and said he would write home to his wife and his mother.

He had made it, Tucker thought as he had his insignia put on his new uniform. In boot camp they had thrown him a uniform that would fit a man five feet ten inches and he was six foot four. He had spent an hour looking for someone small given a large uniform and never did find one that fit perfect. But that was behind him, now he was a Warrant officer and things would be much easier and better for him.

"I hear you were assigned to the USS Nora," his roommate came in just as he was finishing up with his new uniform. "Holy cow, you changed fast." Tucker smiled at him and told him yes, he was going on the Nora and he needed to write home to his mother, she would be so proud of him, and Jessie, he wondered if she would care.

Late November
Riverbend, Florida

Tucker had been gone almost six full months, Allen thought as he read another letter from his grandson. He had also asked to read the letters Tucker was writing to Bethany as he seemed to be less formal with his daughter than he was with his Grandpa. Many times there would only come two letters a week, one addressed to everyone and the other just for Jessie, Allen never asked to read the letters he wrote to Jessie. He looked up and saw his wife Alicia in the doorway and he waved for her to come in.

"Reading a letter from our Tucker?" she asked as she closed the door and he nodded his head.

"He just left Hawaii on his new ship, the USS Northampton. Can you believe his rank? He really is smart, I had no idea," Allen said in an impressed tone of voice.

"Here's something else you had no idea about," Alicia came and sat down on his lap and he held her close. "Shaun Allen is planning on joining the Navy as well." Allen sat forward so quickly that he almost dropped Alicia on the floor and she cried out grabbing him around the neck.

"No, it's bad enough I've lost one of my boys," Allen said as he stood up holding Alicia in his arms and she smiled that at his age he could still carry her around.

"Allen, let him go," she said in her gentle way. "He needs to find himself and it's only a few years." Allen looked down into his beautiful wife's eyes and nodded his head. She was right, Shaun Allen would come back and work the sawmill for him just like Tucker someday, they would never stay off this river for long.

"So when was Shaun Allen going to tell me?" Allen put Alicia down and went to the fireplace, the fire was dying and he added more logs. "Damn, I'm going to have to start chopping my own wood at this rate. We only have Thomas left and he's working full time as a deputy and Taylor is our Minister."

"Chopping our wood will keep you in shape, Allen and we have the gas heat in this place now," Alicia sat down in one of the lovely overstuffed chairs and snuggled up. "I read all of Lang and Holly's story, A Return of Innocence," she saw her husband flinch when she said the name Lang and was sorry that she had said anything. "I love how you're writing our story, Allen. But I hope you'll read my typewritten work, you put in only your feelings, it's very one sided whereas Cecily and Levi wrote their story together as did Holly and Lang and it's both sides."

"We'll why don't we write our story together?" he asked and came and picked her up sitting down in the chair and pulling her onto his lap. "I helped Shaun and Shane with their stories last month, they didn't know about all Blackburn men being hell on an ax handle and how I put the ax through our front door in a fit of temper." Alicia laughed and snuggled up closer to him.

"I was wondering how Jessie is doing managing the books for the mill and the cattle and the planting? She's so quiet I never know what she's thinking. I caught her crying again yesterday morning." Allen made a face over the news of Jessie crying, he knew it was tears of relief that she wasn't going to have a baby by the monster Ludlow but only he knew that because she'd left a letter to Tucker in one of the accounting ledgers and she had written to him her relief and her just wanting to cry forever over not having that happen to her. Allen knew he shouldn't have read her letter and he didn't mean too, it just had happened. And he knew she hadn't mailed the letter to Tucker, she never gave him one letter to mail out ever and Tucker had written to him telling him Jessie never wrote him. Allen couldn't understand why Jessie wrote Tucker but never sent the letters and he had left stamps on her desk but she hadn't touched even one.

"She's amazing with figures and she's fast too," Allen said looking into the bright fire. "Isn't it almost someone's birthday?"

"Mine is tomorrow and you know that too, Allen Blackburn." He hugged her tight and laughed before pointing to the corner of the room, he had been waiting for her to see his gift since she had come into his study. "What is that?" she asked and got up going to look at it.

"You can't look," Allen said and got up to prevent her from lifting the blanket. "Bethany made the cake and I invited everyone up to help us eat it and watch you open your gift. But that's not all

I got for you." He smiled and had her come sit at his desk. "I had to pay a hundred dollars to get the line run way out here, but its past time my wife had one." Alicia looked at the odd thing he handed to her and then up at him with a questioning look. "It's a telephone," he said with a smile.

"Allen, I don't know another living soul with one of these. Who would I call?" Allen smiled and lifted her chin to place a kiss on her lips.

"I didn't just pay one hundred dollars for this to be run out to our place, Seth and Mary have one now too and Bethany and Ethan and the twins at Twin River and Levi had one run for Cecily. So now all of us can talk without running or walking a mile.'"

"We're living in a modern age now. Do you remember when we married there was only horses and buggies and lantern light. Now there's electricity and cars and planes and so much progress. They're even paving roads now." Alicia looked in the corner of the room and had an idea of her birthday gift.

"I remember riding out to that run down old dirt farm on my horse and finding you in that shack all those years ago, Alicia. I was so young and fit and had twice the hair. I didn't want to get old on you. I wanted us to be young like that together in love forever."

"We've had a wonderful life, Allen. Every minute with you has been a minute of joy and peace. Even when you've been putting your fist through our wall." Alicia went back over the overstuffed chair and waited for him to come back and sit down and hold her.

"I don't want my time to be up," Allen said as he pulled her into his lap. "I've had you in my life forty years tomorrow." Alicia leaned into him. "We've lost babies, we lost one another for a time, and we've made love in and on the river. I've seen you with your hair up day in and day out and now it's long and loose and I love it both ways. I'm so thankful I met you and have had you in my life."

"Forty years now, and it feels like yesterday. Remember our wedding night?" Allen gave a laugh like sound and held her close.

"Yes, but our real wedding night was the night you forgave me."

"We're losing Shaun Allen," Alicia cried into his shirt and Allen looked down at her with a look of wonder.

"Wasn't it you who was just telling me we had to let him go find himself? It's only a few years?"

"I was only saying that because I wanted to be brave for you." Allen hugged her and laughed. "Can I look at the new radio?" Allen looked down at her in wonder. "I knew, how could I not know when it's something that big? And I'll act all surprised tomorrow night, I promise." She jumped up and went to the blanket and Allen came and adjusted the knob until he found a station and they listened to some man reading a story that wasn't that good. But it was a fun way to spend the afternoon and he was with his best friend, his lover, his wife.

Allen and Alicia Blackburn took their only son to the bus station, like his nephew Tucker; he was going to San Diego, California for boot camp. "I won't make Warrant officer like Tucker did," Shaun Allen said to his parents, but I'll be in the Navy and I can help our country and see the world." Shaun Allen fell silent when his father hugged him, and he patted him on the back. "Don't worry Dad, I'll come home. Nothing can keep me from the river for long. Or from you and Mama." He turned to his mother who looked like she was going to faint and gave her a kiss on the cheek. "I love my parents. Nothing can keep me from you both for long. I'm so thankful you guys love me."

"I kept losing babies," Alicia said touching her only son's cheek. "And then I struggled with you. You're Uncle Andrew, you don't remember him, he died in nineteen twenty four of a heart attack, he is the reason you came to us. He took me to his home and put me to bed for months and we waited. Your Daddy had to be away from his river, it was hard on him, but he got his only son." Shaun Allen kissed his mother on the cheek again and she hugged him. "Just come home to us, son. That's all I ask of you. Don't stay away too long."

"Mama, the time will fly. And thank you for going to bed for months just to have me," he laughed and looked at his father, "and you Dad, thanks for leaving your river to have me."

"You were worth it, son. My only son, you'll be the one that carries on our name." Allen walked his son to the bus and saw him climb on.

"Dad," Shaun Allen called out from a window half way down the bus. "There are a lot of Blackburn boys to go on for us. Shaun and Shane and Michael have a passel of boys."

"But you're my direct line," Allen called out and followed the bus while it drove away. "You're mine, you're a piece of me boy."

"I'll be home soon, three years isn't forever, Dad. Take care of yourself and Mama!" The bus rounded the corner and Allen stood still in the middle of the road. A piece of his heart was going away from him, Tucker had already gone. He struggled to swallow and felt Alicia come up to him and saw her crying hard.

"We're all right, Alicia. We have Jessie at the house and Bethany and Ethan are right there close. Let's go home and have some dinner and then cuddle." Allen kept his arm around her and she had both her arms around his waist as they walked to the car.

"It's been a year of loss," Alicia said. "I'll be glad when we're through the month of December and into the New Year. We've lost Lang and Holly, Tucker's gone and now our Shaun Allen."

"Lang and Holly," Allen said and got into the car with his wife feeling as though a hand were squeezing around his heart, he would miss his best friend forever.

Tucker sat in his bunk on the USS Northampton with pencil and paper writing home, he decided to write everyone one letter instead of writing so many separate letters. Except Jessie. He would write Jessie a short letter each week. He wrote telling her where he was and what it was like onboard a ship and he asked her how she was doing, knowing she wouldn't write back and tell him. It was Grandma that told him Jessie was still withdrawn, but she was working with Grandpa on the accounting for their estate and doing a fine job. Tucker knew Jessie was smart and well read, there was no reason why she couldn't write him back, even a few lines to say how she was doing. He was becoming frustrated with her, she couldn't even write a few lines; he thought feeling almost angry with her.

"I'm on the Northampton out of Pearl Harbor and we're screening the USS Enterprise, the admiral here is suppose to be the best the Navy has, his name is Bill Halsey but they call him Bull. He gets a nickname while I'm called Allen. Of course I've not met him, my rank won't allow for that, but all the fellows are saying he's the best and a stand up guy. Honestly, I'm glad I'm here, I'm doing something different with my life, but Grandpa Allen is right, I belong on that river running the banks barefooted and fishing and hunting. I sure miss all of you so much. I read from Thomas that he and Elise are married now and even expecting a baby, another Blackburn. We'll populate the whole south end of the county soon, probably before I'm back home as I heard from Hannah and Michael that they're having another one in the spring. Tell Aunt Mary I miss her rolls and Grandpa Allen, don't put anymore holes in the hallway wall without me. Love you all. Mama and Daddy, I'm fine, real good in fact. Hug my Grandparents for me and eat some of those rolls of Aunt Mary's for me. Love, Tucker."

If he hurried, Tucker knew he could get this in the ships mail today and it would be home within the week. Grandpa had written that Shaun Allen was joining the Navy and Tucker was hoping he would be on a ship that was in the same base he was in someday soon. He missed home more than he had let on in his letter, he was so homesick at times that he would struggle to breathe. And when he thought of Jessie, of walking with her on the river bank and the times he kissed her and he ached all over to be home. But Jessie needed time to grow up, to sort out what she wanted and he knew, the marriage couldn't be annulled now even if he wanted that to be the case, he had stayed the night with her. He sometimes wondered if he had done what he did so she would have to stay with him and he feared he had. He put his letter home and his letter to Jessie in the outgoing mail just before the seaman picked it up to put on a transport out. His family would know how he was and where he was by the first of December and maybe he would get leave in the coming months and get to go home for a few weeks, with the planes flying as they were now, he could be home in days.

"What do you think Sarah and Charlotte are running here like that for, and in their Sunday best dresses too?" Alicia asked Bethany from where she stood at the window. "We have these new phones, they could have called. For goodness sake, we just saw them both in church this morning." She turned and saw her husband had joined her looking out the window at their beautiful nieces running toward the house.

"Shaun and Shane are coming too," Allen added when he saw his nephews jump the ditch from behind their wives. "Something is wrong," Allen said seriously. "Bad wrong because they didn't use the phone. And look, Sarah's waving her hat." Allen took Alicia's hand and pulled her out the front door and onto the porch closely followed by Bethany and Ethan. "What's the matter?" Allen yelled as Shaun beat everyone to the porch.

"What ship was Tucker on?" Shaun asked between gasps of air and Shane joined him looking up at Allen and Ethan on the porch with Levi coming to stand behind them. "What ship?" Shaun demanded to know.

"The USS Northampton out of Pearl Harbor," Levi was the one to answer seeing Cecily with her arm around Jessie who looked afraid.

"What's happened?" Allen demanded to know.

"Uncle Allen," Shane said pulling Charlotte close. "We were listening to the radio in the Cartledge store when it came on that Pearl Harbor has been attacked, all the ships were sunk and thousands are believed to be dead."

Allen turned quickly and caught his daughter before she hit the porch and saw his wife grab a hold of him and Bethany. Ethan put his hands on each side of his head and paced the porch while Jessie stood staring at nothing.

"Let's turn on the radio," Levi said and hurried into the house to do so. Allen picked his daughter up and carried her into the house followed by his wife and Cecily and Jessie. Shane and Shaun went to Ethan as he bent forward still holding his head. Well aware that Tucker was Ethan's son and that Ethan still suffered from shell-shock from his battle in the Great War the twins stayed with their best friend Ethan Tucker and always would support him.

"Let's go listen to the radio Ethan," Shaun said waiting for Ethan to stand up straight and seeing his wife Sarah beside him.

"He's a strong man, Ethan. Tucker is big like you," Shane said and let Charlotte take Ethan's hand down and away from his face.

"You're fine," Charlotte said and pulled him into the house knowing he needed someone to guide him right now and to care for him.

Cecily left Jessie in a chair near the fireplace while Levi turned on the radio and waited for it to warm up. She went to her beautiful son so damaged by a war and put her arm around him seeing Bethany was crying on the sofa where her father had laid her. "Bethany needs you Ethan," Cecily said and they all watched as Ethan came back to himself and hurried to his wife.

"I'm here," Ethan said and lifted his sobbing wife in his arms to cradle. "Tucker's tough, he'll come home to us. He promised." The radio finally sprang to life and Levi backed away from the thing after turning the knob for the volume all the way up. No one saw

Seth and Mary come in the porch double doors and sit on a chair listening to the radio as well.

Pearl Harbor had been destroyed while they had all sat in church this morning, they knew by the time night fell. Ships were sunk and planes destroyed but that seemed nothing compared to the reports of men lost. It was unreal and yet it was real. The threat had been there, Japan had been taking over the Pacific for a long time, they now had control of some of the most important things on the earth from minerals to rubber. The United States had been snuck up on and attacked with no warning, Pearl Harbor just destroyed in one big sweep by a surprise attack.

"And we don't know where Tucker is," Bethany moaned. "Do you think the newspaper will give a list of the names of ships lost? If we could see if Tucker's ship is on the list," Bethany's voice trailed off as her father touched her shoulder and assured her would go to town in the morning for a paper.

Late into the evening they listened to the radio and finally learned nineteen ships had gone down, there were more than forty five thousand men missing or dead, and nearly fifty planes had been completely destroyed. But no news if the USS Northampton had gone down. "I think we should all go to bed and get some rest," Allen said seeing Thomas and Elise had come in sometime after Seth and Mary and Taylor was sitting on the sofa next to Aaron and Jenny and four of their children and he saw Julie in the doorway with her husband Jon Brooks, his middle daughter lived over in Jefferson County and didn't get home often, he knew her being here was a sign that this was bad. They were all here for one reason, because they loved Tucker.

"Our Tucker was at Pearl Harbor?" Julie asked and her father nodded his head. "We had to come," she moved and all five of her children came into the room. Allen almost felt better seeing ten of his grandchildren in the room as Bethany and Ethan's daughter Ali had come in as well. But that one grandchild missing, his Tucker, hurt him to the bone, he wanted his Tucker here safe and sound and seeing how much his family loved him.

"Aaron, you and Jenny can take the upstairs bedroom at the end of the hall and the kids can sleep in the room next to you. Julie, you and Jon can take the room on the other side with your children beside you. Seth, you and Mary can have your old room. Bethany, I need you and Ethan close, don't go home tonight." He saw his eldest daughter nod her head and reach for his hand which he gave to her. "We all need to take hands and pray," he reached for Alicia's hand and within the minute they were all holding hands, even the children. "We need Lang here to do this for us," Allen's voice broke and he looked and saw Shane take a breath and nod.

"I've got this Uncle Allen," Shane said and looked at Shaun before bowing his head. "Dear Father in Heaven, we come to you now as a family deeply concerned for our Tucker and ask you Lord to please, keep him safe and bring him home to us."

"In Christ's holy and loving name we pray this prayer, Amen," Shaun finished for his brother and the family broke apart going their separate ways be it upstairs to bed or home.

"Levi," Allen said before Levi took Cecily's hand, "Don't go. There's one more room upstairs. Please, let's Grandpas stick together." Levi reached out and patted Allen's shoulder.

"Dad!" Allen heard Shane yell and saw Charlotte move as Mary cried out and Allen saw his younger brother fall to the floor.

"I'm all right," Seth said as Aaron reached him and eased him down to the floor. "Mary, I don't feel well." He saw his wife kneel down beside him, touch his face and he closed his eyes; he needed some rest, just a little rest.

"Seth," Mary said his name softly and looked up at Aaron. "No, Seth." Mary cried and kissed her husband's pale lips. She had been married to her Seth for almost forty five years; they had never been apart except one time in all those years and now here he had left her for heaven, who would she love now? He was everything to her.

Allen fell into a chair not believing this was happening and yet it was happening. He saw Alicia coming to him and holding him tight, he was aware he was crying and he was aware that Shaun was crying holding on to Sarah while Shane was on the floor holding his mother. This had happened so fast, so suddenly, he thought and while they were all worried about Tucker.

Levi Tucker took charge and drove to Tallahassee in the dark to get a coffin for Seth and to pick up Seth's youngest son Michael. Aaron had stayed with Mary while his family went upstairs to bed. Mary wouldn't leave Seth for hours and her twins stayed with her as well as their wives Charlotte and Sarah. Allen sat in the overstuffed chair with Alicia on his lap and they cried for Seth and for Mary and for their three boys.

"Remember the time he punched me in the face?" Allen asked both Mary and Alicia and Mary looked up from her husband and nodded her head. "He was always the one joking around and ready for fun. But that day he was serious."

"He had been serious that whole year," Mary said brushing Seth's hair back and away from his face knowing this was going to be one of the last times she ever touched her husband. "Allen, will you and Alicia write about Seth and my love in your book? We never got around to writing our story." Allen nodded his head knowing he would include all of his family in his story.

"Dad," Allen heard Shane say and reach out for his father before looking at Allen. "He said we weren't just his sons," Shane said to Allen and saw Shaun nod his head in agreement. "Dad said we belonged as much to you, Uncle Allen. He said you helped him raise us up to be the men we are. He was a good father to share us with his family like he did."

"He didn't share you boys just with me," Allen said looking from one twin to the other. "Heath, your Uncle Heath wanted boys in the worst way and Seth told him one day that he had two boys, and he pointed to you both."

"We were blessed to have three fathers," Shaun said. "Now two are gone. Please, stay strong and well Uncle Allen. This has been a bad year for our family." Allen felt like he was dying right now, like he was too old to have lost his little brother. All the times they played on the river as children. They had grown up in one another's shadow and had always remained more than brothers, more than friends, they were as close as the twins, they even thought alike.

"I'll miss my brother all the rest of my days," Allen laid his head in hands and sobbed like a baby. He had lost Lang and now Seth and Tucker was God knew where in the Pacific and probably at Pearl Harbor where all those dead military men now lay.

Allen felt a small hand touch his head and knew it wasn't his Alicia; she was sitting on his lap crying. He looked up and saw Jessie, her golden hair and blue eyes making her appear like an angel through his tears. "Tucker will be fine," she said softly, "he's a hero and heroes don't die." Allen took her hand and held it to his cheek hoping that she was right.

Levi returned with the coffin before eight in the morning and told Allen that the President was going to speak later that morning and they needed to stay near the radio. "There was no newspapers with word on what ships went down," Levi said to Allen as he watched Michael go to his father Seth's body and lay his head on Seth's unmoving chest. "Like this family hasn't had enough tragedy."

"He was only sixty two years old," Allen said in a broken voice. He hadn't slept all night nor had Alicia. "Can you watch over everyone for me, Levi? I know you're worn out and worried but I need to take a walk." He saw Levi nod before settling into one of the comfortable chairs.

As Allen was walking out the River porch view doors he saw Alicia come toward him and held out his hand. "Down to the river,

Alicia." He broke, his voice, his heart, his whole body and he held her close as they moved closer and closer to the river and he cried out for Seth. "I lost two men that were brothers to me." Alicia wrapped both arms around him and was without words of comfort, she had adored Seth as well. She remembered the time he had put the mistletoe over her head at Christmas and she had been kissed by Allen, a real kiss that had shaken her to the core of her being. Seth was always ready for fun and he breathed life into their family and now he was gone. Alicia looked back at the house and felt she saw him, Seth on the upstairs porch dropping a snake over the rail right before he turned to his beautiful Mary and kiss her. Alicia could have sworn she heard him laughing.

"A light just went out in our lives," Alicia said to her husband. "If we were like Shaun and Sarah, we would get into the water, take off all our clothes and let that river make us clean and new." Allen pulled her close and smiled through his tears.

"It's December," he pulled her close. "Even Sarah and Shaun wouldn't get in the river this time of year."

"I think I fell in love with you standing right here," Alicia said and showed him how she had seen him riding his horse that day long ago and he had gotten off at the house and bent forward looking ill. And then she had gone inside and he had given her everything with the intent to leave and she didn't want him to go, she never wanted him to leave her. "Oh God, did we have a rough start to our marriage?" she cried and thought how Mary and Seth and Emily and Heath had supported them through those difficult days, and Aunt Julia and Greg. And now everyone was gone except Mary and the two of them. "Don't leave me Allen," she cried softly. "Let me go ahead of you in death and you follow me."

"We'll go together, Alicia. I won't last long without you if I do stay behind." He bent his head and kissed her thinking of Lang and Holly going together and how hard losing them was and still was. "Let's decide to grow really old together, you and I. I'm sixty four and you're fifty seven. Let's try to make it until Tucker and Jessie have at least four children." He saw Alicia looking up into his eyes, he loved her aqua eyes beyond word.

"At the rate our Tucker and Jessie are going, we'll be one hundred before the first one comes." Alicia saw him shake his head.

"Alicia, they're in love, they might not know it yet, but wait until he comes home, three years from now we'll be chasing another Tucker on the banks." He turned back to the river and for a moment he almost saw Tucker standing there waving to him a string of fish in his hands. "Tucker's fine. Soon Tucker will be coming home."

Tucker was on a ship that had returned to Pearl Harbor the day after the attack that killed so many and was now cruising looking for the enemy going first to the south and Johnston Island then to the northeast of Oahu and finally to the west of Lisianski Island and Midway. On the eleventh of December the Northampton also known as the Nora collided with the Craven and was damaged during a refueling. Tucker was safe, but for Tucker, he was now at war as was the United States of America and he feared he wouldn't see his river, his parents or his Grandparents for a long time. And Jessie, he wouldn't get to see his Jessie and all he wanted was to see her, to find out why she wasn't writing him. He was broken hearted by her silence and he told her so in his letters. He pleaded with her to write him and she never did, all he ever knew of her was what his family wrote to him about her.

Tucker wished he had a way to call home, he knew that his family had a phone now but being on ship he couldn't call home or anywhere for that matter. He was so busy he really didn't have time to think about home though he wrote detailed letters to his father and Grandfathers of what he was doing and what was happening from his vantage point of the war. All he could do was wait for them to get his letters and wait to read their letters and hope they knew that he was safe, that the Nora had been at sea when Pearl Harbor was attacked.

Chapter Twelve

"The Nora is safe, Mama," Bethany called out as she ran to the house with the newspaper she had gone to town to get that morning with her father. Allen stepped out of the car and lifted his hand to his wife on the porch, their grandson was safe. He saw Mary standing next to Alicia and wished Seth's body weren't in the coffin in his drawing room. They were going to have his funeral in the morning and he had ordered a headstone while in town, Mary had asked for a heart with her name on one side and Seth's on the other. Allen saw Levi and Cecily and wondered how old they would grow and he and Alicia, this year had seen too much death.

"We're at war," Allen said as he came up the steps, "but for right now our grandson is safe," he patted Levi on the back and they all walked into the house, Allen had an arm around Alicia and an arm around Mary. "I know the twins have asked you to come to Twin River to live, Mary." Allen went into his office with everyone close in front or behind him all going to the radio. "But Alicia and Jessie and I talked it over last night and we want you to consider moving here with us. Riverbend needs you." Mary turned her face into Allen's shirt and almost cried but didn't, she had cried too much these past few days.

"I belong here," she said and reached for Alicia. "I can't go home without Seth, I told the boys to clean the place out and if they want to go there, they can. But I won't ever go back, not without Seth." Allen understood how she felt, he knew everywhere he went on this river he would see shadows of Seth Blackburn, his little brother.

"He was a good brother and husband and a better father," Allen said looking out at the river. "Let's all carry on for him, Mary. This is your home, his childhood bedroom is your room. And anything you might want or need you only have to ask for." He kissed her head and saw her reach and hug Alicia.

"We've always been sisters," Alicia said and they went and sat down in front of the radio.

"Tucker," Allen said going to look out at the river. "I sure wish our Grand boy was here," he said to Levi and saw Levi nod his head. "But he's safe. And Shaun Allen is also. We have a lot of prayers to say for those two."

"The military isn't going to take Thomas, now with that missing eye," Levi said and looked up at Shaun coming into the room. "His only son is safe from the war, thank God." Shane followed his brother with Taylor who was ready to go and Minister to the US Army. "Pray God that one stays out of harm's way," Levi nodded to Taylor. There stands a piece of Blackburn and a piece of Taylor, Lang and Allen and Seth all combined."

"Don't forget Michael and Hannah's children," Allen said seeing Charlotte come in with her four other children, two girls and two boys. "Nine children that tie me to Lang and then Aaron and my daughter Jenny, another five. And you and I tied by Tucker and Ali."

"We're a family," Levi smiled. "And as a family we'll get through this war. And through Seth's funeral tomorrow," he added. "I sure wish our Tucker were home."

Jessie stood looking at the huge Blackburn family thinking she didn't belong here, she wasn't family. Her sister was because she was married to Thomas, but Jessie really didn't have a husband, her husband had left her and gone to the Navy. She was mad at him, she had needed him to stay and yet he left her. She was alone and afraid all the time and uncertain what to do with her life. And she kept thinking of the night he had stayed with her in her room, the way he had touched her. He was nothing like that disgusting monster had touched her, he touched her the way a hero would. She wished he would come home and she feared he would be killed and she would never see him again.

Jessie saw Allen Blackburn looking at her and she looked away from him. He had taken her in like she was his own child as he said he would. And Alicia, his wife, they loved her and she knew that without doubt. They included her in everything; they visited with her and told her of their lives together, they even had her typing up their story together to leave to their great grandchildren and beyond someday, something that was Lang Taylor's idea.

Jessie tried hard not to think of Lang and Holly Taylor, she tried hard not to remember that day and sometimes it was all she could think about. The way Lang Taylor had turned and looked at Holly and Holly had said they wouldn't let her mother hurt her sister and they stood in front of Elise. Elise talked of them all the time, how they had saved her, they hardly knew her beyond church and Sunday school and yet they died to keep her safe. Jessie remembered how Tucker had held her in his arms protecting her and then tossed her to the porch like a rag doll while he tackled her mother and the gun went off and hit Holly and she fell onto her husband. Jessie closed her eyes fighting not to see how Lang had tried to reach for his wife, mortally wounded and then Uncle Allen had put Holly gently into Lang's arms. It was awful watching them die like that and it shouldn't have happened. It was her fault. Had Allen Blackburn and Tucker not come and saved her, Lang and Holly Taylor would be here right now.

Jessie wandered down the hall to the drawing room and went to look at Seth. In death he was as handsome as in life. A smaller version of his brother, he was a Blackburn in looks. All of them shared the same basic features. Seth's sons Shane and Shaun and Michael all strongly favored him and Allen and Tucker, Taylor and Thomas and there were several little ones that had the same face and the same cowlick and hair. There would be no surprise in what Tucker looked like in forty years from now, Jessie thought.

"He was a good man," Alicia said coming up behind Jessie who nodded her head.

"So was Lang Taylor and his wife Holly," Jessie said and let Alicia hug her as they looked down at Seth. "He taught me how to do the ledgers at the sawmill. He took time to go over everything with me, very patient," Jessie spoke of Seth before she looked at Alicia and felt weak and stupid. "Why do we have to die?"

"The price of the sin in the world," Alicia said. "And because all things must end in this life for us to obtain heaven. Seth, Lang, Holly, all our loved ones gone before us that knew and loved Jesus as their Savior are there waiting for us, Jessie just as Jesus promised all those years ago."

"But what if we die and that's it, we're just dead?" Alicia hugged her closer wishing she had the answer.

"A long time ago," Allen came up to stand with them and spoke. "A really long time ago a man came to us and told the world of Heaven and his Father that lived there and that we are all sinners and we all must die. But we can know everlasting life through him." He saw Jessie looking at him and he gave her a smile of assurance that he was right. "That man died on the cross for all of us Jessie, so that we all could be forgiven for our sins. And he came back from the dead, he rose up and he was here teaching his followers about his love and heaven. And Jessie, that story has survived over nineteen hundred years. Something happened that day in the upper room where people believed so strongly in Him that they went out and told of him to the world and most were put to death for having done so. For me, to know men died to tell about

Jesus, knowing they would die for telling of him, they had to have seen something that day that left no doubt in them that there is a heaven." Allen saw Alicia smiling at him, and he took them both by the hand and led them to the doors looking out at the river.

"Look at that girls," he breathed. "Look at the trees and the grass and the white soft sand, the river in the distance. Someone made that, none of this just magically appeared. This is the work of God; we all are the work of God. Seth's body is in a box, tomorrow we put his body in the ground, but Seth is in heaven with Jesus seeing what those men saw all those years ago that made them die for what they had seen by telling others because it was that real." Alicia leaned into him and he smiled when Jessie did as well.

"I belong here with your family," Mary said from behind them and Allen turned with Alicia and Jessie still holding on to him and pulled her close.

"A family, always a family. In heaven we'll be reunited and there will be no more pain nor sorrow nor death. And Lang and Holly will be kissing somewhere that we can all see and not caring that we can see." He laughed and looked at Mary. "I hope they have a good oven up there, Mary. You're known for your rolls, everyone I eat makes me think of heaven." Mary hugged Allen closer, he was a good big brother, he always had been.

Tucker was so busy aboard the USS Northampton he barely had time to miss home or think of home. They had mail call and he had gotten a letter from his mother and both Grandfathers but he had only had time to read his mother's letter and he knew that his Uncle Seth had died suddenly on the day Pearl Harbor was attacked. Tucker felt a chill run through him, if his Uncle Seth could die then one of his Grandfather's might. He stopped and prayed that they would grow old and stay with him for years after his return home and he hoped this war wouldn't last long.

The Pacific was huge and the Japanese ruled the whole ocean, Tucker knew that it would be a long time before they won this war, but he was on a ship that was supporting other ships to do what needed to be done to get him home safe and to his river that he loved so much and to his Grandpa Allen and Jessie, he really wanted to be with his Jessie.

In January after the bombing of Pearl Harbor the Northampton joined the USS Salt Lake City to bombard Wotje and on February the first they had demolished buildings and fuel tanks on the island and sank two Japanese ships. By the end of February Tucker had also been to Wake Island and even seen his ship under heavy attack, the guns of the Nora had done heavy damage there and though it was in part frightening, Tucker was also excited that he was a part of protecting others and his county in this war. The Nora hadn't left Wake Island until enemy seaplanes attacked, but within time the United States Navy had seen them all destroyed. The Nora was doing a good job in helping end this war, Tucker thought and yet, he felt no closer to getting home. And he missed home more with each passing day.

Every week Tucker would sit in his bunk and write to Jessie. The one photo he had of her was pinned to the wall and all the fellows teased him about how cute she was and how lucky he was to have her waiting for him at home. But he knew, she wasn't waiting for him, she was waiting for an annulment from him and he grieved because he loved her so much. Every mail drop he hoped and prayed for a letter from her, a letter telling him she hoped he was safe, or a letter asking how he was. She couldn't even write a letter that gave him news of home or a letter just responding to all his letters to her. But no letter came. He was rejected, he meant nothing to her. Their beautiful night together with him making love to her beautiful body with his hands and mouth were of no importance to her, he wasn't even worth the value of one single letter to him. And she was every thought he had, she was every dream he had come true and she was as out of reach for him as his river was and he wanted to cry but knew crying would do no good, so he focused on the war, on keeping the lights burning on the Nora so that the men could see and hoping for a higher rank.

In April the Nora joined the Enterprise's task force and along with the USS Hornet they helped support the Doolittle Raid on Tokyo. Tucker was excited to be a part of this important piece of history in the making in front of his eyes. More than fifteen planes, B-25B bombers were launched from the USS Hornet and made it to China, though it hadn't been the success that was expected, this act would lift the moral of the military men and all Americans. Thought not the success they wanted it did make the military leaders in Japan know that they might not have the ability to defend their own homes and islands soon.

The Nora returned to Pearl Harbor and Tucker was finally able to get to a phone and call home, he was so anxious to hear his mother's voice that when his Grandpa Allen answered the phone he actually screamed making sure he was heard. "Grandpa! It's me Tucker." He then heard his Grandpa's scream,

"It's Tucker!" and he knew that since it was a Sunday afternoon at home most of his family was probably there at Riverbend having lunch. "Tucker!" Allen called out into the phone. "Are you all right? We're following everything the Nora is doing that we can find in the newspapers. We even went to a movie in Tallahassee at the Florida Theater and saw movies of what's happening out there in the ocean you're in."

Tucker smiled listening to his Grandpa and leaned into the phone. He could stay here all day and talk to his Grandpa. "How's Aunt Mary?" Tucker asked and heard Allen say she was living with them now at Riverbend. "I miss my river something awful, Grandpa. And Jessie."

Bethany ran into the room and Allen knew his time on the phone was done; it was so precious to hear Tucker's voice. "Your Mama is here, Tucker," Allen said laughing as Bethany pulled on his arm trying to take away the phone. "She's going to hit me if I don't hand this phone to her. I love you, Tucker. We all love you," he said looking at the large family now in his office.

"Love you too, Grandpa." Tucker heard his mother crying into the phone and saying his name over and over again. "I'm all right Mama, I'm taking care of the lights on the Nora, that's what we're calling the USS Northampton. She's a good ship Mama, she'll support me until I get home to you."

"Please, be safe Tucker," she begged before telling him she loved him and handing the phone to his father. There was a line behind Ethan and Tucker told his father he had only a few minutes left. Ethan pulled Cecily and Alicia forward and bent down with the phone so they could all talk. Then in the last minute Levi was handed the phone and he grabbed Jessie and pulled her to phone with him where he talked to his grandson but Jessie said nothing, she only listened to Tucker's voice.

"Jessie!" Tucker called and she still said nothing. "Are you there, Jessie?"

"She's here Tucker, she just can't speak at the moment," Levi said looking at the stricken look in Jessie's eyes and saw huge tears falling from her eyes. "She's crying Tucker and can't talk."

"I love you Jessie!" Tucker yelled. "I've always only loved you," Levi had the ear piece up to Jessie's ear and she was sobbing hysterically and saying nothing. "If I die out here, please know I loved you more than my own life." He heard nothing and his time on the phone was up, the men waiting to call home were a mile long behind him. "Bye Jessie," he said and heard his mother yelling goodbye and his Grandmothers.

Tucker walked away from the phone wondering why Jessie wasn't talking to him. Why she wasn't writing him. Grandpa Levi had said she was crying and he didn't know why she would be crying, her actions or lack of actions in writing him was telling him that she didn't care anything about him. He looked up at the beautiful sky and then out to the beautiful ocean. This part of the world was beautiful beyond words and he was glad he was getting to see the beauty, but it wasn't home, it wasn't his river with the purple poppy flowers on huge green lily pads. There were no alligators sliding into the clear water or a limestone bottom in this sea. The sand at home was white as snow but it made bare feet muddy and he laughed closing his eyes remembering the heavy clay dirt roads, red for as far as the eye could see. Home, he thought, he just had to survive this war and go home.

The Nora was again screening the Enterprise and on the fourth and fifth of June, the USS Enterprise which was an aircraft carrier launched planes in the battle at Midway and won a huge victory against the Japanese. The battle was so great and so successful that four Japanese aircraft carriers were sunk. In mid June the Nora returned to Pearl Harbor undamaged and Tucker again called home but it was a Monday afternoon in Florida, late afternoon and only Grandpa Allen and Grandma Alicia were home, Jessie was working full time at the mill with the shipping accounts. No matter what, Grandpa said, the world always needs lumber. Grandma assured him Jessie was doing well but that the girl was still withdrawn and easily upset; they were treating her gently and giving her time to grow into the family. Tucker knew she had been in the family for a year now and he had been gone almost all of that year. He remembered how Uncle Lang had told him that he would need to be careful of her and give her time to forget her past, that's what he was doing out here in the Pacific, he was giving Jessie time to heal and grow and see that she could be strong and love him someday. And he was working hard to see his ship was safe, to see that he did what he needed to do to help end this war.

"We stay out to sea a lot, Grandpa," Tucker said into the phone. "Tell Mama I think of her every day and tell Daddy I'm doing well, no shell shock on this ship. I know he worries the war will hurt me like it did him, but I'm holding up fine."

"I'll tell your parents Tucker, they're going to be sick they missed your call. I'll write you tonight son. We love you," as Allen said this Alicia leaned into the phone and said it with him.

"Remember, we're out to sea so you might not hear from me for a while," Tucker said before he hung up and his thoughts turned to Jessie working at the mill and finding her own place. She had wanted to work and never marry, he thought. She had told him everyone came to hate her in time or were mad at her. He knew that she learned that from her mother. And the thought of how he admired her, she had gone off with Ludlow and allowed the man to harm her in order to save her sister and then to learn her sister was dead, that her own mother had killed her and then buried her in the backyard of their home, what a horrible thing to know after having allowed herself to be used in that way.

Yes, Tucker felt sorry for Jessie but he was also angry with her and knew she was right when she had told him that she would make him mad at her. She never wrote him, she wouldn't talk to him on the phone, she wanted nothing to do with him and he thought this a million different times a day. It was tearing him apart, if only she would just say hello on the telephone to him.

He saw his shipmates boarding and knew it was time to go back to work. The Nora was going to the southwestern Pacific Ocean and would be a part of the Guadalcanal operation. In mid September the force that was with the Nora was attacked and several ships were badly damaged, the Nora herself was almost taken down at the port beam but managed to get through undamaged and safe.

By October Tucker was seeing more and more sea, it was endless waves and islands and he was wishing this war would end; they were coming up on almost ten months since Pearl Harbor was attacked and with Admiral Bull Halsey they were making good headway in regaining the Pacific. They were now attacking the Bougainville Island sailing along with the USS Hornet and

Tucker's main focus was on keeping the lights burning on the ship so the men could see day and night to do their jobs.

On October twenty six the Nora rushed to the aid of the USS Hornet, they were at the Santa Cruz Islands and had just been in a battle when the Hornet was mortally wounded by enemy aircraft. The Nora attempted to take the Hornet in tow but it was destroyed by both gunfire and torpedoes and Tucker felt bad, the Hornet had done so much in the effort of the war, far more than what he was doing in his job aboard the Nora and again he wished this war would end, he was tired and wanted to go home he thought as the Hornet sank in the sea.

"Mama!" Bethany cried out waving the newspaper above her hand and Alicia ran out onto the porch along with Allen and Levi. "Mama!! The Northampton sunk!" Allen fell back and Levi caught him, no one moved to catch Alicia as she fell to her knees in tears. And Bethany stood in the yard yelling over and over that the Nora had sank.

Cecily and Mary had gone to Alicia and helped her into the house, Allen was lifted up by Levi Tucker and the two men supporting one another went into the house while Bethany cried coming up the porch stairs. "He's all right," Jessie said in a still small voice to everyone that entered the hall and all eyes turned toward her as though she might really have information that Tucker was alive and well. "He's a hero, heroes can get through everything. And he's coming home, he promised he would." She spoke with such an air of confidence that everyone settled down and regained their calm as they knew yet again they had to wait.

"Any word on the USS Saratoga?" Allen pleaded to know as Bethany handed the newspaper to Mary. "Shaun Allen is on the Saratoga," he almost cried.

"There's nothing here concerning about that ship Allen," Mary said in a calm voice and handed the paper to Levi as Ethan walked in to find Bethany fall apart.

"We have to pray," Levi said and took the hands of those nearest him. "All heads bow for our boy," he said and saw everyone did. He knew Allen couldn't lead the prayer and he breathed a sigh of relief when Mary began to pray and Cecily ended the prayer. "Now we wait," Levi said looking at his family and Allen who was looking all of his sixty four years, this war was taking a heavy toll on the man.

"We have to keep these lights going, boys," he called out as the battle began, it would become known as the Battle of Tassafaronga and it was happening in the middle of the night when it was vital that the lights burn on for the crew to fight and win. There had been three American destroyers that made a surprise attack on the Japanese when all three ships had opened fire with no warning, the torpedoes hit over and over and over again every minute for ten full minutes, the Nora along with many destroyers fought with the single minded purpose of winning and were doing so. And then the worst happened, enemy torpedoes ripped through the port side of the ship; decks and bulkhead alike were torn away and flaming oil sprayed up and over the ship causing her to take on water quickly and Tucker's beautiful Nora began to list. Despite all they were doing things grew worse by the hour and she was sinking stern first and the men had no choice, they had to abandon their ship.

"We keep the lights on while they get off, fellows!" Tucker called out and heard all the men calling out the same. There had been men that the blast had thrown in the water and the men on the ship soon joined them, the lights burned bright until every man was off the ship and in the water and the ship slowly sank with her lights still burning and the loss of life was not great, in fact it was amazing that so many of the crew lived.

Tucker tread water as he waited for help to come, for another ship to pluck them out of the sea. He closed his eyes and pretended he was home, home in his river with Thomas and Taylor and Shaun Allen and even Jessie. The waves weren't bad and had a calming effect on him and he could dream even here of her, of Jessie with her round beautiful breast that he longed to touch again, of making her feel the way he had that last night with her, dreaming of kissing her until he was too tired to kiss her. He wanted to cry knowing that she was at home not thinking of him in anyway, that he meant so little to her that she wouldn't even talk to him on the phone.

When Tucker opened his eyes he saw all the men in the water around him, some of the men were trying to swim toward the islands in hopes the natives would care for them until they could be rescued. Tucker just wanted to be here treading the water and thinking of her and of home and seeing that his ship had sunk and there were no lights to keep burning now, no men that needed to see inside the depths of the ship, he knew he had done his job and done it well.

Toward dawn the destroyers arrived and the men were picked up and taken aboard where they learned that they had been defeated, they had several cruisers that were badly damaged and their Nora as they knew their ship, was lost. The battle had only seen one Japanese destroyer sunk but there was positive news for the men, the Nora hadn't been lost in vain, the battle had denied the Japanese the major reinforcements they had been expecting to arrive.

January 1943
Pearl Harbor

Tucker held the telephone in his hand on a early Sunday afternoon and waited for someone to pick up at his Grandpa's house, he wondered if the church was having dinner on the grounds, if they were then he knew he wouldn't have anyone to talk to on this call.

He had already written his family that he was alive but until now he hadn't been able to get to a phone.

"Hello," he heard his Grandma Alicia call into the phone and he yelled in sheer joy to hear her voice.

"Grandma! It's me Tucker!" he heard her scream his name and he smiled.

"We got your letter that you went down on the USS Northampton," he heard his grandmother crying. "We were so afraid for weeks that we had lost you."

"I'm coming home to my river when this war is over Grandma, I need to be home." He heard her crying and wanted to cry with her.

"Here, talk to your Mama and Daddy," Alicia handed her daughter Bethany and son in law Ethan the phone as Allen's study filled with people listening to this side of the conversation.

Jessie stood in the doorway of the room the family was gathered in not surprised Tucker was alive and well and safe, she had known heroes don't die. She looked around at all the smiling happy faces and wished this war was over, she wished it had never started. She didn't even know what it was about. She saw Grandma Alicia looking at her and nodded her head letting the older woman know that she knew Tucker was safe and she turned and walked out the door going through the drawing room double doors and down to the river. It was a cold day and she didn't take her coat, only her sweater, she wanted to be cold, she wanted to breathe in the crisp air and feel alive.

When he came home, Jessie thought, she would ask him to annul the marriage as quickly as possible. There was no reason for them to stay married, they were strangers now; they would always be strangers. He had grown away from her, seen the world, and she was a country girl. With the knowledge she was getting from the mill she knew that she would find a job in the Capital as a secretary, or she may get on with the library as she wanted to when she was young. She wouldn't be a burden on Tucker or his family forever, she would free him and herself, she just had to wait for this war to end.

Taking a deep breath Jessie knew that she was glad, glad that Tucker was alive, glad that he was doing something so honorable, even proud of him. But she wasn't really his nor did she want to be. "Some people are just meant to be alone in this life," she spoke out loud and wished that she could just flow away like the river. "I'm a loner," Jessie said in a louder voice and went to the edge of the river. If she walked into the river and floated away, no one would miss her. She had never mattered to anyone. She thought of Tucker and how he said he loved her but she knew, he just wanted her body, he wanted to own her and she didn't want that in anyway despite what they had done that night before he left and how he made her feel. The more time that passed since he had kissed her all over like that, the more certain she was that he was doing that for himself and not for her.

Allen Blackburn frowned as he watched Jessie put her feet in the freezing cold river and take several steps into the water. He looked down and saw the alarm on Alicia's face. And then his heard his wife gasp as Jessie went up to her knees in the river. Alicia ran to the river leaving Allen where he was standing and into the water grabbing Jessie by the arm. The two women were almost the same size, one was fifty seven and the other seventeen. The fifty seven year old knew what it was to be desperate to escape life and the seventeen year old was trying to fade away into the river.

"You don't want to do what you're thinking of doing," Alicia said looking Jessie in the eyes and holding her arm.

"I'm a burden," Jessie burst into tears and Alicia took her hand and lead her to Allen on the shore.

"To whom are you a burden?" Alicia asked as Allen took off his coat and put it around her shoulders.

"You both have been so good to me, but I'm not truly Tucker's wife and we all know that." Jessie saw Allen shiver and hurried to the house, she didn't want him to get cold and catch a chill.

"So you're a burden to us because you're not truly Tucker's wife?" Alicia asked as they entered the drawing room and Alicia hurried them all to the fireplace where Allen added more wood and Alicia peeled off her wet shoes and stockings and ordered Jessie to do the same.

"It was my fault that the Taylors were killed," she was crying, for more than a year she had held this guilt inside her. "They were trying to protect Elise and I," she sobbed almost hysterically not seeing Bethany and Ethan enter the room along with Cecily and Levi.

"Jessie," Allen spoke holding her blue eyes with his grass green eyes. "Listen to me and listen well. You didn't really know the Taylors. Lang was a healer and he gave of himself to others freely, he wanted only to help. Holly was the same, they were good, loving and kind people with hearts of gold. If they saw a dog in need of help, they would have died helping that dog." Allen's voice faded away as he choked up but still looked at Jessie.

"It was Betsy Fairchild that killed the Taylors," Cecily said gently, "not you." And she saw Bethany go to the girl and hug her.

"She was my mother," Jessie cried and leaned onto Bethany, the first time the girl had shown any emotion at all toward Bethany.

"She wasn't any kind of a mother to you, sweet girl," Ethan said. "A mother would never do what she did, I can assure you."

"Look, I know you think you're not one of us now, Jessie," Alicia took her hand. "But you are one of us and we want only to love, support and help you. That's what the Taylors would do if they were here right now. Please, please give us a chance. You've been here a year and we've done everything we can to love you."

"Tucker loves you so much, Jessie." Bethany hugged her close. And this war cannot last forever. You went outside before you heard," Bethany pulled away from Jessie and smiled wide. "Because he kept the lights burning on the Nora he's been given the rank of Chief Warrant Officer Fourth class."

"Is that a good thing?" Jessie asked and everyone in the room laughed causing her to laugh as well.

"A very good thing," Bethany said hugging her. "Let's go find something to eat," she said and reached for her mother's hand and saw Alicia reach for her father. "Where are your shoes and stockings?" Bethany asked her mother and then saw Jessie didn't have hers on either.

"We got a little wet in the river," Alicia said. "We needed the cool water to wake us up." She took Jessie's hand and pulled her to the kitchen. "Mary's rolls are fresh out of the oven. Let's go have a slice of heaven."

Tucker couldn't believe his next assignment, he was aboard the USS Saratoga, an aircraft carrier out of San Diego. He was impressed with her size and what she could do. She was the only American fleet aircraft carrier in the South Pacific and being aboard her was an honor, she was the pride of the South Pacific now and he knew that.

Tucker had been aboard ship for over two weeks when he heard someone call out the name 'Tucker' and he was shocked, every since coming into the Navy he had been forced to accept that his name was Allen. He turned with his food tray and saw across the galley his Uncle Shaun Allen. In sheer excitement he dropped his tray and ran to Shaun Allen giving him a big bear hug and lifting him off the floor.

"What are you doing here?" Tucker asked his lifelong friend, his mother's baby brother only two years older than Tucker.

"I've been on this ship since I was done being a boot," Shaun Allen laughed and punched Tucker in the gut. "I can't believe we're on the same ship. Let's get something to eat and talk. I've missed you Tucker."

"I've missed you too Shaun Allen." Tucker walked to where he dropped his tray and picked it up and got in the line to get something to eat. "I'm going to write Grandpa Allen tonight that I'm on the same carrier you are," Tucker held out his tray for the food and watched Shaun Allen do the same.

"Yes, my Dad is in for a shock, his son and Grandson on the same carrier together."

"Anyone ever tell you boys that you look alike?" one of the men at the table said when Tucker and Shaun Allen sat down side by side and they exchanged grins.

"My father is his Grandfather," Shaun Allen said with his mouth full of food and seeing Tucker mix it all up, meat, potatoes and vegetables in a huge pile on his tray, Shaun Allen did the same and they laughed.

"Hey it's all going to get mixed up in the gut," Tucker said and nudged his Uncle. "I sure wish we had some of Aunt Mary's rolls."

"Oh, yeah," Shaun Allen agreed and then saw an officer coming toward them and they both stopped shoving food in their mouths.

"Brothers can't serve on the same carrier together," the officer said looking down at Shaun Allen and Tucker.

"He's not my brother, sir," Shaun Allen said looking at Tucker thinking he really was like a brother; they grew up together and were inseparable as children, if you saw Thomas, Taylor and Tucker, then you saw Shaun Allen, the boys all grew up together.

"You're brothers if I say you're brothers," the officer stated and Tucker had to fight to keep from laughing.

"Yes, sir," Shaun Allen said respectfully.

"He's my Uncle," Tucker said calmly while looking the officer in the eyes. "My mother is his sister."

"Farm boys," the officer said and Tucker looked at Shaun Allen knowing they had never once ever in their lives thought of themselves as farm boys. River pirates or musketeers yes, but never farm boys.

"Actually," Tucker said in a cool yet respectful voice, "we're Floridians, our Great Grandfather was awarded land for services rendered in the Indian wars by our then President, Andrew Jackson on the Saint Marks River near the Capital City of Tallahassee. Our fathers own and operate a lumber supply business there and we raise Texas long horn cattle. We have a proud heritage, sir and never considered ourselves boys, we were born to be men and we are men serving our country with great honor and pride. And we're not brothers but thank you for mistaking us as such, if I had a brother, I would want him to be just like Uncle," he pointed his thumb to Shaun Allen and saw that the officer wasn't upset with his candor or his straightforward words, in fact, the officer looked impressed.

"I hear Florida is beautiful," the Officer said and Shaun Allen smiled and looked at his nephew.

"Most beautiful place you can imagine, but in July and August you don't want to be there," he laughed and looked at Tucker both saying at the same time, "Muggy and buggy."

"You two could be twins," the officer said seeing the only difference was one had green eyes and the other had a shade of green but it was a clear blue green.

"We have cousins that are identical twins," Tucker said with pride. "They along with my Dad served in the Great War. My father has the scar to prove his service."

"Well, take care of yourselves, we're in for some rough seas, this carrier is going to be busy. No shore leave or trips home anytime soon."

"It's been almost two years since I was home," Tucker said seriously. "I joined months before the war started and then Pearl Harbor was attacked while I was on the USS Northampton."

"You were on the Nora?" The officer asked sounding impressed. "How long were you in the drink?" he asked and Tucker knew the drink was in reference to his being in the sea treading water.

"Too many hours, sir," he laughed but didn't find what he had gone through in the ocean that night really funny. Thinking of Jessie and his river was all that got him through. "I sure wish this war would end."

"The tide is turning in our favor here; we'll be done in another year, two at the most." Tucker watched the officer walk away wishing they were done now.

"Let's go find paper and pencil and write home together," Shaun Allen said once they were done with their food. "By the way, did you know you outrank me?

"I won't tell if you don't tell," Tucker said and went to find writing material, they would write to everyone tonight. He wasn't alone now, Tucker thought. He was feeling horribly homesick and blue but now he was feeling stronger, more like he could go on and make it through this war.

Allen Blackburn looked down at the letter in his hand and sighed in relief. Tucker and his son Shaun Allen were together. Nothing would happen to Shaun Allen now, Tucker would watch out for him. Allen knew that Shaun Allen was the older one and probably even the stronger one of the pair, but Tucker had wits about him that Shaun Allen didn't have. Tucker thought on his feet and thought fast. He was like Allen in a lot of ways, he could plan for the future; he set goals to reach. Yes, Tucker was wild and free running along those river banks, he was the boy that climbed trees and swung from branches in the heavy current and then fought his way to shore. He was amazing in his boundless energy and he wasn't a quitter.

Allen thought of his son, Shaun Allen with a lot of pride. His son would come back here and take over the mill and the trees, he knew that Tucker was going to do things differently and he was all right with that. At first he was upset because he wanted a different life for Tucker than the one Tucker wanted for himself, but he had

Shaun Allen to carry on the legacy, and to carry on the Blackburn name for him. He didn't mind having girls, Allen thought and knew at one time he didn't mind having a house full of girls, but now in his old age, he wanted that boy, that son to carry out his legacy.

"Grandpa," Allen heard Jessie speaking from the doorway and he motioned for her to come in.

"What do you need, Jessie?" Allen asked and pointed to a chair.

"We're now into nineteen forty four, this war has gone on forever. Do you see any end in sight and Tucker coming home?" Allen shook his head, that was a million dollar question being asked by families all over this country.

"I need to know how much help I am for you," Jessie said and leaned forward in her chair.

"Jessie, you're not a burden. You have to stop thinking that way. It's time, past time for you to see that you're a gift to our family and we love you so much." Allen saw Mary walk into his office and he smiled at her and offered for her to sit down and join them.

"If you're a burden, then I am as well," Mary said smiling at Jessie. "You at least work hard at the mill and do a good job with the books. All I do is make my rolls."

"Everyone loves your rolls," Jessie said and looked down at Mary holding her hand.

"You've been in our family almost three full years, when are you going to open up and let us see you smile and enjoy us? You're such a kind person Jessie but you're closed off and you shouldn't be. Let your light shine," Mary said and looked at Allen. "Like our Seth, he was always having a laugh at someone or something. I miss his laugh so much. Let's try and be happy in this house. No one is a bother or a burden, we're all family."

Jessie couldn't make this family understand how she felt, no one knew and no one would ever really know what she was thinking. She was meant to be alone, she wasn't meant to be a part of something so large and loving and good. She belonged out in the world with no one and nothing, if she loved, if she opened herself up as Aunt Mary was advising, then she was going to get hurt, and the fact was, Jessie had been hurt enough. She was living for Tucker's return, for Tucker to annul the marriage, to go her own way. Every penny Grandpa Allen was paying her she was putting away so she would have a means to support herself. And she was never, not ever going to love anyone.

Allen saw the look on Jessie's face and knew she wasn't going to take Mary's advice, she had a part of herself locked away and here it was more than three years of her with them and she was still shut up inside of herself. All they could do was wait for her to trust them, to love them and know that she was safe and always would be. She was a Blackburn now, she was his family and he would pray for her and comfort her and wait on her to get over the hurt she held inside.

The telephone on his desk rang and they all jumped in surprise before Allen reached for the thing. "Tucker!" he yelled into the phone and Mary called out for Alicia and Cecily seeing Levi already coming into the room with Ethan and Bethany. "Shaun Allen!" Allen called out and laughed. "My two favorite boys are together."

No one saw Jessie slip out of the room. No one realized that Tucker didn't ask how she was doing in this phone call. Everyone spoke at once to the boys, their handsome boys and Jessie faded away up into her room.

In March the Saratoga was in an escort with three destroyers and assigned to the Eastern Fleet in the Indian Ocean, things were calm and Shaun Allen spent most of his free time with Tucker. The men would surround the carrier on one side with netting to keep sharks from coming at them and then from the deck of the ship, usually only in their undershorts, they would dive eighty feet into the water and swim. It was relaxing and it was fun and it didn't feel so much like they were at war.

In October of nineteen forty four there was an accident aboard the ship when the plane guard destroyer USS Clark ran into the port side of the Saratoga's hull, everything was put to a stop while temporary repairs were made, it wasn't until January of nineteen forty five that she was permanently repaired and she could continue her training.

Tucker and Shaun Allen called home in January of nineteen forty five before the Saratoga left Pearl Harbor to meet the USS Enterprise and talked as long as they could to their family. They knew things weren't going to be as they had been for them on the Saratoga; they knew they were going to conduct a night attack over Iwo Jima with fifty three hellcats and about seventeen avengers on the Carrier. Shaun Allen was excited and worried, Tucker just wanted this over with, as he had been thinking for years, he just wanted this war over and to be home, he couldn't get home soon enough.

The Saratoga had been assigned to provide cover while the carriers launched several strikes on Japan and Shaun Allen told Tucker the war was going to end soon, they were winning. Tucker didn't think so, he felt every day he was out here and away from home, he was losing.

Shaun Allen was on deck as was Tucker when the crew was taking advantage of low cloud cover when suddenly Japanese planes started dropping bombs, within three minutes five bombs hit the Saratoga's flight deck and Tucker felt himself flying in the air and an intense pain in his leg, a pain like he had never known. He hit the water and went down deep having to fight his way up, his right leg not working as it should have making him afraid he wasn't going to reach the surface.

Shaun Allen went up when the bomb hit the flight deck and then over the side seeing Tucker hit the water before he did. He screamed when he hit the water, something hurt but he wasn't sure what hurt, he only knew he had to reach Tucker. He saw his nephew fighting to swim up and saw something dark coming from his pants. Shaun Allen pushed with all of his might and swam down grabbing Tucker by the arm and pulled him up.

"We're all right," Shaun said as he hit the surface and saw more bombs dropping. "Good Lord," he prayed as a Kamikaze plane hit the ship and exploded. "Talk to me Tuck," he ordered and Tucker had a hold of him now treading water with his good leg.

"How bad hurt are you?" Tucker asked and Shaun Allen shook his head.

"I'm not hurt," and then he went limp in Tucker's arms. "I can't swim," he said in a low voice. "I think maybe I am hurt."

"Help!" Tucker screamed and screamed until he saw the men on the carrier had seen him in the water and were coming to get him and Shaun Allen. It wasn't until they were lifting him back on board that he saw all the men in the water, most face down and realized he and his Uncle weren't the only ones out there fighting to stay afloat.

"Oh man," Shaun Allen breathed as Tucker fell onto him once they were safely out of the water. "I feel so numb, Tuck." Tucker pushed himself up despite the horrible pain in his leg and saw the hole in Shaun Allen's side.

"You're going to be all right," Tucker stated and then started screaming for help almost hysterically. Men rushed to him and put Shaun Allen on a cot and Tucker fought to stand and couldn't. Several men rushed to lift him up and he was following Shaun Allen on the cot. "I'm coming, Shaun Allen," he called out. "Talk to me!" he demanded as they were taken away from the flames and to where they could get help.

"Tucker," Shaun Allen said looking up at his best friend. "Tell Daddy I'm sorry. And tell Mama I love her. I'm going home now, Tuck."

"You stop talking like that," Tucker ordered in a loud voice. "We're going home together." Tucker saw the Officer that had called them brothers come into the room and only then noticed the medical insignia. "Please," he looked the officer in the eyes. "Please, he's my Grandpa's only son. Save him, please. I promised Grandpa I wouldn't let anything happen to him." He saw the officer's empathy and compassion and he ignored Shaun Allen and came to look at Tucker's leg.

"I'm sorry, son. You're Uncle is already gone." He cut open Tucker's pants and saw how badly he was wounded. "And you're going home."

Tucker sat up realizing Shaun Allen's fate and he became hysterical. "You can't bury him at sea," Tucker felt the tears pouring down his face. "Please, I have to take him home. He's my Grandpa's only son and he has to go home to our river in Florida. You can't let them bury him at sea."

Tucker heard another crash above on deck and knew the attacks on the carrier weren't over. "Sir, we have over three hundred men either dead or missing," a seaman came to the door and said and Tucker knew the war for him was over, he was among the wounded. The officer looked at Tucker and knew he would be on a plane out of here within the hour, he needed more medical attention than he could get aboard ship. "I'll put your Uncle on the plane with you; pretend he is alive and can be helped. After then it's up to you to see he gets home." He saw Tucker nod his head and lean back still crying. "I'm sorry you lost him, son."

"I just have to get him home, I'll pay his way. I'll do anything." The officer nodded in understanding.

"Because he's the only son in the family, they do show compassion from time to time." The officer motioned to four seamen to come to him. "Get these two on the next flight out, they need more care than I can give them." The Officer took Tucker's hand and shook it hard. "You'll make it back to your river in Florida now. And him as well."

Tucker was forever grateful for that Officer and he had been right, once Tucker had explained that Shaun Allen was an only son, they had made arrangements to get him home and Tucker was going with him. The war was over for Tucker with a severely wounded leg, he had been warned he would probably never walk without support for the rest of his life. But Tucker knew, he had a river to swim in and banks to run on, he didn't have time to stand still, he was going home and Shaun Allen was going with him.

Tucker looked at the coffin that held his Uncle and best friend. Shaun Allen's presence had gotten him through this war, they had a bond stronger than brothers and he was taking his body home to lie in the family cemetery always. "Has some one notified my Grandparents?" Tucker asked as he boarded the plane and fought not to cry. He wanted to be home but he felt bad, inside he felt he had failed Shaun Allen. And he kept hearing his Grandpa years ago ask him to watch out for Shaun Allen.

An officer helped Tucker up from his wheelchair and onto a seat of the plane and he looked up at the man with pleading eyes. "Does my family know yet?" the officer put his hand on his shoulder and nodded his head.

"While you had surgery on your leg, they were notified." Tucker knew that notification usually came in a telegram and he lowered his head fearing that this might have killed his Grandparents. He didn't know what he would find when he got home, and all he wanted was to get home.

Allen was in the yard chopping wood for the fireplace aware that winter was fading and spring was on the way. He had the whole house done in gas heat but he still liked it the way it was in the old days. Alicia was on the porch watching him and he lifted his arm in a wave. She had been right years ago, chopping the wood was keeping him in shape.

Mary had come out on the porch to stand next to his wife and he felt peace that she was here with them. She would always stay with them, he knew. She was really his little sister. He saw Jessie come out the door and bring him a glass of sweet tea. She still kept to herself, she was still withdrawn, he wished she could learn to laugh or even just smile, she was far too serious.

"Thomas is here," Jessie pointed to Allen's nephew and he saw him getting out of the car tall and lean so much like Allen use to be in his younger years.

"What do you know?" Allen teasingly asked Thomas and saw his serious face, so like Thomas, Allen thought. He should have been a judge.

"Uncle Allen," Thomas choked and looked to see his Mama and Daddy driving into the yard along with his Uncle Shane and Aunt Charlotte. He had also called Bethany and Ethan to meet him here but they weren't in sight yet.

Allen dropped his ax and saw his twin nephews getting out of their cars with serious faces and he knew, it was about Tucker or his son. Alicia didn't move, she knew it was bad news. And then Bethany ran around the corner of the house with Ethan beside her. "Is it my Tucker?" she cried out and grabbed her father.

Thomas swallowed hard and looked back at his father, his cousin Shaun Allen had been named for his Daddy. He handed his father the telegram and watched him open it as Bethany cried. No matter what she was going to cry, it was her brother. "The USS Saratoga was bombed," Thomas said and saw his Aunt Alicia sit down on the step with his Grandmother Mary sitting down beside her.

"It's not our Tucker," Shaun said handing the telegram to his Uncle Allen. "It's our Shaun Allen." Thomas and Shaun moved together and caught Allen.

"No," Allen breathed as the boys lowered him to the ground unable to look at Alicia. She had fought for that boy to be born, she had loved him all his life and now he was gone. It couldn't be true.

Allen put his face in his hands and held perfectly still. This was a dream, this was not real. Shaun Allen was with Tucker; Tucker was smart and stable and as Jessie said, a hero. Tucker wouldn't let anything happen to his son. He had asked Tucker to watch over Shaun Allen years ago.

Alicia sat on the steps for a full minute and then she stood and went to Allen sitting on the ground. "Get up," she said in a tone of voice no one in the family had ever heard her use; she sounded nothing like the gentle, fragile Alicia Blackburn. "Get up," she said again and Allen looked at her not realizing it was his wife was talking to him.

"I can't Alicia," Allen looked up at his wife, still beautiful after all these years and looking younger than her age. "All those babies we lost," he almost cried and saw her looking at him with a fierce look he had never seen from her ever before.

"Get up, Allen," she said in the same tone and didn't realize her family stood in shock at her tone and the way she was treating her husband when they had just lost their son. "Do you remember that night at Aunt Julia's? What you did to the door? And you've done it to our hallway wall for over forty years. I need you to come do that for me right now, Allen. I need you to hit that wall and hit it hard. For me. For me, Allen." Alicia saw Allen push himself up and his nephews reach to help him and he looked at his small wife that rarely asked anything of him knowing she had lost their son today as well.

"I love you Alicia Blackburn," he took her hand and went up the porch steps, his heart was in his throat. He didn't notice everyone following him and his wife.

"Hit it Allen," Alicia demanded. "Hit it hard, Allen."

Before he could make a move to beat up his hallway wall, Allen watched in shocked disbelief as Alicia hit the wall. She was screaming when she did and with both fists pounding the wall and causing no harm, leaving no mark. Allen took a deep breath and punched with all his might breaking a hole the size of fist.

"Look Alicia," he took hold of her. "I've not put a hole in a wall that good since Aunt Julia's house." He was crying and Alicia fell into him, her arms around his neck and her sobs loud in the hall. Allen looked up and saw Levi standing in the doorway with Cecily and handed him the telegram. "Shaun Allen is dead," he said and heard his wife cry out. "Tucker's hurt and is coming home to heal." Allen hugged Alicia and her feet left the floor as he held her against him. "My son," he cried and started for the stairs, Alicia held close and her feet not touching the floor as he walked up the stairs and to their room, everyone hearing the door close.

"Levi," Mary moved closer to him and Cecily. "Does it say when Tucker will be home?" Levi shook his head and handed her the telegram.

"It only says he's on his way home. Doesn't even say how he's getting here. What do we do?" Levi looked at everyone in the room and Thomas stepped forward.

"Let me call the Sheriff, he might can find out for us." Levi followed Thomas to the phone in Allen's study while the rest of the family listened to Aunt Alicia sob and Uncle Allen sobbing with her. Bethany was holding on to Ethan and no one noticed Jessie in a corner of the hall, safely alone and separated from the family as she had been all these years.

Allen didn't move from the bed. He held Alicia in his arms and cried with her as she cried. He then started talking, reminding Alicia of all the things Shaun Allen had done in his life, of how the boy had made their life so much sweeter. He could see himself standing on the porch holding Shaun Allen when he was only two years, how proud he had been to have his son. He could see himself teaching him how to bait a hook and shoot a gun, and helping him clean the first deer he had shot. He lay in the bed remembering the happy days with his only son.

"I prayed so hard he would be safe," Alicia said finally when she was able to stop crying. "I was so certain God heard me." Allen said nothing; he could only look up at the ceiling and think of Shaun Allen.

A knock sounded at the door and Allen didn't want to sit up, he didn't want to move so he just called out for whoever it was to come in. "Daddy," Bethany said softly looking at her mama. "Tucker is arriving tomorrow afternoon by train. He flew into New Orleans and caught the train there."

"Good," Allen said in a cold voice. He didn't care Tucker was coming home right now, his son wasn't coming home.

"Do you and Mama want to come with us to get him?" she heard her mother crying again and knew the answer. "I understand." Bethany went to leave the room but met her father's eyes; they were still full of tears. "Shaun Allen was loved by all of us Daddy. He was a wonderful man." She saw her father's head nod and he swallowed hard. "I love you both." She left the door and came onto the bed where she kissed her mother's forehead and her father's cheek.

"We love you too, baby girl," her mother said before hiding her face in Allen's neck.

"We need time alone," Allen said seriously and Bethany stood up and went to the door, she didn't want to leave them like this, she wanted to make things better and stay with them but saw her father lift his hand and shoo her out the door.

"They're broken hearted," Bethany said knowing that if it had been Tucker killed she and Ethan would have been in an agony right now.

"Your daddy will take care of Alicia," Mary said. "He always has. Though I don't know how they're going to get over this. It's the worst, Shaun Allen was so young. So full of life."

"He was special," Cecily added and they all looked up the stairs. "Jessie," Cecily called her grandson's wife's name after seeing her in a corner. "Are you coming with us tomorrow to pick up Tucker?" Cecily saw Jessie shake her head and then run out the front door. "I cannot understand that child, she's so silent and still, we all forget to notice her. She needs to go with us to pick up her husband."

"Let her be, Mama," Ethan said in a kind way to his mother. "She needs to find Tucker on her own, and Tucker needs to come home and find her. But right now, Shaun, Shane, can you lead us in prayer for Aunt Alicia and Uncle Allen and Tucker and Jessie?" The family clasped hands and bowed their heads in prayer, Shane starting the prayer and Shaun finishing the prayer as Alicia's cries floated down the stairs well and Allen's calming voice was saying his son's name over and over and over again.

PART THREE

Tucker's Return
The End of a Dynasty

Chapter Thirteen

March 1945
Tallahassee, Florida

Tucker was helped off the train by the conductor and put in his wheelchair. There was no way he could walk or even attempt to stand on his leg as it was. He was hoping Doctor Aaron Taylor could help him know for certain that he was going to get the full use of his leg back. He pushed himself to the back of the train and stopped next to the coffin that held his Uncle and wondered how he was going to get them both home.

"Tucker!" he heard his Mama call his name and gasped seeing her running toward him. She was the most beautiful thing he had seen in years. His father was beside his mother pulling her toward him and he saw his Grandpa Levi and Grandma Cecily, they hadn't changed a bit in the four years he had been gone from home.

"Mama," he cried, really cried real tears and fell into her arms as she bent down to him. He could feel his father's hand on his shoulder and reached up to take a hold of his father's hand. "Shaun Allen," he sobbed and touched the coffin. "I fought like hell to bring him home to our river." His mother pulled away and saw the coffin that held her brother, her sweet little baby brother that had been her father's pride and joy along side of her own son.

"Ethan, how are going to get him home?" Bethany asked about both her brother and Tucker in his wheelchair.

"My chair folds up Mama. I already talked to the conductor and he's gone to the local funeral home to make arrangements to get Shaun Allen to Riverbend." Tucker saw the conductor coming back toward them with a man in a nice suit and his Grandfather Levi Tucker went to meet the man.

"It's good you're home," Cecily came to her grandson and hugged him close.

"Grandpa Allen and Grandma Alicia didn't come with you?" Cecily shook her head.

"They weren't up to it, son. They're both broken up over the loss of our Shaun Allen." Cecily turned when she saw her husband come back to them and hug Tucker.

"The undertaker will bring Shaun Allen out to the house this afternoon," Levi said. "Let's get you home." Between the four of them they were able to get Tucker into the car along with his chair and his sea bag. He sat in the back seat with his mother on one side and his father on the other and his Grandmother turned looking at him from the front seat.

"Grandpa Allen," Tucker took a deep breath and worked up the courage to say what he was thinking. "He's mad at me for coming home without Shaun Allen. He asked me to watch out for him years ago and I failed him." Tucker broke down in tears and his mother hugged him.

And where was Jessie, Tucker wanted to asked but he didn't dare. All these years and not one word from her or out of her and she wasn't even here for him now. All this time he had loved her and waited to come home to her and now she was nowhere near him. He felt sick thinking of her rejection and then cried harder because he knew if she hadn't wanted him whole, she certainly wouldn't want him like this. He couldn't even stand and walk.

"Can we go to our home, Mama? I can't face Grandma and Grandpa yet. Please, can we go to our home?" Bethany looked at Ethan and saw Ethan was looking at her. They both remembered all too well when he had come home from war and how he had needed tender care and support to heal.

"Yes, we'll go quietly to our house and you take your time, you need to get well some." Tucker nodded his head and leaned back into his parents. He felt safe, he felt like he wasn't going to hate himself for Shaun Allen's death, he would just be angry with himself for not saving him.

"We were together for two years, Mama. He was my best friend." Ethan heard Tucker breaking down again and knew it was for the best. To keep everything inside only made you feel worse, Ethan knew that to be true as he had lived through hell once long ago.

Tucker didn't look up as they drove past the cemetery, he didn't look in the direction of his Grandpa Allen's house. He kept thinking of his home, with his parents, safe and sitting on the porch watching the river flow by. He could think right again once he was on that porch. This fog he was in would lift and he would feel better. He just needed to see the river.

Jessie saw the car turn down the road going to Ethan and Bethany's house and knew they weren't coming here to Riverbend. She breathed a sigh of relief and started back to the mill, she had work to do and she was bringing a jug of sweet tea she had made to Shaun and Shane. They were working extra hard because Ethan wasn't there to help them.

Jessie didn't see Allen Blackburn looking out the window as he saw Levi Tucker turn down the road toward his daughter's house and didn't come here to his house. He was relieved; he and Alicia weren't up to a happy home coming when their son was coming home in a box. Tucker had his other Grandparents and his parents, he didn't need them.

"Allen," Alicia said coming down the stairs. "I need to see Tucker," she said pulling on her sweater. "I saw them not come this way. I'm going to Bethany's. Come with me." Alicia saw Allen shaking his head and she reached for his hand but he pulled it away.

"Don't ask me too," he cried and she backed away from him.

"Allen, you aren't mad at Tucker for living and coming home are you?" She saw her husband shake his head and turn away from her.

"I asked Tucker to take care of him. I told Tucker Shaun Allen was weak and need him to protect him." Alicia put her hand over her mouth and shook her head.

"Tucker is younger than Shaun Allen. And it was a war, they were in battle. How dare you be this way Allen. How dare you." Allen saw his wife turn on her heals and leave him standing in the hall. He went to the stairs and sat down on the bottom step, his face in his hands.

"It's not like you think, Alicia. I just can't face him." Allen cried and Alicia turned back to him.

"He is our grandson, he has always loved you best and everyone knows that too, Allen Blackburn. And you've always adored him and I know you're hurting, I'm hurting as well. You have one day, Allen. One day is all I'm giving you to get over your hurt toward Tucker and see him. Do you understand me?"

"You've gotten bossy, Alicia," Allen said looking at her pointing her finger at him.

"I have not. I just lost my only son and my husband is acting like he's the only one hurting in this house and looking for someone to blame. And our poor hurt Grandson isn't the one to blame. It's this war. Blaming and being like you are right now, well that's just not who you are Allen Blackburn. You're the finest man I've ever known in my life. Even better than Lang Taylor and we all know that man was an angel right down from heaven. One day to get over being upset with Tucker for living when our son died.

I know my Tuck, he's upset right now that he lived." Alicia saw Allen look up at her and she knew he realized that to be the truth.

"Give me a minute," Allen stood up and reached for his hat and coat and then came to take his wife's hand. "I'll drive us," he said and pulled her outside and to the car. "And by the way," he looked down into her beautiful eyes. "Thank you."

"You're welcome," Alicia said as she sat right next to him on the car seat, her head on his shoulder. She knew her husband; Allen Roston Blackburn was the finest man in the whole world.

Levi carried the chair up the front porch steps while Ethan and Bethany got Tucker up the steps, realizing there was no way he could use his leg, he crawled up the steps and into the chair dragging his poor blown up leg behind him. "I need Doctor Taylor to come look at this Mama, can you call him?" He saw his mother nod her head and go into the house. "I just want to sit here and look at my river," Tucker said and saw his father sit in a rocking chair near him and his Grandparents sit on the porch swing.

He was home, Tucker thought as he looked at his river. And he couldn't even hobble to the banks of his river, he was trapped in this chair. And poor Shaun Allen was in a box waiting to be planted like a tree in the ground. He saw a deer in the distance near the spring and breathed in deeply and then he heard the car, saw his Grandpa Allen and Grandma Alicia getting out, and he choked on air and fought to breath.

"Are you all right Tucker?" he heard his father ask and he choked again.

Allen Blackburn saw his beautiful grandson on the porch; he hadn't seen him in four years. He saw the battle going on in his Tucker and he left Alicia and went to him. "I'm sorry Grandpa," Tucker cried out and threw his face in his hands. "I'm so sorry Grandpa," he cried louder and harder as Allen cried with him and pulled him into his arms.

"My Tucker is home," Allen cried and kissed his head and Tucker clung to him saying he was sorry over and over. "I love you so much."

Alicia walked up to the two of them, her beautiful husband she'd loved for so long and her handsome grandson. "Tucker," she said in her gentle way and he looked at her as she took his hand and Allen held his other hand. "Thank you for taking care of our son. He wrote home many times in the past two years how well you watched out for him and how close you two had grown. Closer than brothers, he said." Alicia fell forward into Tucker's arm and held him while he sobbed, her husband Allen holding them both and many minutes passed as the three stayed just this way.

Later, Tucker looked at his Grandmother and then his Grandfather and said, "There's something you both should know," and he saw them pull up chairs to sit next to him. He knew his mother was standing behind him and his father was watching him close along with Levi and Cecily. "The bombs hit our carrier and Shaun Allen and I were on deck. It happened so fast, we were blasted off the deck and up into the air and then into the water. I couldn't swim, Grandpa, my leg was too messed up. I was fighting like mad to get to the surface; I was drowning there in the Pacific when all I wanted was to just come home to our river. And then Shaun Allen was there pulling me up and holding on to me and treading water for us both. He saved me. And within a few minutes, I saw how badly he was hurt and I was holding him and treading water with one leg and an arm. They pulled us back on deck, so many dead men in the water and we were alive. But Shaun Allen, he was dying. I couldn't save him." Tucker broke down into tears again. "I should have saved him."

"My son saved my grandson, Tucker. Shaun Allen wouldn't want you blaming yourself. And I don't want that either. Thank you for being there for him at the last, son. We love you." Allen pulled Tucker close again and let him cry and while he did, Allen wondered where Jessie was.

Aaron Taylor, the son of Lang and Holly Taylor arrived with his wife, Jenny Blackburn at Jenny's sister Bethany's home. He knew Tucker, Bethany's son was home from the war and injured and that they had lost Jenny and Bethany's younger brother Shaun Allen. "How are you doing, Tucker?" Aaron asked his nephew and sat on the edge of the bed Tucker was lying on.

"My uncle, the doctor," Tucker teased and lifted the blanket revealing his lower thigh and the damage that had been done when the bombs went off on the aircraft carrier he was stationed on. "The Navy doctors assured me I'd never walk without the aid of crutches again and that the leg would never heal. But I wanted you to tell me that Uncle Aaron." Tucker looked up into brown eyes that stared at him with a serious look and thought that the older Aaron got, the more he looked like Lang Taylor. He had seen Aaron's sister Charlotte earlier that morning when she stopped by and had been surprised at how much she looked like her mother Holly Taylor as she grew older. All these Taylor children married to Blackburn children, Tucker thought with a smile, it made him know that though the Taylors were dead, they had left a blood line that would grow on.

Aaron saw the damage done to Tucker's leg, it wasn't minor and he knew this would be months healing if not a full year. He cleaned the wound and changed the bandage before pulling the covers back up and over Tucker's leg. "It's not good, Tucker. But I think in time you'll heal, you just need time. I don't want you lying in bed all day while this heals, you'll grow weak and you need to stay as strong as possible. The wheelchair is good using for long distances but short walks I want you up on the crutches. Give yourself another week, I'll come out daily and change the bandages, and then we'll try and take a walk down to the river with the crutches."

This was good news, Tucker thought and almost laughed. He could use another week of lying around in bed and resting, he hadn't had much rest in the past four years. He wasn't going back to the war, he had hopes that if his leg would heal, he could stay in the reserves, but right now he knew he wasn't going to rejoin the war efforts and in a way he was sad, Tucker wanted to finish what he had started and he felt since he had been based at Pearl Harbor when this war began, he should see it all the way through.

"Thank you for bringing Shaun Allen home," his Aunt Jenny said from the doorway. "Daddy and Mama would have been even more broken had my brother not been brought back to his river." Jenny saw Tucker cover his eyes and came into the room to sit on his bed. Tucker saw his parents standing in the doorway.

"They bury the men that die at sea," Tucker said looking up at his mother's sister Jenny. "I begged them to let me bring him home, I even paid for the trip," Tucker looked at his parents, they were now at the foot of the bed and he saw Grandpa Levi and Grandma Cecily in the doorway. "There was this medical officer on board the ship, he knew I needed to be flown out, he signed Shaun Allen on as still alive in need of immediate medical attention. He was dead, he had been dead for an hour. I held his hand on the flight so I wouldn't lose him. And when we landed they took me in to surgery and I kept screaming at this little nurse to not let them bury my Uncle, that I had to take him home. She made sure he was embalmed and put in a coffin, her father was an undertaker and she had called him to help. She found me after the surgery and told me that my Uncle was at her father's funeral home and would stay there until I got well enough to leave." Tucker looked up at his family surrounding him and felt better that he had told this. "When are we going to have his funeral?" he asked everyone in the room.

"Mama has it planned for Sunday after church services," Jenny said still sitting on Tucker's bed but now holding her husband's hand. "You just focus on getting well Tucker, don't worry about anything else. You did real good getting Shaun Allen home too. I'm proud of you."

Tucker looked around the room and was comforted, he was glad he had told this little piece of information to his family. Much of the war and what he had seen and been through, Tucker felt he would never tell anyone, but this needed to be told. "Can someone tell me where Jessie is? If she's gone, if she didn't wait for me to come home, I understand. But I need to know that she's safe at least."

Bethany looked at Ethan and Levi and motioned for everyone else to leave the room; she would make coffee and had some of Aunt Mary's rolls they could eat. Levi sat in a chair in the corner while Ethan went and sat on his son's bed. "I guess Jessie's gone," Tucker grieved, he had lost too much to this war, he had seen too much taken away.

"No, Tucker," his father said shaking his head and knew he had to explain Jessie to Tucker. "She's still up at Allen and Alicia's house. She's been working at the mill now since you left years ago."

"She's still here," Tucker gave a sigh of relief and leaned back into the pillows behind him. He still had a chance with her to make their marriage right. He would do what Uncle Lang had done with Aunt Holly years and years ago, he would take it slow and easy with her, win her love and they would have the future he had long wanted.

"She's not like the rest of us, Tucker," his Grandpa Levi said leaning back in the chair he was sitting in. She's closed off inside of herself, she is with us in the room, but she's not with us. The girl doesn't laugh or even break a smile; she just goes through the motions of getting up, going to work, working hard coming home and going to bed. What was done to her all those years ago, she's never gotten over son. I just don't want you to plan a future with her. If she wakes up now that you're home, good. But I don't see that happening."

"Dad's right," Ethan said. "She's locked up inside of herself and I don't think she loves or cares about anyone. Allen and Alicia have loved her well and supported her but she shows no gratitude in any way. She just is silent and accepting. There's been a few times I've thought they reached her or even your mother had, but she'll only peek out the door and then go back and close herself off."

"Jessie's always been that way, Dad. Honest she has. She will open up when it's just the two of us, but she's very reserved around others. At least she's still here, I still have time to make things right and good between us. But first this leg has to heal." Tucker was tired of waiting to be with Jessie but he knew, like this, with his leg hurt, he couldn't walk on the river banks with her, he couldn't swim in the river with her, and then he thought of making love to her and knew that wouldn't happen with him hurt like this, Jessie would have time yet to stay locked away inside of herself while he healed. "Another thing the family needs to know," Tucker said feeling tired and wanting a nap. "My whole military career of the past four years, only Shaun Allen called me Tucker. I was called Allen, so if I don't respond to my name, I just need time to adjust."

"Allen is a fine and good name," Levi said with a smile and stood up from his chair. "And you're worn out Allen Tucker, get some sleep. I'll have your Mama bring in some lunch in an hour for you." Levi looked at Ethan as he stood up from the edge of his son's bed and they left the room not knowing that Tucker had slid down in the bed and turned his head and was allowing hot tears to fall.

She hadn't once written him in all these years. She hadn't spoken to him on the telephone. He had been home for almost a full day and she hadn't even stopped by to see him. She was his wife. He was her husband and yes, according to her, in name only but they had known one another almost their whole lives, and still he didn't matter to her in the least. And no matter where he went, no matter what he did, no matter that she completely rejected him, Tucker loved her and he wanted her love in return.

Chapter Fourteen

Levi and Ethan had taken the wheelchair out of the car and placed it on the top step of the church entrance way, they saw Tucker looking up at the chair and leaning on his crutches and they both knew that he was wondering if there was any way he was going to make it up those steps and into that chair. Shaun and Shane came up beside Tucker and they smiled at him before Shaun handed his crutches to Sarah and the twins bent and lifted him up, one on each side grabbing a leg and Tucker's arm wrapped around their necks. "It's a good thing you fellows are as big as me," Tucker laughed as they hauled him up the stairs and put him in the chair.

"We're just helping a fellow veteran," Shaun said as he followed Tucker into church seeing the coffin in front of the pulpit.

"Taylor is going to get us through this," Shane said putting a hand on Tucker's shoulder.

"I don't want anyone staring at me," Tucker spoke in a low tone to Shane and Shaun and his father Ethan who was standing next to him. "Dad, put me in a back corner please. I really don't want anyone staring at me." Ethan moved quickly and wheeled his son to the back corner of the church and then stood beside him. "Um Dad," he tugged on Ethan's arm and Ethan looked down at him. "Go sit with Mama, I want to be alone back here."

Ethan Tucker didn't want to leave his son in the back of the church alone, he knew his son was fragile still and needed others around him to help him stay strong. But he respected Tucker, and he loved him, so he honored his request and went to Bethany who was sitting next to her sisters and her parents, surrounded by the family in a front pew and he held his wife's hand.

"Where's our Tuck?" Bethany asked and Ethan nodded to the back of the church. "He should be with us," she whispered and her husband shook his head.

"He can't be, Bethany," Ethan said softly. "He's grieving in a way we aren't. He held Shaun Allen as he died. He fought to get him home to us. This is probably one of the hardest days of his whole life." Ethan looked around for Jessie wishing the girl were here, wishing she would comfort his son. Tucker needed someone he could connect with and share things with and be with, the way he had been with Bethany when he returned home from the war. He looked at his wife and remembered that first night on her father's porch, his face scarred and half ruined and he had tried to break off their engagement and she had demanded that he kiss her and he had, for more than an hour. She had brought the part of him the war had hurt back to life and he wanted Tucker to have that as well.

"Where's Jessie?" Ethan asked Alicia who was sitting next to Bethany.

"She stayed home to organize and prepare food for everyone that comes by after the funeral," Alicia whispered and looked for her grandson. "Where's our Tucker?" she asked and Ethan nodded to the back of the church just as Taylor stepped up to the pulpit. Alicia saw her grandson with his face covered by his hands already sobbing, he was crying so hard his whole body was shaking and she looked and saw her husband had seen Tucker and was like she was now, not looking at Taylor and hearing what he was saying, but looking back at their surviving grandson, and he had survived the war and come home wounded making sure his Uncle was laid to rest with his family.

Taylor Blackburn led the services seeing his cousin Tucker in the back of the church shaking apart. They had grown up together, best friends, him and Thomas and Shaun Allen and Tucker. They had played in river and on the banks, they had been more than cousins, more than friends, and now they were bidding one of their own a final farewell while another one was falling apart. Taylor knew that Tucker had fought to save Shaun Allen's life and he had lost that battle, they had all lost Shaun Allen.

Thomas Blackburn had turned to see his cousin shaking apart, his face covered as Taylor spoke of the fun they had growing up, the love they knew from their large family, that Shaun Allen would never be forgotten and Thomas moved to the back pew near Tucker and forced an elderly woman to move so he could sit and support his friend and his cousin. Tucker didn't look up at him and Thomas didn't think that he would, Tucker wouldn't want anyone to know he was crying and that's why his face was covered.

Allen Blackburn had sat and watched his grandson; caught between looking at Taylor and the coffin and hearing Taylor's words; unable to keep his eyes off of Tucker more than a full minute he finally stood up and went to the back of the church not caring that Taylor had fallen silent and that all eyes were on him. "Tucker," he knelt down before his grandson who sat in the wheelchair. "You did good," he said and felt Tucker fall forward and wrap his arms around Allen.

Taylor saw the scene of Allen going to Tucker, of hearing his Uncle Allen's words to Tucker and then Tucker holding on to his Grandpa for dear life. Taylor also saw Jessie standing in the doorway of the church watching her husband and knew from family gossip it was the first time she had seen her husband since he came home.

Jessie stood still as a stone watching her husband for all of five minutes, he didn't see her, he was too busy holding on to his Grandfather, but she saw how hurt he was and backed out the church door not knowing what to do. She couldn't ask him for the annulment now; he was too hurt by all he'd been through. She would have to carry on and wait on him to get better before she approached him.

The funeral services came to an end and Tucker stayed in the car at the cemetery, his cousin Thomas sat in the backseat with him as they watched their friend being lowered into the ground. "We'll never be the same again, Thomas." Tucker leaned back and frowned when he saw her leaning against an oak tree just beyond the cemetery. Her hair was a long dark blond and wavy; her skin was so pale she looked white against the tree. Her lips were so full and thick he could see them even at this distance. She was all women, he thought as he stared at her, her figure was amazing, tiny waist with beautiful hips, the dress she wore revealed her body's beauty in a way that Tucker found impressive. "My God," he breathed and then took a sharp deep breath. "Who is she?" he asked Thomas and pointed to the woman he was staring at leaning against the tree.

Thomas Blackburn followed Tucker's finger and saw her leaning there, they all knew she was a great beauty, his wife's sister. "You've been gone away too long cousin," Thomas whistled. "That's your wife. That's Jessie." Tucker's mouth fell open and he leaned forward.

"No," he said and saw her turn toward him, saw her almost look at him but not quite see him in the darkness of the car. "She grew up while I was gone," he said swallowing hard. Her breast had been round and beautiful when he was with her that one night, but in that dress, he grabbed a breath and shook his head hard. "My God, that's really my wife?"

Thomas laughed at the look on Tucker's face. "Yeah, Elise is more beautiful as well. The Fairchild girls were never plain though. I want to warn you Tucker," he saw Tucker look away from Jessie as she disappeared behind the tree. "Jessie's still hurt. She's all closed up inside of herself. She doesn't even talk much to Elise. She's different Tucker."

"She always was different," Tucker said and took a deep breath trying to find her beyond the trees. "She never once wrote me." He leaned back in the seat as he saw his family coming back to the car and knew they were going home, the funeral was over but the pain would never go away.

"We're all going to Uncle Allen and Aunt Alicia's for dinner," Thomas said and rode in the car with Tucker, his wife and children were with his own parents. "Jessie will be there, I hope she'll at least attempt to speak to you."

"I doubt she will," Tucker said as his father turned into the yard at Riverbend. "Dad, can you and Shaun and Shane set me in a rocking chair on the porch? I don't want to sit in that wheelchair. And Mama, can you please bring my crutches?" His parents did as Tucker asked but it was Thomas and Taylor that had lifted him up onto the porch and into a rocking chair and he felt relieved that he was home with his family.

Jessie knew he was there. She knew he was surrounded by his family and she knew she wouldn't bother him. She poured tea into glasses and mixed up lemonade while she saw Grandma Alicia and Aunt Mary making sure everyone had something to eat and drink. The sun shone in the kitchen window and she saw the river beyond and thought to get away from all these people, she didn't belong here. Elise did, she was married to Thomas and had his children, but she was nothing to any of them, and soon, she would have the annulment and be alone and Tucker could move on with his life.

Tucker stood with the crutches and hobbled on to the porch that faced his river. He longed to go down there and wondered if he dare try. Everyone was busy inside eating and talking and being together, he was alone at last and he carefully took the steps with his crutches. The river was a lot farther away from the house on crutches than it was when he ran down to it as a child and young man, Tucker thought and was frustrated that he was so slow and that he hurt so much.

With all of his effort and the last of his energy, Tucker lowered himself on the grassy bank and kicked off his shoes and pulled off his socks before putting his feet in the water. Now he was home, he thought and leaned back letting the sun touch his face. He worried for a few minutes of how he would get back up and make the long walk up to the house, he hoped someone missed him and saw him out here. Maybe someone sitting on the porch would look down this way. And then he felt as though he weren't alone, as though someone were watching him and he knew, in his heart, his gut and his mind, he knew. It was her. It was Jessie.

"I know you're there," he said softly and heard the leaves nearby make a rustling sound. "I'm all right if you don't want to talk to me. But it would be nice if you'd just say hello." Tucker lay back in the grass certain she wouldn't say anything, waiting to hear her running away from him.

"I was here first," Jessie said in a soft voice and stayed back behind Tucker so he couldn't see her.

"I'm sure you were. As slow as I am getting anywhere, everyone will be where I want to be first." He kicked with his one good foot at the water and just lay still waiting to regain his strength so he could walk back to the house.

"I'm sorry you got hurt," Tucker heard Jessie say from behind him and thought her voice didn't sound sorry, she sounded like she was just trying to fill the silence by saying what she had.

"You know me," Tucker said and forced himself to sit back up. "I never stay hurt for long. And it's okay if you want to run away," he said in a softer voice. He suddenly felt like he wasn't man enough for her. He wanted to cry again. Cry for everything and nothing, he thought and all at the same time. He looked at his limp leg and knew like this, even if she wanted him, he couldn't make love to her. And then he knew, he wanted to cry because he couldn't even attempt to seduce her, he couldn't even go to her now and pull her into his arms and kiss her.

"I don't run away," Jessie said in a voice filled with the tone of denial and stepped closer to Tucker being careful to stay behind him. "I waited like you asked me too. And now you're here and I know your hurt and all, but I want the annulment as soon as you're strong." Tucker took a deep breath and closed his eyes before he spoke being careful in what he said.

"Jessie, you have my word, I'll get well as fast as I can and we'll work this whole situation out. I just got home and I just buried my Uncle. Give me some time to get my leg where I can at least stand on it, please." He was tried, tired of fighting, tired of being pushed into doing things, tired of having no choices and battling in some war. He broke again, he knew he was going too and he felt the tears flooding his face as he covered his eyes, he had spent his whole life never crying and now he couldn't stop crying.

Jessie stood behind Tucker and saw him crying. She couldn't just stand here and not do something. She thought of how Grandpa Allen had hugged him in church and Thomas had sat with him and slowly, hesitantly and not wanting to do so, Jessie went to Tucker and sat down beside him. He didn't see her there and she closed her eyes and took a deep breath thinking what she should do, she didn't want her hero to cry, it was agony enough to see him on the crutches and in that chair. She opened her eyes and looked out at the river, the river that he loved and that he said was the blood of his family and she wanted to be a part of something that beautiful, like he was but she knew she never would be.

Tucker silently sobbed, his body shaking apart, his hand over his eyes fighting to get control of himself and to not feel the way he was feeling. And then he felt something brush against his mouth, slowly and gently he felt her breath on his mouth and he removed his hands from his eyes looking up at Jessie only inches away from him. She had changed since he had last seen her, she was even more beautiful, her long hair loose and spilling over her shoulders. He felt the tears stop, he wasn't shaking any longer and he reached up a hand and touched her cheek.

She just wanted to be alone, Jessie thought. She just wanted to be away from everyone and everything and be totally alone. Until right this moment. Looking at him, his perfect nose; his wide eyes so green, as green as the grass and his lips so thick she just had to touch them. She put her fingers on his lips feeling them and then her eyes were staring into his as he reached and put his fingers onto her mouth, and then into her mouth and she sucked on the tips as he went farther into her mouth and she sucked more and realized that he was sucking on her finger tips the same way.

He wanted her. She made him forget his leg pain, she made him forget his hurt over his loss and all he had been through, only she could take away the ache he had had for her, she owned him because he loved her that much. "Kiss me," he pleaded when she pulled her fingers from his mouth. "Please, I need you to kiss me." Jessie leaned forward and put her lips onto Tucker's, she wasn't sure what to do; he had always kissed her. And then she knew she didn't have anything to do, he had her pulled down on top of him and his tongue was in her mouth and he was moaning and crying in the back of her throat and she felt like she was climbing higher and higher and couldn't stop and if she didn't stop, she was going to come crashing down to the earth.

"Tucker," she said his name in a pleading voice trying to stop the spiraling out of control feeling that was consuming every inch of her body. "Help," she said and he pulled her back to him, his mouth covering her ear and breathing hot and heavy there and making her hurt in a good way, a longing for him that she hadn't known since their one night together.

"Give me time to heal," he pleaded as he moved back to her lips and Jessie knew that she would carry on as she had been, she was alone here in this crowd the Blackburn family called a clan; she could be just as alone with him. Even with him kissing the breath from her lungs.

Allen Blackburn pulled Alicia onto the porch and pointed to the river and was smiling from ear to ear. He heard his wife laugh as he ran into the house amazed that either of them were able to laugh with the loss they had suffered. But Tucker was really home, they could smile for Tucker.

"Boys!" Allen called out to Ethan, Shane and Shaun while grabbing Aaron and Michael and Thomas and Taylor. "Get upstairs and pull one of the double beds up there apart and get it into my study now, today."

"What do you need a bed in your study for Uncle Allen?" Shaun asked and he ran to the double doors and pointed to the river.

"Oh, Tucker's moving in with Jessie," Ethan knew and they all raced up the stairs to get a bed down into the study knowing Tucker, with his leg hurt, could not climb the stairs.

"I wanted Tucker to stay with us," Bethany cried out as she came from the kitchen. Her father guided her to the double doors looking out at the river and she saw Jessie on top of Tucker and they were very intimately kissing. She quickly turned away and blushed glancing up at her father and then turning back to look at her son on the grassy bank of the river that was their home, Bethany smiled in relief. She just wanted her Tucker happy.

"Don't play innocent," Allen teased his daughter as she turned her face away and blushed. Allen also looked at Jenny who stood with his wife staring at the young lovers kissing. "I know you girls did your fair share of kissing down there," Allen laughed and saw

Jenny gasp. "And one of you slapped her future husband down there," Allen winked at Jenny as she turned blood red.

"Jessie has been so distant with us all these years," Bethany said looking at Jessie lying next to her son, his arm around her holding her close and Jessie's cheek on his chest.

"Maybe Tucker can open her up," Allen said looking at Alicia. "Love can save a soul," he whispered just for his wife and she nodded her head. "Some people are naturally silent," Allen added for his daughters.

Allen watched the boys put the bed together in a corner of his study and asked Aaron about Tucker's leg and how bad he thought it was. Aaron had stood watching Tucker kissing Jessie for a long while and then turned to Allen with a serious expression. "Yesterday I would have said there was no way with crutches he could walk to the river," he pointed and said, "I was obviously wrong in my thinking." He saw Jessie lift up over Tucker and pull him up and Tucker, with Jessie's help stand. "I also didn't know he was going to have a helpmate."

Allen rubbed his hands together and smiled. "We'll have that boy well in no time and he'll be back to running along the river." Aaron laughed softly and believed Allen Blackburn was right.

"You and Alicia haven't taken my parents place," Aaron said softly. "No one can. But these past years I want to thank you for filling in for them to me and Charlotte and Hannah." Allen looked down into Aaron's face, a face so much like Lang's face and nodded his head.

"Your Daddy blessed my life and made it better," Allen put an arm around Aaron and they looked at Tucker slowly walking and struggling to make it to the house with Jessie there in case he fell. And then he saw Shane and Shaun running toward Tucker and lifting him up, Thomas and Taylor were with them and Ethan, he could see Ethan laughing and was glad that his son in law had learned to laugh with ease again. "You've blessed my life as well,"

Allen said to Aaron and then Aaron laughed and ran out the door to the others grabbing a ball in the yard and throwing it to Taylor who jumped and caught the thing.

"I love my boys," Allen said to Levi who agreed with him. "We have a good family."

"You need to stay here with your grandparents," Bethany said to her son Tucker as she plumped a pillow on the bed in her father's office for him and looked at Jessie looking worried. "They've lost their son, they need their grandson. And Jessie is here to help you." Bethany reached and took Jessie's hand. "You'll come for me if he needs me."

"Yes, ma'am," Jessie said softly and then hurried from the room. She was almost on the verge of panic as she paced the hall and wrung her hands. Tucker was going to be just down the stairs from her room, she would see him all the time. This isn't what she wanted. She was going to get the annulment and leave here and live out her life alone. And that kissing at the river, she touched her finger tips to her lips and remembered how he had sucked on them and how that had made her feel, he might want more of that she almost panicked.

Jessie turned at the end of the hall she was pacing and slammed into Allen Blackburn. "See that wall?" he asked and pointed the hallway wall and she nodded. "It helps me to punch a hole in it from time to time." Jessie took a step back and looked at Grandpa Allen. Was he serious? She wanted to ask him. Did he really think she wanted to hit the wall? "Go ahead, give it a try. I've been hitting walls all my life. It helps."

Jessie went to the wall and slapped at it and then shook her head at Allen Blackburn. "That did nothing for me," she sounded very disappointed and Allen touched her head like a father would a child.

"You'll find something to do to ease your tension. Hitting a wall isn't for you, I guess." Jessie nodded and walked upstairs to her room where she sat worrying more on her bed.

She hadn't meant for the kissing to get so out of control today. She hadn't meant to give Tucker any ideas and now here he was right under foot and the way he made her feel wasn't helping her in any way. She groaned that she wanted to kiss him again and she got up from the bed pacing the floor. Ever since the night he had made love to her body with his mouth, she couldn't remember what the monster had done to her, the monster was forgotten and all she remembered was Tucker's mouth on her, caressing her in places she never dreamed a man would touch in that way and now today.

Jessie made up her mind she wasn't going near Grandpa Allen's study. She would stay every minute in this room and only go down to eat. She had spent the last four years being separate from the family; she needed to go on in that way, keeping herself apart from everyone. But she didn't want to be a part from Tucker, Jessie almost cried in agony. What he made her feel made her want to be with him.

She flung open the double doors leading to the upstairs porch outside her bedroom and sat down. Up here she was safe, he couldn't come up here, she just had to stay here and she would be safe. She would be alone and soon, his leg would heal and she could leave him and she could leave here. She just had to stay focused on her plans as she had the past four years.

Tucker lay on the bed in his Grandpa's study and thought of kissing Jessie. If only he could spend every day kissing her, he thought and felt an ache deep inside of himself, a feeling as though he were missing something that he shouldn't be missing. It was almost like his leg, it wouldn't work right and when he was kissing Jessie, everything seemed to be working right and he wasn't missing anything.

He couldn't roll over on his side to look out the doors where the moonlight was streaming in because of his leg and Tucker felt frustrated. He was forced to lay on his back looking at the ceiling and all he could think was that above him was his wife sleeping alone in her bed, so close to him and yet she might as well be million miles away. He couldn't get to her and if he did get to her, he wouldn't be able to do anything beyond kiss her. And he was dying to kiss her.

Jessie slipped into Grandpa Allen's office feeling like there was a knot in the pit of her stomach. She didn't want to be here, but she had to be here. She was conflicted and horribly so. She wanted to stop herself and she couldn't stop herself. Certain that Tucker was asleep she tiptoed to his bed and looked down at him gasping when she did as he was awake and looking right at her.

"I was just thinking of you," Tucker said and reached for his wife's hand. All she could do was think of him, ever since he had sucked her fingertips into his mouth, he had made her ache for him, to be with him. "I wasn't thinking of you," Tucker confessed as he saw Jessie standing beside his bed looking lost and alone and frightened. "I was dying to have you here with me."

Jessie pulled her hand from her husband's hand and he watched as she reached down and pulled her nightgown up and over her head and drop it on the floor. He lost his breath when the moonlight revealed her beautiful breasts and he grieved his leg was hurt. Jessie reached for his hand and put it on her breast and he sucked in air fast and hard.

"The night before you left," she said softly and he knew what she was saying.

"Help me sit up," he said in a hoarse whisper and she pulled on his hands until he was sitting on the edge of the bed. "I won't hurt you," he said gently and stood up to drop his shorts on the floor and saw her eyes get large. "I won't hurt you, Jessie girl." He used a pet name similar to the one his Uncle Lang had used for his wife Holly and the pet name sounded right.

"I don't know what to do," she said softly and he pulled her between his legs and took her breast into his mouth. Jessie cried out as he touched her other breast with his mouth and then sucked on it as he had her fingers. "Tucker," she sighed his name and he ran his hands onto her nude bottom and pulled her closer. "Tucker," she almost cried and he looked up to her removing his mouth from her breast.

"I won't hurt you," he said again in a gentle voice. "Ever."

"I don't think you'll fit," she pointed to the part that made him different from her and he realized her concern.

"Let's not worry about that right now," he put his mouth back on her breast and felt her relax into him, he wanted her to relax, he wanted to just touch her all night long.

Jessie kept trying to breathe, and her breath came in gasps as Tucker moved from one breast to the other slowly making her feel an agony of desire for him, far more than what he had at the river today and that night four years ago. She almost passed out when his finger went between her legs and gasped holding on to his head as he kept his mouth on her breast. "Help," she said in a small voice as her knees buckled and his finger went up inside of her. And then he was stroking her and she was almost crying begging him not to stop what he was doing, pleading with him to help her and she felt like she fell to bits and pieces on his hand.

"Jessie," he said her name when she was able to support herself again. "Put your knees on either side of me here," he showed her. "Like when you ride a horse." He saw that she was willing to do anything he asked of her and she climbed up onto the bed straddling him and worrying over his leg. "You won't touch where my leg is hurt," he said as he guided himself into her and heard her gasp and sigh at the same time. "I told you I would fit." Holding her to him and lay back on the bed unable to finish this task of love making to her, he couldn't move with his leg hurt and he was throbbing in an agony of desire for her.

"I don't know what to do," Jessie said as she sat up on him and felt his finger come back between them and stroke her making her lose her breath again. After a few minutes he reached and lifted her up and toward him and had her come back down, his mouth on her mouth and his tongue plunging in and out of her mouth as he helped her lift up.

"If my leg weren't hurt, I could do this without your help," Tucker said as he lifted her up again and guided her back down. "You feel so hot," he cried and covered her mouth with his own again.

Jessie knew what to do, she saw him lifting her up and down and she sat up on him and moved hearing his gasp and he almost cried out. He sounded good crying out beneath her, Jessie thought and realized the control over him that she had. He wasn't making love to her now; she was making love to him. She moved again and again and again seeing him holding his breath, knowing that she was going to make him feel what he had made her feel with his fingers.

"I love you, Jessie," he cried as she fell onto his chest and he lost himself inside her. "I love you forever," he said and held her close to him as he throbbed inside of her

Much later, holding her still in his arms, Tucker kissed her ear and knew he had to confess to her what he had been through and how she had saved him. "When I was in the sea when the Nora sank, thinking of you made me survive and come home. When I was blasted into the sea with Shaun Allen and he pulled me up and saved me all I could think was 'thank God, I'm going to make it home to Jessie.' You're all I've ever wanted my whole life."

Jessie was quiet above him and lay still in his arms. This isn't how her life was meant to go. She loved the way Tucker made her feel. She loved this between them but she was meant to be alone.

She wasn't meant to spend her life with anyone other than herself. Her silence went on for nearly a half hour, she didn't move from him, he was still inside of her and she was still on top of him. She was meant to be alone and she would be, but first, she had to be with him all that she could be, she couldn't leave him yet, she had to have more of him.

Tucker felt Jessie put her lips on his ear, breath in as he had done with her and he was breathing deeply and felt himself coming back to life within her. "Don't move," he pleaded as he throbbed deep within her. "Jessie," he lifted her up and she knew what to do and he was almost crying because he felt so good. And he had to make sure she was feeling what he was, it was important to him that she was with him in this. He reached down with his hand and stroked her, felt her tense up and his free hand took her breast and held it gently. He was trying to breath, trying to touch her, trying to have her reach for and find what he was reaching for and finding. And then he felt her shutter and shake above him and fall forward and he fell with her.

Allen grabbed Alicia's hand and shook his head hard and she looked confused. "I heard noise downstairs last night, in my office." He winked at her and she nodded her head. "Look and see if Jessie is in her bed." He saw his wife open the bedroom door that Jessie slept in and shake her head sadly.

"Jessie's tucked up tight sleeping away," Alicia said and both disappointed they went down to get breakfast.

"Good morning," Allen said as he walked into his office and saw his grandson looking up at the ceiling. And then he saw on the floor his grandson's shorts and Jessie's nightgown and his face was all of a sudden covered with a big smile.

"Grandpa," Tucker looked at him with a puzzled frown. "Are all women confusing?" Allen looked back at the door to make sure they were alone.

"Most of the time," he answered. "But it's a good thing; they keep us on our toes." He reached down picked up the clothes off the floor. "Seems you lost something," he dropped Jessie's nightgown on Tucker and then his shorts. "No annulment now for certain." He smiled.

"Three times in one night," Tucker said and then turned blood red at what he'd just said out loud in front of his Grandpa Allen.

"Tucker, don't be embarrassed. How do you think you got here? Your Grandma Alicia and I were young once. Three times in one night is impressive." He patted Tucker's arm and stood up. "You're probably starved to death. Let me help you get dressed while we're alone." Allen reached for Tucker's clothes in a corner of the room, his pants were in one pile and his shirts in another and his shorts between. "How is your leg this morning?" He helped Tucker get his shorts on and he ruffled his hair like he use to when he was a little boy. "I wish we could go back to when you were little," Allen thought of Heath and Seth and Lang. "We had some happy times. Promise me you'll take care of the books that we wrote and your Grandpa Levi and Grandma Cecily and don't forget or lose Lang and Holly's book." Tucker nodded his head.

"I know where the box is that they're in Grandpa. I think you should put the box in your safe in case the house catches fire. And why don't we have Jessie type up another copy? Oh that reminds me, Shaun and Shane said they're working on their story to add to the family collection."

"Maybe you should think of writing your story," Allen suggested. "When you figure out all of your story." He smiled and saw Tucker buttoning up his shirt.

"My story will have all of you as a part of it, a big part Grandpa. I've had a blessed life surrounded by my family." Tucker stood when Allen handed him his crutches and went into the hall. "Good morning," he said to Jessie as she hurried past him acting like she didn't even know who he was. "No telling how my story will end. Hell, Grandpa, it's barely begun."

Jessie sat in the office next to the saw mill and watched through the window as Ethan worked on a huge order with Shaun. She had just finished the books and knew she could go back home, but she didn't really want to go back home. He was there and when she was near him, she had to be with him, she had to be touching him. She took a deep breath and remembered the night before and knew she should be tired, but she wasn't. She wanted more of last night. She wanted more of Tucker.

"Hey," Grandpa Allen came into the room with a brand new typewriter. "Do you have spare time to type some things up for me?" He saw Jessie nod her head and he handed her the typewriter with several boxes of extra ribbon and left to go back to his car. Jessie watched Allen come back in with a huge box of paper and wondered just what he wanted her to type up.

"Wow Grandpa," she said in a surprised voice. "That's a lot of paper and ribbon."

"Well, you'll be busy." Jessie watched him go back out to his car. "Don't worry, I'll pay you extra for this." He said and put a large box on the table. "When you get done for the day typing, lock this box in the safe, I don't want anything to happen to this." He patted the box and Jessie nodded her head thankful that she was good typist. "Don't stay past four every day," Allen ordered and knowing that Jessie wasn't a talkative person, he left her alone with one last look before he closed the door. "Make sure you lock those up in the safe every single day." Jessie nodded knowing he would ask her when she got home if she had locked them up.

Ethan saw Jessie working at the typewriter later that afternoon and nudged Shaun and Shane. "You guys have your stories done?" he asked and saw them nod their heads. "I want to add mine to yours because we all were in the same place at the same time and you guys are in my story."

"So we'll put it on the desk for Jessie in the morning," Shane said and they went back to work not seeing Jessie wiping her face.

She knew she would type up the stories as they were written first, but she would rewrite them later, when she finished and she would write them from her view and make the stories more like stories but with all the reality that was written in them by the people that lived those lives. At the end of the day, Jessie put them in the safe and locked them up, they were more precious than money, she realized. The story of Lang and Holly was beyond beautiful. Holly had survived a nightmare and Lang had helped her live. She thought of Tucker and her life together and what had happened to her and knew, she felt like Holly did; deep shame and a desire to punish herself for what she allowed to be done. And Maggie, she put her head in her hands and closed her eyes; everything she had done was to keep Maggie safe and all that time Maggie was buried in the back yard dead.

"Hey," Ethan poked his head into the office, "you ready to go home?" He saw Jessie nod and wondered at the look on her face, he knew if he asked her if she were all right she would say yes or she would say nothing at all, but he had to ask, it was the right thing to do. "You all right Jessie?" She looked up at him and shocked him by speaking.

"I need Tucker," she said in a broken voice and Ethan saw tears fall on her face.

"We know where he is," Ethan said kindly and reached for Jessie's hand and she surprised him again by taking his hand.

Ethan watched Jessie jump out of the car at the house and run inside, he had never seen her like this, and he liked her like this. She was finally showing some emotion, maybe she was going to learn to live now, the last years with the family he felt like she had only been existing the way he had been when he first came home from the Great War. He bowed his head and prayed for her and his son's happiness.

Jessie ran up the steps and onto the porch passing both Alicia and Mary without a word and they looked after her with worried frowns. Allen sat at his desk watching Tucker lay in the bed, they had been talking about the future of the saw mill and with Shaun Allen gone who would take over running the business from Ethan, Shane and Shaun when they grew too old. Thomas was a deputy and had no time for the mill, Taylor was with the church, that left only Tucker.

The office doors flew open and Jessie ran into the room and to Tucker on the bed, he had sat up when the doors open and saw his wife looking frightened out of her mind. "What is it?" he asked in concern and Jessie climbed into his bed and kissed him. With his eyes open he saw his Grandpa Allen wink at him go to the open doors pulling them closed.

"I have to be alone," Jessie said in a serious tone. "I was meant to be alone. I told you about the peck order years ago." Tucker nodded his head feeling confused over what she was saying; he didn't understand her at all. "You have to give me the annulment, no matter what we do together. Promise me," she started pulling off his shirt and kissing him all over as he had kissed her the night before. "Promise."

In this moment, Tucker would have promised her the river, the sea along with the moon and the stars. She had pulled off most of his clothes and her own and was on top of him gasping and trying to figure out how to put him within her. "I got this, Jessie girl," he said in a husky voice trying to breath when she lifted up and came down on his. "No one better walk through that door," he said as she fell onto him lifting up and down as she said his name over and over.

Allen stood outside his office door smiling from ear to ear and guarding the door when Bethany came into the hallway with Alicia and Mary. "How's Tucker this afternoon?" Bethany asked and tried to go past her father who shook his head hard and blocked the door. Ethan was looking at him with the same frown as his wife had.

"He's with his wife at the moment," Allen said and grinned even more. "And he's just fine this afternoon."

Tucker worked hard to get better. Every day Aaron came out to the house and changed his bandage and encouraged him to walk a little more. Aaron assured him exercises would keep his muscles strong and promote healing. "He's getting exercise," Allen said with a wink to Tucker letting the younger man know that everyone in the house knew Jessie was sneaking down stairs almost every single night. Allen saw his grandson smile and knew that at last his Tucker was happy.

Levi had sat down with Allen and asked if they should give Tucker advice on how to make his marriage happy at which point Allen told Levi that Jessie was now typing his and Cecily's story and had just finished Lang and Holly's.

"Jessie is a smart girl," Allen said to Levi. "She's using carbon paper and making three copies at once. Levi nodded his head as he saw Jessie running up the porch steps. "She's not changed toward us, still distant as always," Allen said as Jessie ran past him and into the house.

"She looks like she's running to a fire," Levi said as the front screen door slammed.

"She's running to start a fire," Allen said while laughing. "She runs home every single day to Tucker and they lock themselves in the study."

"I see," Levi said looking at Allen with a wink. "Damn, aren't we too young to be Great Grandpas?"

"I still feel like I'm thirty when I'm with my Alicia," Allen said as his wife stepped out onto the porch and came to him, followed by Cecily. "Why don't we give the children the house and take a walk down to the river?" Allen asked and took Alicia's hand. "Come on Mary, we'd be lost without you." He saw his sister in law force a smile and knew she was missing his brother still, she always would. "Are we having rolls for dinner, Mary?" he asked and took her hand as well.

"Every night, Allen." Mary said and felt Cecily take her hand, their circle had been broken with the loss of Lang and Holly and Seth, but they were still together and part of a circle together. Mary was grateful for her family.

Chapter Fifteen

The war was over, all the men were coming home and everyone knew that Tucker wouldn't have to go back to war when he healed, though he was still planning on being a part of the reserves and share his knowledge with the Navy. His leg was getting better but not healing as fast as he wanted it to heal. He still couldn't manage the stairs, he wasn't up and running but he was getting better at making love to his wife. He loved being with Jessie intimately and he knew she was happy with him. Now, in the night after they made love they would lay talking, he told her all about the war and what had happened to him and all he had seen. She told him that she was working on the stories of his family and he knew she had read Lang and Holly's story. He wanted to know what he thought of their story but she never said. She was still Jessie, she kept a part of herself closed off and he knew she kept more closed off with his family.

Tucker had been home more than two months, every day was spent with Jessie and he loved her more now than he had before. He saw her walk into his Grandfather's study with a box in her hands late one afternoon and Tucker saw her hand that box to his Grandpa. "I made three copies like you wanted of each story you gave me." She didn't look at Allen as he sat on the sofa holding the box looking grateful toward her. "And I made three more copies my own way." She handed him another box and he looked up at her wondering what she meant. "I wrote the stories over in the third party. All three of them, Grandpa Allen. I'm behind in the accounting books but now that I'm done my days can go to working on the bookkeeping."

"I have been doing the bookkeeping for you," Allen confessed and picked up Lang and Holly's story and saw that it was written as though it were a novel in one box and in the other, the way Lang and Holly wrote their story. "You did this with all out stories, Jessie?" he asked and saw her nod her. "Thank you Jessie. I'll start reading them tonight with Alicia. He picked up the story he had written with Alicia and then the story Jessie had written. "This means a lot, Jessie. I'll give Levi and Cecily their story to read."

Jessie watched Grandpa Allen leave the room and looked to see Tucker staring up at her with a look that let her know he wanted something of her. "Do you want to try and walk to the river, just the two of us and your crutches?" she asked and saw him shake his head staring hard at her and she wondered just what he wanted of her. "What is it you want, Tucker?" Jessie asked in frustration of the look on his face.

"I want you forever, Jessie." He saw her take a step back and away from him and shake her head.

"We've been together too much Tucker in that way," Jessie said and then blushed red to her neck. "You agreed to an annulment months ago. You can't want me forever. You said as soon as you're well we could end our marriage. I'm only staying here until you're well, you have to get well so I can be alone."

"I'll never get well Jessie, not if it means I'm going to lose you," he said softly and reached for her hand but she snatched it from his reach.

"Then I'll leave now," she cried and Tucker sat back in shock at the change in her behavior. They had grown so close; they were together every minute she wasn't working. Why did she still wanting to leave him? "I cannot and will not stay with you like Uncle Lang and Aunt Holly," she said firmly. "I'm different from those love stories of your family. I'm bad and stupid and wrong and you don't deserve someone like me, you deserve an angel like you are." Jessie turned and ran from him and out of the room.

Tucker tried to stand up and his leg gave out and he fell onto the sofa. "Jessie girl," he called out for her but she didn't come back. Shaking his head in confusion, Jessie kept him in a state of confusion he thought, he pushed himself up off the sofa. "Stupid crutches," he said as they were across the room from where he was on the sofa. He put his weight on his leg and nearly cried out but he kept pushing himself to move.

"What's going on?" Alicia came into her husband's office and saw her grandson struggling to walk and looking upset. "Jessie's upstairs throwing everything she owns into a suitcase, Tucker. Where in the world is she going?" Alicia saw her grandson put weight on his leg impressed that he could and watched him move past her.

"I don't understand you women," Tucker said to his Grandmother as he hobbled past his grandmother and into the hall. "Jessie girl," he called up the stairs that looked a mile long for him to climb with his hurt leg. Alicia jumped when his fist connected with the wall and he saw his Grandpa Allen looking at him with a smile.

"How badly do you want her son?" Allen asked and Tucker grabbed the stair rail and pulled himself up forcing his leg to work despite the agony of pain he was in. "That bad," Allen put his arm around Alicia and they watched Tucker pull himself up the stairs and disappear from their sight.

"He doesn't understand women," Alicia said to her husband with a smile and he laughed while he hugged her close.

"No man does, Alicia. Let's go read a book."

"You can't get an annulment from me," Tucker said as he entered the bedroom that belonged to his wife. "We've been making this marriage real for two full months."

"Then we'll divorce," Jessie said seriously. "You don't understand me Tucker. I've tried to tell you over and over and over again that I'm meant to be alone. I hurt people."

"No, you don't hurt people," Tucker said and sat on the bed rubbing his leg. "People hurt you so you've closed yourself off and pulled inward and won't let anyone reach you." He saw Jessie stand up staring at him for a full minute before she shook her head.

"I'm a bad person," she cried out and saw Tucker pulling her clothes out of her suitcase. "What are you doing?"

"I'm not letting you leave me," he said and threw her clothes out of the suitcase.

Jessie ran to him and grabbed up her clothes he had thrown out. "You can't make me stay, Tucker." She threw the clothes back in the suitcase.

"You want to stay," Tucker dumped the suitcase out and heard Jessie cry out before she reached and put the clothes back inside. "I love you," he screamed as he threw the suitcase and clothes toward the open door of the porch.

"Well I don't love you!" Jessie screamed out and ran for her suitcase and clothes shoving them inside again.

"You think I don't know that?" Tucker cried out and Jessie slowly turned around. "You've made it clear for years how you really feel about me. And I've stayed true to you. I married you knowing you didn't love me. I wrote you every single week for four years knowing you didn't love me. I came home after nearly dying with my Uncle and saw you and knew you didn't love me." Tucker lowered his head and stood up on his poor bad leg and hobbled to the suitcase on the floor knowing he was crying and hating that he was. "Here, you want to leave me." He put her things in the suitcase and then handed it to her. "But leave knowing this; even though you've hurt me time after time after time, I still love you. I never hurt you back Jessie. I'll die loving you. You're all I ever wanted."

Jessie watched her husband hobble back to the bed and fall down before reaching the bed. She swallowed hard and ran to him putting her arms around his waist and holding on to him tight. "I never meant to hurt you," she said with all honesty. "I'm not good enough for you Tucker. My mother killed the Taylors."

"Your mother's crimes have nothing to do with you, Jessie," Tucker said in a tired voice and leaned back onto the bed. "No one here blamed you or ever thought to blame you because of your mother. We all know you and Elise were her victims. That's why Uncle Lang and Aunt Holly stood in front of Elise, to protect her from further harm. And they did, Jessie. They didn't die in vain." He saw her looking at him with wide blue eyes and he shook his head. "You'll have to divorce me. But go, get out, I'm tired of your rejection when there's no damn reason."

Jessie saw Tucker lean forward on the edge of the bed and put his head in his hands as she reached down and put the last of her things in her suitcase and set it on the chest of drawer. She opened the top drawer and looked inside, this she wouldn't take with her. This was meant for him. "Here," Jessie said and saw Tucker lift his head and move his hands to see what she had for him. "I did write you. Almost every single day," he saw the huge stack of letters a foot thick and tied together with string. "I didn't know I hurt you by not sending these to you."

Tucker looked at the letters and took them from his wife and closed his eyes. "You really do love me, you know." He saw her shaking her head and he reached and pulled her toward him. "Don't leave me. Don't leave me. Please, don't leave me."

Those beautiful aqua eyes were looking up into her eyes and she knew she could get lost in his eyes, his nose was perfect, his jaw line, even his hair was perfect. "Don't leave me," he pleaded again. "I don't want to live without you Jessie girl."

"I don't want to love you or anyone," she whispered and this Tucker understood.

"If you open your heart, then you'll get hurt," Tucker said pulling her down onto the bed. "I can't promise you that I won't ever hurt you. I hope I don't. But we belong together." He pulled her on top of his chest and looked up into her eyes. "Don't leave me."

"Oh Tucker," Jessie shook her head. "Can I trust you?"

"With your whole life, with your body, with your heart, you can trust me completely."

March 1951
Riverbend, Florida

Tucker sat at the table with his four year old daughter Cecily on one knee and his cousin Taylor Blackburn's six year old son Allen on the other knee and watched his wife cooking dinner while Taylor told him of his new church in Tallahassee. Taylor had bought a new home in a brand new subdivision in Tallahassee called Indian Head Acres and his Methodist church was very near to his home. Taylor's Grandfather Seth Blackburn was Tucker's Grandfather Allen Blackburn's brother, they shared the same Great Grandparents and had grown up together. Now their children Cecily and Allen were growing up together.

"You won't be able to keep driving from way out here to Tallahassee now that you have the job at the University teaching Engineering, Tuck," Taylor said seeing Jessie turn from the stove and stare at him. "The house next door to Lydia and I is for sale," Taylor was looking at Jessie knowing that his wife and Jessie had become best friends. "And Thomas and your sister, Elise only live two blocks away from us. Our children can grow up together the way we grew up on that old river out there."

"I know you're right Taylor," Tucker said and looked from his cousin to his wife. "I saw the house yesterday, Jessie and it's perfect for our family, it also has an apartment built onto the back, my Mama and Daddy can move in with us," as Tucker said this his mother Bethany walked into the room carrying a platter of fried chicken.

"Move in with you where?" Bethany asked Tucker as she bent and kissed the children he held on his knee.

"Well, we won't be moving as long as Grandpa Allen and Grandma Alicia are alive," Tucker kissed his mother's cheek. "But I was telling Jessie and Taylor, I went ahead and bought the house next door to Taylor and down the street from Thomas in Indian Head Acres. I can't keep driving back and forth to Tallahassee for work every day, Mama." He saw his Daddy Ethan peek around the corner; his Daddy knew he had already bought the house.

"Bethany," Ethan came into the room and took his wife from behind, his arms around her waist. "The house has a two bedroom apartment built on the back of it." He kissed her neck and she leaned into him. "We can watch our grandchildren grow up, and your cousins Thomas and Taylor's children as well. Best of all, Thomas and Taylor's parents will be visiting often."

"My mama and Daddy are moving in with Lydia and I," Taylor said and smiled when Shane, his father came in followed by his mother Charlotte carrying a pot of beans. "And Thomas is building an apartment on the back of his house now for Shaun and Sarah. We'll all be together."

"Someone said my name," Thomas asked as he came into the kitchen with his wife Elise and his parents Shaun and Sarah, Shaun was carrying cornbread and his wife had a pot of lima beans.

"I sure wish we could have just one more of your Grandma Mary's yeast rolls," Tucker said to Taylor and then wished he hadn't said anything for the sorrow that covered Shane and Shaun's face. Mary Blackburn had died in the spring of nineteen forty six.

His Grandmother Cecily went to Jesus in the late summer of the same year and Grandpa Levi followed her two weeks later. Tucker had found his Grandpa Levi sitting on the porch here at Grandpa Allen's house looking out at the river, or he had thought he was looking out the river. Grandpa Levi had passed brokenheartedly missing his wife, he was with her now, Tucker knew and felt at peace with Levi Tucker's passing.

The generation of Allen and Alicia's in their family was all gone except for Grandpa Allen and Grandma Alicia. All of their stories were locked up in the safe and Tucker was in charge of seeing they were handed down through the generations along with photos. He and Jessie had just finished with their story and had it locked away along with his father and mother's story that was a part of Shane and Shaun's story.

"Grandma Alicia wasn't feeling well again this morning," Jessie said to Tucker as she put mashed potatoes and gravy on the table and a pitcher of tea. "Grandpa Allen doesn't want to leave her so I made him a plate of food already. Can you take it up to him after we eat?"

"Keep it in the warmer," Bethany said to Jessie. "I can't believe my parents are the only parents left to us," Bethany said taking Shane and Shaun's hand to say the blessing. "We grew up together. And now we're going to be moving to Tallahassee and living near one another after my Mama and Daddy pass on. And Thomas, Tucker and Taylor will be together. I just hate the thought that we're going to lose my parents before too much longer." Bethany looked down at the children on her son's knee and said, "Allen and Cecily will grow up together, that's a good thing, Daddy and Mama will be happy to know we'll keep our children together."

"Another Allen Blackburn and another Cecily Tucker," Shane teased. "And my grandson Allen is the great grandson of Doctor Lang and Holly Taylor. We can't ever forget those two." He looked at his beautiful wife Charlotte and knew she still grieved the loss of her parents, they all did.

"I'll be sad to leave this place," Tucker said. "I'm worried about losing Grandma Alicia, she's just been so unwell."

Allen Blackburn stood in the hallway listening to the conversation in the kitchen. He knew that his boys weren't going to be able to work his and Levi's sawmill much longer, they were all growing old now. He leaned against the wall as he thought of his son Shaun Allen. If his son had lived, he would have kept the mill going, but Shaun Allen had been killed in the war. The river would soon be empty of Blackburns and Taylors and Tuckers, Allen thought. But the memories would live on, the memories were a part of that old river and this land they lived on.

Allen went to the hallway wall and looked at the years of damage he had done here. He remembered many of the reasons he had hit this wall, the senseless murder of his best friend Lang Taylor and his wife Holly, the loss of his only son Shaun Allen, the cruelties of a man over the child he had once saved from drowning, his Eddie. On and on down that long hall were holes put there by his frustration over the decades of his life. And now he wanted to punch the wall again. His Alicia was ill, no one could figure out what was wrong with her; they only knew that she was getting weaker. She was as beautiful now as she had been the day he had first laid eyes on her and he loved her more every day. All the years they had been together had been happy and filled with love. They had lived a good life, built a strong family, and loved their river. He wouldn't change one thing between them. The only thing he would change was the loss of their son, Shaun Allen.

Allen went up the stairs and to his bedroom, Alicia lay in the bed looking pale and ill. She reached up her hand to him and he hurried to take her hand. "Allen, my necklace," she pleaded and he knew what she was asking for. Once, a long time ago, he had to leave her and he feared he would never see her again. He had given

Seth a locket to give to her and inside was a painting he had done of himself. When he returned home, he had a painting done of her on the other side. He pulled the necklace out of her jewelry box and saw there were two. "Alicia?" he pulled them both out and brought them to the bed.

"When Cecily was born to our Tucker," she said to her husband seeing the two lockets he held in his hands that were identical, "I had another locket made Allen. One for Bethany after were gone and one for Cecily for when she grows up." She saw her husband nod his head and smile down at you. "I want Cecily to have a piece of us."

"You always think of others," Allen said still holding the lockets.

"I want you to write a note right now and wrap those lockets up in the note and tonight give them to Bethany for me. I want her to put them somewhere safe and she can wear hers to remember us by after we're gone." Alicia saw Allen go the dresser and pull out paper and pencil.

"Do you want me to just tell Bethany the one locket is for her and the other for our granddaughter Cecily?" he turned and asked his sweet wife and saw his Alicia nod her head. He stood sideways so that she could watch him write the note and he put both lockets in an envelope and he left them for now on his dresser. He would put them in the safe in the morning.

"I love you Allen Blackburn. Thank you for finding me. Thank you for marrying me, thank you for loving me all these years."

"It should be me thanking you," Allen said to his wife as he climbed into bed beside her and pulled her into his arms holding her close. Her small hand lay on his cheek, her head on his shoulder and he pressed his lips to the top of her head.

"Forever, Allen, forever," Allen heard his wife say on a sigh.

"She came at last and my heart can see, she came and loved someone like me," Allen breathed against her hair, his lips still near her head. "Forever Alicia," he whispered as he closed his eyes.

Tucker went to the stairs intent on checking on his Grandparents, but he stopped in the hall and saw all the holes that his Grandpa had made through the years and smiled. His Grandfather was a wonderful man, the glue that held their family together. And the man could punch a hole in the wall, Tucker smiled. He had a good family, Tucker thought and loving Grandparents. He went up the stairs and knocked on the bedroom door twice and there was no answer so he peeked into the room and saw them as he had often seen his Grandparents, together. His Grandpa held his Grandma in his arms; she was turned with her head on his chest and her hand resting on his cheek. They had lived that way, in love for fifty years and he knew their story told by them and then told again by his wife Jessie when she wrote it in the third party. He was so thankful to God that they had been in his life, that he had grown up with the two of them teaching him what true love was.

"Grandpa," he said softly and then he just knew, he wouldn't get an answer from his Grandfather again. He touched his grandmother and found her cold and he fought not to cry. They had passed away together in one another's arms. Tears pooled in his eyes and he had to catch his breath, he had never known his life without his Grandpa in his life guiding him, guarding him and protecting him. For a moment he was afraid, afraid of his future without this strong man and then he knew, his Grandpa Allen had prepared him for his future, he could and would go on, but he would never be the leader of his family that Allen Blackburn had been.

Bethany looked up at her son as he entered the kitchen and sat down hard on a chair. "Mama," he took her hand. "Grandma and Grandpa, they're together. They're in the bed together and they've passed over." Bethany shook her head and hurried for the stairs with Ethan close behind her. Jessie had turned from the stove and picked up their daughter, her eyes meeting her husband's eyes before he looked and saw Shaun and Shane looking like they both were going to cry and Sarah was hugging Charlotte.

"They were so kind and good. And always so in love," Shaun said and saw Tucker pull Jessie into his arms as she was crying.

"We need to be just like them," Tucker said to Jessie seeing Shane go to Charlotte and Shaun reach for Sarah. He could hear his mother crying upstairs but he knew, Grandma and Grandpa's story was just beginning, they were now in heaven reunited with so many that went on before them that they loved so much. He could see Grandpa; young again running along the banks of the Saint Marks river, they would both always be young and free of all suffering and pain now. And there was Shaun Allen with them, he thought. Their grief over Shaun Allen was at an end.

"We'll love as well as they did Jessie girl. Forever; you and me; even in heaven together." Tucker saw the others in the room all nodding their heads and crying with him.

"Forever Tucker. I'll love you forever," Jessie whispered as she clung tight to her husband.

April 1952
Near where Riverbend use to be

Tucker stood by the car with Jessie knowing they were leaving the river for the last time. A storm had come through and washed the church and store away in Rockhaven, the city was no more. Uncle Seth and Aunt Mary's house had burned down the year before, Lang and Holly's house was still standing but the roof had caved in and it wasn't safe to even go near now. Shane, Shaun and Tucker's father Ethan had taken their homes apart and moved them to the city of Woodville where they put them back together again and sold them to local families. The saw mill was closed, the land was now a full time tree farm and they had workers come out and plant and cut the trees, no Blackburn worked this land now and never would again, though it would continue to support many of the family for generations to come.

The huge beautiful house that had belonged to his Grandpa Allen had been taken apart and used to make five new homes in Woodville that his cousin Michael and Uncle Aaron's children were now living in. Heather had long ago abandoned her parents' home and it had gone to ruin, no one ever knew what became of Heather. There was nothing left but the land and the caving in house of Lang and Holly's and the river, the river would always be here Tucker knew. He watched his daughter and son playing nearby and knew it was time to leave here. He had to live near where he worked at the University in Tallahassee as an Engineer and he was also in the Navy Reserves as he had wanted to be. He was starting a whole new life, but he would never forget where he came from or those that raised him. He swallowed the lump in his throat, and fought the tears in his eyes; his life had changed so much since his Grandpa Allen had died.

"I wonder what this place will be like when our grandchildren are grown." Jessie said taking his hand. "Will anyone remember the river we love so much?" her heart was in her throat as she looked out at the river that had been the Blackburn home for five generations. "Will anyone remember the love that could be found here? Really, the love that was made here."

"We have the stories typed up, several copies. We'll pass them on and share them with the cousins," Tucker put his arm around Jessie and called to his children to get into the car. "As long as we love as deeply as they did. As long as we live life to the fullest as they did, our family will go on."

"We can still come out here fishing," Jessie said as she got in the car and watched Tucker look around one last time.

"Yes, we'll still come out here for picnics and family reunions." He got into the car and started down the road stopping to get out to look back and knew Jessie had gotten out and was looking back as well. "I can see Grandpa on his horse in the distance, a young man again and Grandma in front of him, him holding her like he wrote in his story."

"Allen Blackburn will always be here," Jessie said. "Love stories never end."

Tucker lifted up his arm and waved goodbye one final time, the white sandy road behind him was all that was left showing anyone had ever lived here. "I love you Grandpa Allen," he whispered, his words caught on the wind and taken down to the river's edge where he use to play, where Grandpa Allen made love to his beautiful Alicia.

Summer 2010

"Mama said Grandma wrote the stories that we just read for our Great Great Grandparents," Holly Blackburn said to her twin sister Alicia.

"Would you slow down? You're going too fast and we're not in a hurry." Alicia Blackburn and her sister strongly favored one another. The difference was Alicia had aqua eyes and her sister had a lovely shade of green. They both had cowlicks in the front of their hair and perfect noses. Our Great Great Grandparents were beautiful," Alicia said looking through the photos her mother had given her that were on the front seat of the car between she and Holly. Alicia saw Holly touch the locket her mother had given to her and she reached for hers that was identical to Holly's and opened it up seeing their beautiful Great Great Grandparents. "We have Allen Blackburn's nose and hair, you have Allen Blackburn's green eyes and I have Alicia Blackburn's name and eyes."

Alicia and Holly were the daughters of Cecily Tucker and Allen Blackburn. Their mother had been the daughter of Allen Roston Tuck Tucker and Jessie Fairchild. Their father was the son of Taylor Blackburn and Lydia and yes, they were aware their parents were cousins, but they didn't understand the relationship until the started becoming interested in genealogy.

"I think I have it all sorted out in my mind," Alicia said looking at her sister. "Or I would if you would slow down. You're driving too fast, Holly. We aren't going to fire."

"Our ancestors aren't that hard to understand Alicia," Holly said shaking her head. "Mama was the daughter of Allen Roston Tuck Tucker and Jessie, Tucker was the son of Bethany Blackburn and Ethan Tucker. Bethany was the daughter of Allen Blackburn and Alicia and Ethan was the son of Levi and Cecily Tucker. And Allen Blackburn is the one who built the estate that is now our tree farm and he was the son of Jarred and Bethany Blackburn. That's Mama's side of the family.

"For our Daddy," Holly continued, "Daddy was the son of Taylor Blackburn and Taylor was the son of Shane Blackburn and Charlotte Taylor. Shane was the son of Seth and Mary Blackburn and Charlotte was the daughter of Lang and Holly Taylor and Seth Blackburn was the brother of Allen Blackburn and the son of Jarred and Bethany Blackburn."

"Making us share our three Great Grandparents Jarred and Bethany Blackburn through both Mama and Daddy and I'm still confused." Alicia saw Holly turn off the Woodville Highway and onto the Natural Bridge Road. "I wish you'd slow down, Holly," she said in frustration and Holly laughed as she rounded a corner.

"Nothing but woods out here now," she said looking at both sides of the road and seeing only trees. "I sure hope my car doesn't break down, it'll take a tow truck an hour at least to get out here to us."

"Is your car acting up?" Alicia asked in a worried tone as they passed The Old Plank Road.

"No, just trying to freak you out," Holly laughed and finally slowed down as they passed the pavement and hit clay dirt road.

They traveled over the Natural Bridge where the Saint Marks River went underground for a long way and came back up on the other side. The Natural Bridge Battle site for the civil war remembrance was the last bit of civilization they saw as they went deeper into the woods.

"Mama said after we cross the Natural Bridge there's a sandy road to the right," Alicia said and pointed to the right. "There's the gate, she gave me the combination." Alicia jumped out wishing their Grandpa Tucker were here with them, sadly he had died at the age of eighty in nineteen ninety nine missing the turn of the century. Grandma Jessie had died of cancer the year before. When they were little their Grandparents brought them out here a few times, but Grandpa Taylor Blackburn said it made him sad for the old way of life. Alicia and Holly knew their Grandfather's were cousins and very close friends, they had grown up out here on this river. Both were gone now and there was no one to share the memories of this place with beyond the books the girls had read.

Alicia picked up the books her grandmother Jessie had long ago typed up, they were sitting in a box on the floor at her feet in the car and she smiled. "We come from a long line of Romantics," she said in a teasing tone. "I love the names our Great Great Grandparents gave their stories," she heard Holly laugh and she did as well. "They're awesome names, Holly, and you know it."

Alicia looked down at the story written by Lang and Holly Taylor, this was the first story she had read, A Return of Innocence. Levi and Cecily Tucker named their story, No Sound the Silence Makes and the third book she read was of her Great Great Grandfather Allen Blackburn and his wife Alicia, they had named their story, Come Love Someone Like Me. Also in the box was the story of their Great Grandparents, Shane Blackburn and Charlotte Taylor and Ethan Tucker and Bethany Blackburn, they had named their story, Come Save Someone Like Me. And the last story in the box, the one that was her favorite was her Grandpa Tucker and

Grandma Jessie's story, they had named their story, Come Tame Someone Like Me.

"A long line of romantics," Holly said looking at her sister as she reached to hand Alicia the map her mother had made.

"I hope we can find the cemetery," Alicia fretted as she looked at the map. The roads were logging roads made by trucks that came in and took out the cut trees, they were bumpy and Alicia wished they had a truck instead of her sister's car. "Just around this curve," Alicia said looking for a cemetery but she only saw sandy roads and palmetto bushes and pine trees.

"It should be right here," Holly said and then saw the bleached headstone, bleached by the sun and rain and wind and she stopped the car. "Look out for snakes," she called to her sister and grabbed her digital camera.

"I found our Great Great Grandfathers, they're all buried together," Alicia called out from several yards away from Holly. "Seth and Mary Blackburn," she read out loud. "Lang and Holly Taylor, Levi and Cecily Tucker and here, look Allen Blackburn still has two headstones." Alicia pointed and remembered in the book he had written that he had died as a young man. "Allen and Alicia Blackburn." Holly came and joined her sister looking at the headstones.

"Our Great Grandparents," Alicia said feeling sad. "Shane and Charlotte Blackburn and he's buried next to his twin Shaun and his wife Sarah, Ethan and Bethany Tucker, Grandpa's mama and Daddy. Mama said they had markers put out here for Grandpa Tucker and Grandma Jessie but both had their ashes scattered on the river and she said Grandpa Taylor Blackburn is actually buried out here with Grandma Lydia."

Walking together the girls found their family from the stories left behind and held hands wishing the families were still close. They had all grown apart and many had moved away from the Tallahassee area. The family that Allen Blackburn had brought together and created with Lang Taylor and Levi Tucker were gone forever; only markers in an old cemetery were left. "It's really sad," Holly said to her sister leaning her head on Alicia's shoulder. "This whole place was a city with houses and people and even a business only sixty years ago and one hundred years ago almost all of our family lived here and now there's nothing left except those stories in the books our Grandma Jessie typed up."

"Allen Blackburn was born in a time of horse and buggy and no phones and when he met Grandma Alicia women wore their hair up and were innocent and sweet." Alicia pulled out her cell phone and saw she had no signal. "And we carry a phone with us everywhere. I'd be lost without mine."

"We have to go down to the river, Alicia. We have to see Grandpa's river, the one where Allen Blackburn made love to Alicia, his wife." The girls left their car and felt they had stepped back in time to one hundred years before right now. The place was so beautiful, huge cypress trees with Spanish moss hanging from the branches and reaching to the ground, towering oak trees and pine trees and the ground was soft as they got near the river. There were no grassy banks, the weeds and trees had taken over everything.

"Holly, there's the sulfur spring, let's go see if it's cold like in the book," Alicia pulled her sister to the spring and put her hand in. "Icy, just like in the story Come Love Someone Like Me."

"This place is haunted," Holly looked around and wanted to cry. "More so since I read those stories." Alicia pulled her to the river and they saw all the lime stones on the bottom and knew, this was the pool where their Great Great Grandfather Allen made love to his beautiful wife Alicia. "Look," Holly pointed up to an old rope tied high up in the tree. "Maybe that's where he and his brother Seth swung from."

Alicia did a full turn around looking up and out at everything and saw Holly do the same thing. "It's beautiful here," they said at the same time and laughed at one another.

It was late in the afternoon by the time the girls got back to their car and as Holly was getting in she saw someone off in the distance. "Hey, Mama said no one lived out here. Who's that man waving to us?" She pointed down the road and Alicia looked at what her sister saw.

"I bet his truck broke down and with no cell signal out here, he's in trouble," Alicia pulled her car door closed after she was in and put on her seatbelt.

"You're probably right, he's waving hard. I wonder why he's not yelling at us to come help him," Holly got in the car and cranked up intent on going to help the man, no one should be stranded out here in the middle of nowhere; it was miles away from anyone that might help.

Holly drove to where the man was and all of sudden, he wasn't there anymore. "Hey, Alicia, where did he go?" Holly stopped the car and got out looking off in the woods in both directions but saw nothing. "I know there was a man here," she said firmly to her sister.

"With all the sand out here, he had to leave footprints," Alicia said and looked down for footprints in the sand walking down the road in one direction and saw Holly going in the other direction.

"Alicia," Holly cried out for her sister and Alicia ran to Holly thinking she had found footprints they could follow but instead she gasped because there, clearly written in the sand she saw in old fashion cursive the words….

"For she came at last, and my heart can see. For she came and loved someone like me."

The End

www.ingramcontent.com/pod-product-compliance
Lightning Source LLC
LaVergne TN
LVHW021233080526
838199LV00088B/4329

www.ingramcontent.com/pod-product-compliance
Lightning Source LLC
LaVergne TN
LVHW021233080526
838199LV00088B/4329